After you have read this research report, please give us your frank opinion on the contents. All comments—large or small, complimentary or caustic—will be gratefully appreciated. Mail them to CADRE/AR, Building 1400, 401 Chennault Circle, Maxwell AFB AL 36112–6004.

The Limits of Friendship

US Security Cooperation in Central Asia

McCarthy

D1466054

Thank you for your assistance.

AIR FORCE FELLOWS

COLLEGE OF AEROSPACE DOCTRINE, RESEARCH AND EDUCATION

AIR UNIVERSITY

The Limits of Friendship

US Security Cooperation in Central Asia

MICHAEL J. MCCARTHY
Lieutenant Colonel, USAF

Walker Paper No. 9

Air University Press
Maxwell Air Force Base, Alabama 36112-5962

October 2007

Muir S. Fairchild Research Information Center Cataloging Data

McCarthy, Michael J., 1962-
    The limits of friendship : US security cooperation in Central Asia / Michael J. McCarthy.
       p. ; cm. – (Walker paper, 1555-7871 ; no. 9)
    Includes bibliographical references.
    ISBN 978-1-58566-172-5
    1. United States—Military relations—Asia, Central. 2. Asia, Central—Military relations—United States. 3. Military assistance, American—Asia, Central. 4. Asia, Central—Strategic aspects. I. Title. II. Series.

    355.0310973058—dc22

Disclaimer

This Walker Paper and others in the series are available electronically at the Air University Research Web site http://research.maxwell.af.mil and the AU Press Web site http://aupress.maxwell.af.mil.

Air Force Fellows

Since 1958 the Air Force has assigned a small number of carefully chosen, experienced officers to serve one-year tours at distinguished civilian institutions studying national security policy and strategy. Beginning with the 1994 academic year, these programs were accorded in-residence credit as part of professional military education at senior service schools. In 2003 these fellowships assumed senior developmental education (SDE) force-development credit for eligible officers.

The SDE-level Air Force Fellows serve as visiting military ambassadors to their centers, devoting effort to expanding their colleagues' understanding of defense matters. As such, candidates for SDE-level fellowships have a broad knowledge of key Department of Defense (DOD) and Air Force issues. SDE-level fellows perform outreach by their presence and voice in sponsoring institutions. They are expected to provide advice as well as promote and explain Air Force and DOD policies, programs, and military-doctrine strategy to nationally recognized scholars, foreign dignitaries, and leading policy analysts. The Air Force Fellows also gain valuable perspectives from the exchange of ideas with these civilian leaders. SDE-level fellows are expected to apprise appropriate Air Force agencies of significant developments and emerging views on defense as well as economic and foreign policy issues within their centers. Each fellow is expected to use the unique access she or he has as grounds for research and writing on important national security issues. The SDE Air Force Fellows include the National Defense Fellows, the RAND Fellows, the National Security Fellows, and the Secretary of Defense Corporate Fellows. In addition, the Air Force Fellows program supports a post-SDE military fellow at the Council on Foreign Relations.

On the level of intermediate developmental education, the chief of staff approved several Air Force Fellowships focused on career broadening for Air Force majors. The Air Force Legislative Fellows program was established in April 1995, with the Foreign Policy Fellowship and Defense Advanced Research Projects Agency Fellowship coming under the Air Force Fellows program in 2003. In 2004 the Air Force Fellows also assumed responsibility for the National Laboratories Technologies Fellows.

Contents

Chapter		Page
	DISCLAIMER	ii
	FOREWORD	ix
	ABOUT THE AUTHOR	xiii
	ABSTRACT	xv
	ACKNOWLEDGEMENTS	xvii
1	INTRODUCTION	1
	Evaluating US Security Cooperation	1
	US National-Security Interests	4
	Defining Security Cooperation	6
	Structure of the Study	9
	Notes	10
2	CONCEPTION	13
	Denuclearization	14
	Democratization	16
	A Modest Beginning	21
	Notes	21
3	EXPANSION	25
	Roots of Expansion	25
	Denuclearization	29
	Proliferation Prevention	30
	Democratization	32
	Regional Cooperation	44
	Reaching the Summit	50
	Notes	52
4	REASSESSMENT	59
	Roots of Reassessment	60
	Denuclearization and Proliferation Prevention	63
	Democratization	65
	Military Contact Program and Education and Training Programs	66
	Regional Cooperation	67

Chapter		*Page*
	Military Capabilities	71
	On the Eve	78
	Notes	79
5	REWARDS AND REBALANCE	83
	High Watermark	84
	New Equilibrium	87
	Military Capabilities	95
	Proliferation Prevention	98
	Regional Cooperation	100
	Democratization	103
	Current Status	104
	Notes	105
6	CONSTRAINTS AND LIMITATIONS	111
	Environmental Constraints	112
	Bureaucratic and Policy Constraints	119
	Programmatic Constraints	125
	Constraints and Limitations in Perspective	145
	Notes	146
7	MEASURING EFFECTIVENESS	153
	Building Relationships	156
	Building Military Capabilities	160
	Gaining Access and Basing Rights	161
	Relative Accomplishments	164
	Notes	165
8	PROSPECTS	167
	Integrate Efforts within the Defense Department	168
	Integrate Efforts within the US Government	171
	Integrate Efforts with NATO and Allied and Partner Nations	172
	Focus Security-Cooperation Efforts on Kazakhstan	175
	Focus Security-Cooperation Efforts on a Limited Range of Objectives	176
	Notes	183
9	CONCLUSION	185

Appendix   *Page*

A   US SECURITY COOPERATION
      FUNDING IN CENTRAL ASIA   187

B   US SECURITY COOPERATION TRAINING
      PROGRAMS IN CENTRAL ASIA   205

C   EXPANDED INTERNATIONAL MILITARY
      EDUCATION AND TRAINING PROGRAM   219

D   ALLIED SECURITY COOPERATION
      EFFORTS IN CENTRAL ASIA   225

      ABBREVIATIONS   235

      SELECTED BIBLIOGRAPHY.   239

Illustrations

Figure

1   Central Asia.   2

2   US-funded English language laboratory   20

3   Kazakhstani Cadet Elena Milyuk with
      US general Richard Myers   43

4   Uzbekistani army contingent of
      CENTRASBAT   48

5   US ambassador Joseph Pressel delivering
      first high mobility multipurpose wheeled
      vehicle (HMMWV)   73

6   Central Asian participants in the
      Regional Cooperation 05 exercise.   102

7   Selected US security-cooperation
      funding in Central Asia, 1993–2006.   105

8   US Military personnel with deputy
      commander of Kazakhstani Air Force   128

CONTENTS

Figure		Page
9	International Counterproliferation Program (ICP) training flowchart	139
10	US and Kazakhstani personnel during a transport aviation military contact event	154

Tables

1	Examples of security-cooperation activities	7
2	State Partnership Program (SPP) agreements	33
3	Partnership for Peace (PfP) program framework documents	34
4	Interoperability programs eligible for Warsaw Initiative Fund (WIF) funding	36
5	Military contact events planned with the Central Asian states, 1996–1999	37
6	Excess defense articles (EDA) deliveries to Central Asia	74
7	Proposed focus areas for US security cooperation in Central Asia	177

Foreword

Looking back 20 years, it is astounding to contemplate the profound changes that have occurred in the political geography of Eurasia. The massive geopolitical shifts witnessed in this period rival those of any previous era in modern history. From the fall of the Berlin Wall in 1989 and the subsequent unraveling of the Warsaw Pact, the collapse of the Union of Soviet Socialist Republics (USSR) in 1991, the birth (or rebirth) of democracy in the states of Central and Eastern Europe, and the expansion of NATO and the enlargement of the European Union into these former communist countries, the pace and scope of political, social, and economic change has been breathtaking. From the wreckage of the Soviet empire there emerged 15 new states, all formerly constituent "republics" of the former USSR. Among them are the five new states of Central Asia: Kazakhstan, Kyrgyzstan, Tajikistan, Turkmenistan, and Uzbekistan. Although far removed from the dramatic events occurring in Central and Eastern Europe, Russia, Ukraine, and other western regions, the terrible events of September 2001 thrust the distant and exotic lands of Central Asia into the center of American strategic thought.

Until then only a small number of academics, human rights activists, and oil company executives were familiar with Central Asian cultural, political, and economic dynamics. However, unknown to most Americans for almost a decade, the US military has been discretely establishing relationships with the armed forces and security services of these nations through a variety of security-cooperation programs. As America's interest in the region grew, so did the volume and range of military activities. But to what ends? Are these programs simply payoffs for access to the region in order to conduct operations in Afghanistan? Or do they represent more complex reasons? What have these programs really accomplished? Have these military-cooperation programs produced tangible, long-term results?

In the first comprehensive study of US security cooperation in Central Asia, Michael J. McCarthy explores these efforts, seeking to understand not only the details of the individual programs but, more importantly, to understand the objectives of those activities and the policies and strategies that drive them. *The Limits of Friendship: US Security Cooperation in Central Asia* unravels 15 years of military activities in this pivotal region, tracing the ebb and flow of the bilateral and multilateral relationships and how they translate into specific security-cooperation programs. In this historical context, McCarthy illuminates the differences between the successful implementations of policy into practice and the unintended consequences when these programs become disconnected from their original intents.

The title, *The Limits of Friendship*, captures the essence of McCarthy's thesis, that there are constraints on security-policy objectives that can be accomplished through security-cooperation programs. Foreign military forces can only absorb a finite amount of assistance, and the US military, for a variety of operational, budgetary, and programmatic reasons, can only provide so much assistance. Further, each type of cooperative activity has its own strengths and weaknesses. The patron-client dichotomy, present in every bilateral relationship, adds friction to even the most well-intentioned programs, especially in countries (such as the Central Asian states), where the political system is not in harmony with democratic principles or transparent governance. McCarthy explores deeply into these limitations, addressing not only how they have shaped the bilateral and regional relationships, but he also draws out methodologies for planning and implementing security-cooperation programs in ways that could help to mitigate the limitations that seem to be inherent in security-cooperation programs.

McCarthy's work crosses many boundaries. *The Limits of Friendship* offers a unique insight into an aspect of US relations in Central Asia that, until now, has not been fully explored. Most academic works on Central Asia address US relations only to the extent of describing how diplomatic initiatives indicate a shift in policy one way or the other. This work provides policy makers a range of concrete proposals for using security cooperation to advance US interests with Kazakhstan, Kyrgyzstan, Tajikistan, Turkmenistan, and Uzbekistan. Recent events underscore the need for informed and in-depth analyses such as those McCarthy provides. The resurgence of Russia as a major player in the region, the creation and strengthening of the Shanghai Cooperation Organization (bringing Russia, China, and the Central Asian countries together into a fledgling, but strengthening military/political alliance), the crucial petroleum and natural gas export routes from Central Asia to the world market, and the potential for further political turmoil in a region plagued by civil war and authoritarianism all demand the attention of both the academic and policy communities.

Finally, many of these policy considerations have value and applicability beyond Central Asia. Policy makers would be well advised to draw from them when crafting guidance for use in other regions. Additionally, *The Limits of Friendship* gives security-cooperation practitioners a valuable set of techniques that, if properly implemented, can help ensure successful results. McCarthy's analysis has already set the framework for the revision of US Central Command's Theater Security Cooperation strategy for Central Asia and the Middle East, and many of his recommendations are being adopted throughout the Department of Defense. This work is the product both of extensive research and a career spent in the field, a combination that makes this a major addition to our knowledge of this increasingly vital region and to the practice of military-security programs. As such, the author is to be commended for his devotion to the subject and the contribution he makes to the furtherance of US national security.

Ralph S. Clem, PhD
Florida International University
Maj Gen, USAFR, Retired

About the Author

Lt Col Michael J. McCarthy, USAF, is chief of the Central and South Asia Branch of the Security Cooperation Division, US Central Command (USCENTCOM), MacDill AFB, Florida. Colonel McCarthy's past operational assignments include squadron intelligence officer in the 309th Tactical Fighter Squadron, and then as chief of both the Intelligence Operations and Target Operations Branches in the 31st Tactical Fighter Wing Intelligence Division, Homestead AFB, Florida; watch officer, Base Warning Office, Ramstein AB, Germany; command intelligence briefer, Headquarters, US Air Forces in Europe; senior analyst for Russian political and military affairs, National Air Intelligence Agency, the Pentagon, Washington, DC; the speechwriter for the Assistant Chief of Staff for Intelligence. He helped establish the Special Programs Office, the Office of the Assistant Chief of Staff for Intelligence, Headquarters, US Air Force (HQ USAF). Other assignments included serving as information warfare requirements officer; the executive officer to the Director of Plans and Programs, Office of the Assistant Chief of Staff for Intelligence, HQ USAF; a plans and exercises officer, Joint Intelligence Center (JIC), Central, USCENTCOM; the chief of the Central Asia Analysis Team, JIC, USCENTCOM; operations officer, 23d Information Operations Squadron, Lackland AFB, Texas; United Nations (UN) military observer, senior liaison officer in the UN Headquarters; and the commander of assigned US forces, UN Observer Mission in Georgia, Tbilisi, Republic of Georgia. Colonel McCarthy also was assigned as country director for Russia, Caucasus, and Central Asia, Office of the Deputy Under Secretary of the Air Force, International Affairs, the Pentagon, Washington, DC; and senior executive officer and military assistant to the Deputy Under Secretary of the Air Force, International Affairs.

Colonel McCarthy was made National Defense Fellow of the Center for International Relations, Queen's University, Kingston, Ontario. He is a graduate of the Air War College, US Marine Corps (USMC) Command and Staff College, the Air Command and Staff College, Squadron Officer School, and Officer Training School. He also holds a bachelor of arts degree in International Studies of the Soviet Union, the Ohio State University; a diploma in Russian Language, Pushkin Institute of the Russian Language, Moscow, Union of Soviet Socialist Republics; and master of science degrees in International Relations, Catholic University, Washington, DC; in Military Science, USMC Command and Staff College, Quantico Marine Corps Base, Virginia; and in Air Warfare, American Military University, Manassas, Virginia.

Colonel McCarthy is married to Col Muriel R. McCarthy, USAF, who currently serves as the mobilization assistant to the Chief of the Air Force Reserve, HQ USAF, the Pentagon, Washington, DC. They have a Yorkshire terrier named Webster.

Abstract

This research paper explores the history of US security-cooperation programs in Central Asia from 1993 to the present, identifying five distinct phases of development as those programs sought to achieve US objectives in *denuclearization and proliferation prevention, democratization and military reform, regional cooperation,* and *improvement of military capabilities.* These security-cooperation efforts were limited by a variety of factors, including the lack of political and economic reform in the region, Russian influence through bilateral cooperation agreements and multilateral security institutions, constrained resources, diffuse objectives and multiplying recipients, and US policies that restrained commitment to Central Asia. Each of the programs available to US planners had strengths and weaknesses, but these programs were not always integrated in a fashion to achieve the best results. The linkages between the specific activities and the ultimate objectives have not always been constant and still may not always be clear. As a result, the United States has had mixed results in building relationships, developing capabilities, and providing access. The United States should focus its efforts on Kazakhstan, more closely integrate the existing security-cooperation programs within the Defense Department and across the US government, leverage the assistance programs of North Atlantic Treaty Organization partners, and seek to employ a strategy of persistent engagement against a limited number of clearly defined objectives.

Acknowledgements

I was first exposed to the complex dynamics of US security cooperation in Central Asia during a tour at USCENTCOM in the late 1990s. A subsequent assignment as a country director in the Office of the Deputy Under Secretary of the Air Force, International Affairs, provided the opportunity to be a part of the process of developing and implementing specific initiatives for the region. When I was selected for a research fellowship, I immediately decided to more rigorously examine and evaluate the role of US security cooperation in Central Asia. That my research identifies limitations inherent in US security-cooperation efforts in Central Asia should in no way detract from the dedication, perseverance, and patriotism of the many civilian and military personnel who plan and execute these programs.

I thank the many people who assisted with my research, most of whom provided information or perspectives that may have seemed inconsequential to them at the time but to me were invaluable. This research was jointly sponsored by the Office of the Secretary of Defense (OSD) and USCENTCOM, and many in those two organizations gave freely of their time to assist me in gathering data and responding to my many questions. In particular, I thank Col Dan Groeschen at USCENTCOM, Col Jon Chicky and Paul Watson of the OSD, and Deborah Bereda at the Defense Security Cooperation Agency for their time, support, and assistance. I also thank Col Michael Howe and Lt Col Eric Nelson who originally promoted the topic as a viable research paper. I simply could not have accomplished this project without their willingness to provide information, answer questions, share their experiences, and invite me to their conferences.

Several others responded to my many requests and questions with the professionalism that is the hallmark of this business. At the risk of omitting someone, I offer my appreciation to the following individuals: William Aseltine, LCDR Rebecca Badders, Hussam Bader, Gregory Baker, Ronald Battaglia, Lt Col Dashdondog Bayarsaikhan, Lt Col Paul Bigelow, Maj Edward Black, Lt Col Taft Blackburn, Jeannie Borden, Barbara Braese, Col Matt Brand, Lt Col David Brigham, Maj Kent Broome, Maj Mark Campbell, Lorain Cardenas, David Cate,

ACKNOWLEDGEMENTS

John Charlton, Leslie Christensen, Maj Padraig Clark, Anna Crockett, Dr. Judy Damewood, Alice Deery, Maj Ted Donnelly, Maj Scott Dullea, Maj Neal Edmonds, Lt Col James Fain, Ronald Fine, Lt Col Helmut Fritsch, Alan Gorowitz, Janice Gould, Lt Col Kelsey Harris-Smith, Maj Daniel Hash, Col Roy Hawkins, Lt Col Russ Hittinger, Maj Amir Hussain, Scott Jasper, Gloria Jenkins, Kay Judkins, Timothy Kelly, Maj Harry Lane, Dr. Amer Latif, Sharon Latzen, Maj Ben Louma, Lt Col Stephen Mariano, David Martin, Kenneth Martin, Cristina Matei, Ken McFarling, John McKane, James McNaughton, Col Assylbek Mendygaliev, Lt Col Kurt Meppen, Walter Monroe, John Moseley, Thomas Nankervis, Steven Peterson, Mark Pirritano, Martin Poffenberger, Allan Polley, Lt Col Jeff Predmore, Heidi Reisinger, Capt Will Santos, Maj Paul Schmitt, Silvia Serben, Terri Smith, Capt Jessica Soderbeck, Lt Col Robert Timm, Dr. Marybeth Peterson Ulrich, Roman Vassilenko, Linda Wesley, Maj Kevin Westley, Col Thomas Wilhelm, Brett Wise, Lt Col Wiu Chaing Yong, Maj Michael Yuschak, Maj Michael Zabrzeski, and Col Albert Zaccor.

I also thank Dr. Ralph Clem (Maj Gen, USAFR, retired.) at Florida International University for his guidance and support on this project. Because of his phenomenal academic background in Russian and Soviet affairs and his extremely successful career as a military intelligence officer, Dr. Clem has been an invaluable mentor for many years. I offer my appreciation as well to Dee Taylor at the College of Aerospace Doctrine Research and Education for the outstanding support she provided during this year.

I offer a special thanks to my parents, Jim and Alice McCarthy of Monument, Colorado, who supported me on this and countless other endeavors. Finally, but most importantly, I thank my wife, Col Muriel McCarthy, for her support, guidance, and encouragement through our many wonderful years together, and for taking care of the thousands of minor crises at home while I was away in Canada on this fellowship. Without her by my side and in my heart, this project would have been impossible.

MICHAEL J. MCCARTHY
Lieutenant Colonel, USAF

Chapter 1

Introduction

In 1999, teams of Green Berets arrived at former Soviet garrisons outside the capital here. They were some of the Army's finest soldiers, they traveled in small groups and in the two years that followed they came and went every few months. The mission was straightforward: to train the army of a former foe, in part to prepare its inexperienced conscripts for skirmishes with the Islamic Movement of Uzbekistan, a terrorist group accused of setting off bombs in Tashkent earlier that year. The long-term goal was more ambitious. The Green Berets were one element of an accelerating security arrangement in which the two nations were laying the groundwork for more extensive military cooperation. In recent weeks this relationship has blossomed into the large-scale American deployment of Special Forces units and aircraft on what was once enemy soil.

—C. J. Chivers, *New York Times*, 25 October 2001

Evaluating US Security Cooperation

In the days and weeks following the terrible terrorist attacks against the World Trade Center in New York and the Pentagon in Washington, DC, American military forces quietly began to deploy to forward bases in Central Asia (fig. 1) to begin combat operations against the Taliban and al-Qaeda in Afghanistan. At the time, few Americans knew anything of these exotic countries in this far off region, but soon Uzbekistan, Kyrgyzstan, Kazakhstan, Tajikistan, and Turkmenistan began to figure prominently in the news reports of the campaign. The "Stans," as they were called, were identified as critical partners in America's new war on terrorism, and the American public began to learn that the seeds of this partnership had actually been planted years before.

1

Figure 1. Central Asia (Reprinted from Central Intelligence Agency [CIA] Web site, https://www.cia.gov/library/publications/cia-maps-publications/maps/802868.jpg.)

The Central Asian nations proved surprisingly willing to support American combat operations in Afghanistan. All five offered overflight privileges, allowing US military aircraft to transit their airspace. Kazakhstan, Kyrgyzstan, Tajikistan, and Uzbekistan also offered the use of their military facilities to station US forces (Turkmenistan permitted refueling privileges for humanitarian flights); ultimately, the Pentagon selected Karshi-Khanabad in Uzbekistan and Manas International Airport in Kyrgyzstan for its deployments (Dushanbe in Tajikistan hosted a small US contingent). Among other nations, France and the United Kingdom deployed combat units to Dushanbe, and Germany deployed to Termez in southern Uzbekistan.[1] The value of this support cannot be overstated: the early successes of Operation Enduring Freedom (OEF) against Taliban and al-Qaeda forces simply would not have been possible without the cooperation of the Central Asian states.

Most observers viewed these deployments as a visible success for US security-cooperation programs in Central Asia. One of the earliest reports, a *New York Times* article by C. J. Chivers published on 25 October 2001, described reunion scenes—"hearty bear hugs and backslaps"—when US Army Green Berets met with their Uzbek counterparts at Karshi-Khanabad. The Green Berets had been rotating through Uzbekistan since 1999, training Uzbek military forces to deal with a growing fundamentalist Islamic insurgency and laying the groundwork for a stronger and deeper relationship between the two militaries.[2] Implied in this article, and others like it, was the belief that the security-cooperation activities the United States had been conducting since the early 1990s directly led to the overflight privileges and basing rights offered by the Central Asian states in late 2001.

Within a few years, however, the situation had dramatically changed. In December 2003, Secretary of State Colin Powell's refusal to certify Uzbekistan as having made progress in respecting human rights put a freeze on most security-cooperation activities between the two countries, and in July 2005, facing condemnation of its response to civil unrest in Andijon, Uzbekistan directed the withdrawal of all US military forces from Karshi-Khanabad. Immediately before Tashkent's ultimatum, the Shanghai Cooperation Organization (SCO), a regional security forum that included Uzbekistan, Kyrgyzstan, Kazakhstan, Tajikistan, Russia, and China, urged the United States to set a specific date for the withdrawal of all American military forces from Central Asia. Kyrgyzstan, not demanding an immediate withdrawal of US forces, was asking millions of dollars as payment for the use of the facilities at Manas; in the wake of the Karshi-Khanabad withdrawal, these demands have escalated with the importance of Manas to the US military that Bishkek perceives. In Turkmenistan, the government publicly denied that the visit of a US commander was the first step in allowing American military forces into the country. The relationships that had seemed so successful in late 2001 appeared to be stumbling badly by late 2005.

The reality of both situations—the apparent successes of 2001 and failures of 2004–2005—may be less dramatic than the media reports would suggest. US security-cooperation efforts in Central Asia began in the early 1990s with a simple goal of eliminating the nuclear weapons left stranded in Kazakhstan as a result of the collapse of the Soviet Union. Over time, additional objectives were added, but gaining basing rights was never one of them. Uzbekistan had offered permanent bases as early as 1998, but US officials politely brushed aside the invitations: until the dramatic attacks on 11 September 2001, few in the US military could conceive of conducting military operations from or in Central Asia. And while security-cooperation efforts with Uzbekistan are currently limited, US military relations with Kazakhstan and Kyrgyzstan are excellent (notwithstanding the current negotiations over Manas), those with Tajikistan are steadily growing, and those with Turkmenistan remain relatively untroubled.

The collapse of the security-cooperation relationship between the United States and Uzbekistan, however, offers the opportunity to evaluate these programs. How did US security-cooperation efforts in Central Asia develop? What are the US national-security interests in Central Asia, and how can security-cooperation initiatives work to achieve them? What were and are the specific objectives of the security-cooperation programs, and how successful has the United States been in achieving them? What changes should the United States implement to improve the effectiveness of these programs? In evaluating US security-cooperation efforts in Central Asia, this paper seeks understanding on how specific activities have and can assist in *building relationships*, *developing capabilities*, and *providing access*; and how they may be limited by internal and external factors. It will do so in the context of evaluating the particular themes that have run through US security-cooperation efforts since 1992: promoting denuclearization, democratization, regional cooperation, and improving military capabilities.

US National-Security Interests

Daniel Fried, assistant secretary of State for European and Eurasian Affairs, offered the most recent official explanation of

US security interests in Central Asia. Testifying in front of the House International Relations Committee on 27 October 2005, Assistant Secretary Fried identified three interconnected sets of interests: *ensuring security*, in which he grouped efforts to counterterrorism and proliferation of weapons of mass destruction; *promoting energy development and economic cooperation*; and *supporting political reform*, including respect for human rights. As these objectives are indivisible, mutually reinforcing, and ultimately interconnected, US policy is to advance all three sets of interests simultaneously, seeking to maintain a balance between them: "failure in one area will undermine the chance of success in another."[3]

The US national-security interests for Central Asia, as outlined by Assistant Secretary Fried, have evolved and expanded over the past 15 years, but the three fundamental objectives were evident as early as 1995. Given the nuclear arsenal in the newly independent Kazakhstan, security issues arose first. As US energy companies began to invest in the region and reform efforts in Eastern Europe began to demonstrate success, more emphasis was placed on economic and political considerations. The terrorist attacks on 11 September 2001, raised the importance of this region in US security planning and brought an increased emphasis on security issues, but they did not fundamentally change the goals that had developed over the 1990s. Concerns generated by the Kyrgyz revolution and the Andijon situation in 2005 have resulted in a new focus on developing integrated strategies for addressing these concerns and ultimately a new balance in pursuing the national-security objectives.

Security cooperation is one of many tools used by the United States to advance its national objectives in Central Asia. These objectives are interrelated and often complementary—programs that contribute toward building capabilities will usually result in stronger relationships, and programs designed to establish relationships can contribute to developing capabilities. However, they can at times be contradictory—for example, creating capabilities for participation in coalition operations can detract from efforts to improve defensive capabilities. These objectives should be directly related to the national-security objectives for the region; but, again, they can be supporting, or, at times, contradictory in the actual execution of the programs.

Defining Security Cooperation

The initial challenge for a study such as this is defining the meaning of *security cooperation*. The Department of Defense (DOD) officially defines *security cooperation* more in terms of what it is supposed to accomplish rather than what it is: "All Department of Defense interactions with foreign defense establishments to build defense relationships that promote specific US security interests, develop allied and friendly military capabilities for self-defense and multinational operations, and provide US forces with peacetime and contingency access to a host nation."[4] In this sense, it addresses and includes those positive activities that strengthen military ties between the US armed forces and those of allied and partner nations. Security cooperation is not altruistic, nor is it conducted without purpose. With this definition, security cooperation has three objectives: to *build relationships* so that the United States can influence other countries and their military forces, to *develop capabilities* of foreign military forces so they can conduct operations on behalf of or in coalition with the United States, and to *provide access* so that the US military has strategic flexibility to conduct its own operations. Security cooperation is, at its core, specifically intended to achieve specific US national-security objectives.

Security cooperation is a relatively new term within the DOD, encompassing the traditional programs of *security assistance* that provide equipment and training to foreign military forces, as well as the programs of *military engagement* such as joint exercises, senior leader visits, and military contact events.[5] Security cooperation also includes a range of other activities which serve to promote defense relationships.[6] Some examples of security-cooperation activities are shown in table 1.

Despite the official definition and examples above, there is still considerable debate within the DOD as to what constitutes security cooperation. Often this challenge comes from bureaucracies, fearing a loss of control over specific programs, which resist having their activities fall under this definition. Col Albert Zaccor, USA, a senior fellow at the Atlantic Council of the United States, relates one example: "Officials in [the Office of the Secretary of Defense's (OSD)] Counter-proliferation Policy office refused to admit that activities intended to improve the mari-

Table 1. Examples of Security-Cooperation Activities

- Appointment of defense attachés
- Appointment of exchange officers, liaison officers, military advisors, or security assistance personnel
- Visits of senior defense and military leaders
- Contact visits of military delegations, including ship visits or air deployments, for orientation or familiarization
- Participation in military workshops, seminars, symposiums, and conferences
- Training of foreign military and civilian defense personnel, including attendance at language schools, technical training, or combat training
- Professional military education of foreign military and civilian defense personnel, including attendance at service academies and war colleges
- Combined exercises
- Sales of defense equipment and material goods, including appropriate logistics support
- Cooperative weapons development or coproduction
- Cooperative logistics support agreements
- Intelligence exchanges
- Cooperative use of military communication and information systems
- Integration and joint command of specific military units
- Provision of permanent basing and port rights and overflight privileges
- Cooperative efforts to reduce or eliminate specific categories of weapon systems

Adapted from Andrew Cottey and Anthony Forster, *Reshaping Defense Diplomacy: New Roles for Military Cooperation and Assistance*, Adelphi Paper 365 (New York: Oxford University Press, 2004), 7; and *Security Cooperation with the United States Army Forces Central Command* Brochure, US Army Forces Central Command, undated.

time security capabilities of Azerbaijan and Kazakhstan in support of counter-proliferation would be included under the definition of Security Cooperation and declined to integrate their program *formally* with other DOD Security Cooperation efforts" (emphasis in original).[7] The result of these types of disagreements over definitions, of course, has been the "proliferation of narrowly focused, redundant, and generally uncoordinated assistance programs," an issue that will be raised later in this paper.[8]

The definition does not specify whether the "interactions with foreign military establishments" include only those that occur in peacetime, or if they embrace the range of cooperative interactions that occur between allied and coalition partners engaged in peacekeeping, humanitarian, or combat operations. Given the history of major security-cooperation efforts, such as the Lend-Lease program and the military assistance programs of the Cold War, and nature of the current war on terrorism, most DOD policy and doctrinal publications imply that security cooperation extends up to, but does not include, actual operations. Likewise, most US security-cooperation practitioners view their role as *preparing for*, rather than *participating in*, combat operations.

Given the rather broad definition, security cooperation cannot be easily defined by the source of funding, known within the US federal budget process as *programs*. Many individual programs lie clearly and completely within the scope of security cooperation: Foreign Military Sales (FMS), Foreign Military Financing (FMF), Excess Defense Articles (EDA), and the international military education and training (IMET) programs are governed by the Foreign Assistance Act of 1961 and are inherently and completely part of security cooperation. However, the funding for other initiatives, such as allowing foreign cadets to attend US military academies or providing flight training under the Aviation Leadership Program (ALP), are absorbed by the DOD within its normal operations budget.

Likewise, security cooperation cannot be easily defined by the organizations which conduct the activities. Some DOD organizations are dedicated to security-cooperation activities, such as the Air Force Security Assistance Center (AFSAC) or the US Army's Security Assistance Training Field Activity (SATFA). Others conduct security-cooperation activities based on functional expertise, such as the Defense Intelligence Agency (DIA) or the Defense Threat Reduction Agency (DTRA). However, almost every organization within the US military has or may be called upon to contribute in security-cooperation efforts, whether it is hosting a foreign military delegation or participating in a combined exercise.

Despite the relatively short period of cooperation and rather limited scope of its engagement, the United States has employed most of the activities described above in its security-cooperation efforts in Central Asia. The definitional debates, wide range of programs and funding sources, and variety of organizations that have participated in security-cooperation events make it difficult to identify all of the activities that have occurred in or with the Central Asian nations. In particular, the historical record is very weak on the details of military contact events, exercises, and training programs. This paper makes no claims to have captured all of those activities, but it includes the majority of them, and certainly a sufficient quantity to allow for an evaluation of their role in meeting US national-security objectives in the region.

It is also important to note the wide variety of other programs executed by other US government agencies that have similar objectives as the DOD's security-cooperation program. The US Coast Guard, for example, has helped develop the maritime security capabilities of Kazakhstan, Turkmenistan, and Uzbekistan; the State Department's export control and related border security (EXBS) program provides equipment and training to border services in the region. Non-DOD security-cooperation efforts comprise almost half of the security and law enforcement funding to Central Asia in recent years.[9] These efforts, while they are often very similar and complement the DOD efforts, lie outside of the scope of this study. In this regard, this paper only addresses *military* security cooperation—generally speaking, those activities conducted by the DOD with other military organizations. The need for greater integration, however, is briefly addressed in the recommendations.

Structure of the Study

US security-cooperation activities with the Central Asian states span just over a dozen years, having started in 1993. Chapters 2, 3, 4, and 5 trace the evolution of those activities, addressing the six stages of development between 1993 and the present, and describing the various programs introduced by US national-security policy makers to meet changing and multiplying national-security objectives for the region. This review is necessary for two reasons: first, security-cooperation efforts take years, sometimes decades, to achieve results, and only a historical perspective can fully illustrate the linkages between the original goals, current programs, and ultimate results. The review will help establish the framework for understanding the current status of US security-cooperation efforts in Central Asia and their prospects for success in the future. Second, a historical review can help identify lessons from previous successes or failures and demonstrate how those lessons may be applied to current programs.

These perspectives influence the execution of current US security-cooperation efforts and shape the development of those for the future. Many observers view Central Asia as a new "Great Game" played with Russia and China; others see these nations as "front-line states" in the long war on terrorism. Chapter 6 examines the external and internal constraints on US security-cooperation programs in Central Asia that limit them from meeting the objectives set by the US government. It explores the different types of programs, describing their strengths and weaknesses in a manner that addresses the best methods for utilizing them. Chapter 7 offers an evaluation of the effectiveness of US security-cooperation programs in Central Asia. Given the absence of accepted measures of effectiveness and the paucity of data from which to make an assessment, this evaluation must be considered tentative. Chapter 8 offers specific recommendations for national-security policy makers and security-cooperation practitioners, and analyzes the prospects for US initiatives in the future.

US security-cooperation efforts in Central Asia are limited by a host of internal and external factors, and the linkages between the specific activities and the ultimate objectives is not always clear. In the years ahead, Central Asia will remain a critical region in America's long war against terrorism. Security cooperation has been and can be a valuable tool in building relationships with allies and partners, developing capabilities of foreign militaries so they can join in this struggle, and providing access so American forces can take the war to the enemy.

Notes

1. Ehsan Ahrari, "The Strategic Future of Central Asia: A View from Washington," *Journal of International Affairs* 56, no. 2 (Spring 2003), 164.

2. C. J. Chivers, "Long Before War, Green Berets Built Military Ties to Uzbekistan," *New York Times*, 25 October 2001.

3. Daniel Fried, *A Strategy for Central Asia: Statement Before the Subcommittee on the Middle East and Central Asia of the House International Relations Committee*, 27 October 2005, http://www.state.gov/p/eur/rls/rm/55766.htm (accessed 14 December 2005).

4. Joint Publication 1-02, *DOD Dictionary of Military and Associated Terms*, as amended through 22 March 2007, http://131.84.1.34/doctrine/jel/doddict/data/s/04830.html.

5. Some have termed this latter category *military diplomacy* or *defense diplomacy*. Andrew Cottey and Anthony Forster, *Reshaping Defense Diplomacy: New Roles for Military Cooperation and Assistance*, Adelphi Paper 365 (New York: Oxford University Press, 2004), 5.

6. The Department of Defense also conducts humanitarian assistance programs, disaster relief, and demining programs which fall under the rubric of security cooperation. However, as the partners and recipients of these activities are generally the civilian population rather than the military forces or political leadership, these activities fall outside the scope of the paper and are not discussed.

7. Col Albert Zaccor, USA, *Security Cooperation and Non-State Threats: A Call for an Integrated Strategy* (Washington, DC: The Atlantic Council of the United States, August 2005), 34.

8. Ibid., 1.

9. In 2004, the last year for which comprehensive figures are available, DOD security-cooperation efforts accounted for $75.48 million, or 57.5 percent, of the $132.63 million of US funds budgeted for security and law enforcement assistance to Central Asia. Non-DOD efforts through the Departments of State, Energy, and Agriculture, US Agency for International Development, National Science Foundation, Environmental Protection Agency, and the Nuclear Regulatory Commission, comprised 42.5 percent. If the funding for DOD's nuclear, chemical, and biological dismantlement programs, which are inherently destructive rather than productive, is excluded, then DOD efforts comprise only 23.9 percent of the total funding. *U.S. Government Assistance to and Cooperative Activities with Eurasia, Fiscal Year 2004* (Washington, DC: US Department of State, 2005), appendix, http://www.state.gov/p/eur/rls/rpt/c16112.htm (accessed 12 January 2006).

Chapter 2

Conception

The Safe, Secure Dismantlement [SSD] *Agreement marks the beginning of an entirely new relationship between Kazakhstan and the United States.*

> —Vice Pres. Al Gore at the signing of the
> SSD Agreement in Almaty, Kazakhstan,
> December 1993

Following the collapse of the Soviet Union in December 1991, Pres. George H. W. Bush sought to develop an aid program for the newly independent states in Eurasia. The resulting Freedom Support Act, signed into law on 24 October 1992, was largely intended for the European states of the former Soviet Union, but it also laid the foundation for a variety of assistance programs, including the beginnings of a security-cooperation relationship, with the new states of Central Asia. Beginning in 1993, when the first programs were officially established, the United States slowly built a web of ties to the military forces of the Central Asian nations. Progress was slow and uneven, largely due to limited funding, multiplying objectives, and the effect of outside factors, such as reversals in democratic reform and the insurgent attacks in the region in 1999 and 2000. This development went through three distinct stages prior to the turning point of 11 September 2001, and two more stages afterward.

In December 1991, when the new states of Central Asia were handed their independence, the United States had little intention of establishing lasting security relationships in the region. Within Eurasia, the foreign and security policy focuses of the Bush administration were on the political, economic, and military disintegration in Russia, and, to a lesser extent, on the dynamic transformation in the emerging democracies in Eastern Europe. Central Asia, tacitly acknowledged to be within Russia's sphere of influence, was an exotic, distant, and strategically unimportant region in which the United States had few national-security interests and even fewer reasons for security cooperation. Equally important, the US military was recrafting its view on the use of security-cooperation tools: instead of the Cold War programs designed to develop foreign military forces capable of defeating Communist threats, military-to-military contacts, exercises, and security-assistance programs were now intended primarily to promote and permit "forward presence"—the stationing or deployment of US troops overseas.[1] With little intention of deploying forces to Central Asia, the US military had little interest in, or need for, security cooperation with these countries.

Denuclearization

The exception to the relative neglect of Central Asia was the critical concern of securing the nuclear weapons stranded in the region, and, as a corollary, eliminating the potential threat of the proliferation of the materials, technology, and knowledge needed to develop nuclear weapons. Even this concern, however, was seen in the larger context of relations with Moscow: Kazakhstan, one of the four successor states that now possessed nuclear weapons, had to be convinced to relinquish them to Russia, and Moscow had to be convinced to accept and destroy them.

Fortunately, the US military had been involved in denuclearization efforts in Kazakhstan since 1988. When the Intermediate-range Nuclear Forces (INF) Treaty was signed by the United States and the Soviet Union in December 1987, it established four points of entry in the former Soviet Union for inspectors, one of which was located in Almaty, Kazakhstan. (In Central Asia, only Kazakhstan, Turkmenistan, and Uzbekistan have facilities subject to inspection under the INF Treaty; the last two have only a single facility each and do not participate in on-site inspection activities or the related meetings.) Beginning in July 1988, US inspection teams from the On-Site Inspection Agency (OSIA) routinely visited the four sites in the Kazakhstan Soviet Socialist Republic that had missile and missile-related facilities subject to inspection under the treaty. For the first few years of inspections in Kazakhstan, these teams most often visited the elimination facility at Saryozek to monitor the destruction of SS-12 and SS-20 missiles. Under the eyes of US military officers, the first SS-12 missiles were destroyed at Saryozek on 1 August

1988; the final missile was destroyed on 27 October 1989, with Capt John Williams, USN, serving as the chief of the American inspection team.[2]

Although short-notice inspections under the INF Treaty continued irregularly after 1989, the primary concern after December 1991 was Kazakhstan's new strategic nuclear arsenal. Almaty had inherited 1,040 nuclear warheads mated to 104 SS-18 intercontinental ballistic missiles (ICBM), 320 nuclear warheads for AS-15 cruise missiles, and 40 TU-95 strategic bombers as launch platforms.[3] Initially, the new Kazakhstani government was reluctant to denuclearize, citing its two nuclear-armed neighbors—Russia and China—as potential threats. Ultimately, with the promise of substantial US aid, Pres. Nursultan Nazarbayev consented to relinquish these weapons. On 13 December 1993, the Kazakhstani parliament ratified the Nuclear Non-Proliferation Treaty as a nonnuclear state. On the same day, Nazarbayev and US vice president Al Gore signed the SSD Framework Agreement and a series of subordinate implementing agreements that established a wide range of efforts between the two nations designed to eliminate the nuclear weapons, the delivery platforms, and the corresponding infrastructure.[4]

The signing of these agreements opened the gates for significant US financial assistance via the cooperative threat reduction (CTR) program. The CTR program, also known as Nunn-Lugar, had been initiated in 1991 by Senators Sam Nunn (D-GA) and Richard Lugar (R-IN) in response to concerns about the control of the nuclear arsenal throughout the former Soviet Union, but primarily in Russia, Ukraine, Belarus, and Kazakhstan. The DOD initially allocated $85 million to fund projects for withdrawing the nuclear weapons and destroying the missile silos, strategic bombers, and weapon storage areas (table A.1, figure A.1, appendix A). The program also provided emergency response equipment for use during the transport of nuclear weapons from Kazakhstan to Russia and established a government-to-government communications link with the Kazakhstani Ministry of Defense (MOD) to manage the arms control notification requirements.[5]

Although these efforts started slow, within 18 months, two highly successful goals had been accomplished: the transport of almost 600 kilograms of highly enriched uranium (HEU), sufficient for at least 20 nuclear weapons, from the Ulbinsky Metallurgy Plant in Ust-Kamenogorsk, Kazakhstan, to the Oak Ridge Plant in Tennessee in November 1994 (an effort known as Project Sapphire); and the final transfer of all deployed nuclear warheads from Kazakhstan to Russia in April 1995. The successes of the CTR program in initially eliminating the nuclear legacy established a solid foundation for security cooperation between Kazakhstan and the United States that continues to the present.

Related denuclearization efforts progressed as well. The first INF inspection in independent Kazakhstan was made at Petropavlovsk in February 1994, although a practice inspection had been conducted at Saryozek earlier to ensure the Kazakhstani side was prepared for the actual event. Short-notice inspections at the four facilities continued irregularly thereafter. Kazakhstan acceded to the Strategic Arms Reduction Treaty (START) on 5 December 1994, and OSIA teams began visiting the five facilities subject to inspection under that agreement soon thereafter. (In Central Asia, only Kazakhstan has facilities subject to inspection under the START and Conventional Forces in Europe [CFE] Treaties.) These denuclearization efforts led to increasing interaction between the armed forces of Kazakhstan and the United States.[6]

Democratization

The CTR program also offered the opportunity for a broader security-cooperation relationship with Kazakhstan. Among the subordinate documents of the SSD Framework Agreement was the "Memorandum of Understanding and Cooperation on Defense and Military Relations" between the MOD and DOD, signed by Kazakhstani minister of defense Gen Sagadat Nurmaganbetov and US secretary of defense William Perry on 14 February 1994.[7] This agreement established a broad program of defense and military contacts (DMC) between the two nations and outlined specific actions that each agreed to undertake. It was the first establishment of a US military-to-military contact program in Central Asia, and it later served as the model for others in the region. The military contact program was designed "to increase understanding and promote more stable military relations between the U.S. and the FSU [former Soviet Union] states, to encourage support for reform and the development of military forces under civilian control which are more responsive to democratically elected officials, to promote denuclearization of forces in the FSU, and to encourage cooperation in regional crises."[8] These military contact events, therefore, were part of an objective much broader but much more nebulous than securing the nuclear weapons: they also were intended to "democratize" the military forces of Kazakhstan. The DOD initially notified Congress of the intent to allocate approximately $1.9 million from the CTR program to the military contact program with Kazakhstan, although much of this funding remained unspent (table A.2, figure A.2, appendix A).[9]

Military Contact Program

During this early period, these military contact events were planned and executed by several different commands and organizations in a rather unsystematic manner and funded through a variety of programs beyond just CTR.[10] Kazakhstan and the rest of Central Asia, like the other regions of the former Soviet Union, were not assigned to any of the geographic unified commands under the US Unified Command Plan, which establishes missions and delineates areas of responsibility to the major commands in the US armed forces. As such, there was no single headquarters tasked to establish and maintain military relationships with these countries. (The Joint Staff retained responsibility, but was unable to provide much more than guidance and oversight.) Based on the success of its Joint Contact Team Program (JCTP) in Eastern Europe, US European Command (USEUCOM), based in Stuttgart, Germany, initiated many of the first contacts with Kazakhstan, but US Pacific Command (USPACOM) in Honolulu, Hawaii; US Atlantic Command (USACOM) in Norfolk, Virginia; the US Coast Guard in Washington, DC; and others also began to conduct military contact activities and establish relationships.[11] Each command funded, planned, and executed the events it perceived as useful, but the program lacked an overall plan or schedule that could coordinate and deconflict the range of events conducted with each country. In all cases, Central Asia was seen as peripheral to the other regions within the commands' areas of interest. The initial military contact events, although few in number and limited in scope, were a patchwork quilt of disparate activities with little integrating strategy beyond the idea that contacts, in and of themselves, would foster open, positive relationships and promote the democratization of these countries. Unfortunately, the ad hoc nature of the military contact program meant few records were kept that would provide details on the number or type of events that were conducted. By October 1995, at least eight military contact events were conducted with Kazakhstan using CTR funds, including visits to Kazakhstan by a US Army general officer and a US Coast Guard aviation assessment team; and visits by Kazakhstani delegations to the United States to participate in defense conversion meetings, a disaster relief conference, and an orientation visit to US Coast Guard facilities.[12]

Training and Education Programs

Along with the military contact program, the Central Asian states also benefited from other security-cooperation initiatives originally designed to promote democratic transitions in the emerging nations in Eastern Europe and the European portion of the former Soviet Union. The final year of the Bush administration brought recognition that security-cooperation activities could do more than promote forward presence, but could also promote the transition process within these countries to democratic governments and market-based economies: "It is time to refashion our security assistance. . . . We need to increase funding for military and defense contact programs and other activities designed to facilitate the successful transition of foreign militaries to democratic systems."[13] The Clinton administration expanded this concept, linking the existing IMET program, funded by the Department of State (DOS) but executed by the Department of Defense, to this goal.[14] The Department of State advocated for these funds under the Freedom Support Act within the broader construct of assisting political- and economic-reform efforts throughout the former Soviet Union. The proposal argued:

> Providing professional education to foreign defense personnel, both civilian and military, particularly in the proper role of the military in a democracy[,] is an effective way to support countries in transition to democracy. This training helps produce a professional and politically neutral armed forces under civilian control. . . . [D]irect civil-military relations training will: 1) promote the development of institutions and processes that will permit a more thorough integration of the armed forces into the larger national society; 2) encourage military personnel to respect their national constitutional framework, and its implications for the role of the military in a democracy; and 3) promote the development of civilian specialists in military affairs.[15]

But this effort was largely for Russia and Eastern Europe; the small amount of funding for Central Asia was included almost as an afterthought. In 1993 Congress first authorized $163 thousand for Kazakhstan, sufficient for the training of only eight students. It approved funding for Kyrgyzstan and Turkmenistan the following year and for Uzbekistan in 1995. (Tajikistan, embroiled in a civil war until 1997, would not receive funding until 2002.) IMET funding remained symbolic for the first few years: in 1995 the State Department requested $900 million for transition assistance in the former Soviet Union, of which $2.375 million was for the IMET program. Only $250 thousand was allocated for Central Asia (table A.5, figure A.4, appendix A).[16] The funds were intended to be used specifically for English language training and for instruction, via orientation tours, professional training, and mobile training teams, on appropriate civil-military relationships.[17] The modest level of funds was sufficient for a single language lab for each defense ministry and the training of a small number of students, most of whom received instruction to be English language teachers (fig. 2). From 1993 through 1995, Kazakhstan had 42 students come to the United States for training, while Uzbekistan had five, Turkmenistan had four, and Kyrgyzstan only three (table B.1 and figure B.1, appendix B).[18] Most of the training was accomplished at the Defense Linguage Institute English Language Center (DLIELC) in San Antonio, Texas (table B.2 and figure B.2, appendix B).

Figure 2. US-funded English language laboratory, Ministry of Defense, Ashgabat, Turkmenistan, July 1998 (Reprinted from Author's Personal Collection.)

The Central Asian states were also included in another initiative designed to promote democratic transitions in Eastern Europe. In June 1993, using the facilities of the US Army's Russian Institute in Garmisch, Germany, USEUCOM established the George C. Marshall European Center for Security Studies "to positively influence the development of security structures appropriate for democratic states." The Marshall Center offered a series of resident educational courses for civilian and military officials, and beginning in 1994, individuals from all five of the Central Asian states began to participate. (Of note, this was one of the very few US security-cooperation programs during the 1990s in which Tajikistan participated.)[19] The original curriculum consisted of a five-month course offered twice a year titled Program in Advanced Security Studies (PASS) on national security and defense planning in democratic societies. (The course is now three months long and offered three times a year.) In 1994 15 military officers and senior defense civilians representing all five Central Asian states attended the Executive PASS course; in 1995 another 26 completed the program (table B.5 and figure B.3, appendix B).[20] The Marshall Center, which also offered a variety of shorter courses and conferences, would play a significant role in the efforts to democratize the armed forces of Central Asia.

A Modest Beginning

Between 1993 and 1995, the US military had taken a few tentative steps toward building security relationships in Central Asia. These first efforts were almost entirely with Kazakhstan, although there were some tenuous ties with the armed forces of the other nations. But these programs, and their objectives, were largely viewed as a subset of the security-cooperation efforts in Eastern Europe and the European portion of the former Soviet Union—an afterthought, small efforts added on to the much larger initiatives conducted elsewhere. The goals—denuclearization and democratization—were ambitious. While the resources for denuclearization were extensive—and probably sufficient for the task—those for democratization were modest: adequate only for a few military contact events and some limited training opportunities. Given the very limited resources, US attempts to promote democratization within the armed forces of Central Asia could have made little progress.

Notes

1. *A National Security Strategy of Engagement and Enlargement* (Washington, DC: The White House, 1991), 9, 27, and 7.

2. George L. Rueckert, *On-Site Inspection in Theory and Practice: A Primer on Modern Arms Control Regimes* (Westport, CT.: Praeger, 1998), 26; Diane L. Smith, *Breaking Away from the Bear* (Carlisle, PA: US Army War College Strategic Studies Institute, 1998), 74–75; and Joseph P. Harahan, *On-Site Inspections under the Intermediate-range Nuclear Forces Treaty* (Washington, DC: Defense Threat Reduction Agency, 1996), http://www.dtra.mil/about/media/historical _documents/books/infbook/ch6e.cfm (accessed 30 March 2006).

3. *Kazakhstan: Reducing Nuclear Dangers, Increasing Global Security* (Washington, DC: Embassy of Kazakhstan and the Nuclear Threat Initiative, 2004), 62.

4. Emily E. Daughtry, "Forging Relationships, Preventing Proliferation: A Decade of Cooperative Threat Reduction [CTR] in Central Asia," *In the Tracks of Tamerlane: Central Asia's Path to the Twenty-First Century*, edited by Daniel L. Burghart and Theresa Sabonis-Helf (Washington, DC: National Defense University Press, 2004), 325.

5. This funding would reach $172.9 million by 31 January 1999. *Kazakhstan: The Cooperative Threat Reduction Program*, "Defense and Military Contracts," http://www.nti.org/db/nisprofs/kazakst/forasst/thectrpr. htm#contacts (accessed 10 February 2006); Daughtry, "Forging Relationships," 325 (see chap. 2, note 4); and Rueckert, *On-Site Inspection*, 193 (see chap. 2, note 2).

6. Rueckert, *On-Site Inspection*, 26 (see chap. 2, note 2); Smith, *Breaking Away*, 74–75 (see chap. 2, note 2); Harahan, *On-Site Inspections* (see chap. 2, note 2); "US Experts Advise Kazakhstan on Implementation of START," Remarks by US ambassador Linton Brooks and nuclear expert Dr. Edward Ifft, 19 August 1994, http://www.fas.org/news/kazakh/940819-357639.htm (accessed 30 March 2006); and "DTRA Fact Sheet: Strategic Arms Reduction Treaty (START) Inspection and Monitoring Sites in the Former Soviet Union, March 2006, http://www.dtra.mil/newsservices/fact_sheets/display.cfm?fs =start-fsu (accessed 30 March 2006).

7. President Nazarbayev signed this agreement in Washington, DC, during a state visit to deposit the signed Nuclear Non-Proliferation Treaty (the United States, United Kingdom, and Russia are the three depository states). Robert V. Barylski, "Kazakhstan: Military Dimensions of State Formation over Central Asia's Civilizational Fault Lines," *Civil-Military Relations in the Soviet and Yugoslav Successor States*, edited by Constantine P. Danopoulos and Daniel Zirker (Boulder, CO: Westview Press, 1996), 136; and Daughtry, "Forging Relationships," 337 (see chap. 2, note 4).

8. Marybeth Peterson Ulrich, *Democratizing Communist Militaries: The Cases of the Czech and Russian Armed Forces* (Ann Arbor, MI: The University of Michigan Press, 1999), 53; and Daughtry, "Forging Relationships," 324 (see chap. 2, note 4).

9. For a number of reasons, the Defense and Military Contact (DMC) program within the CTR program faced challenges in the early years in expending funds, and therefore funding has been erratic: the total 1994 allocation (for all of the former Soviet Union) was $13.6 million; 1995, $5 million; and 1996, $10 million. Katherine E. Johnson, "Sustaining Nuclear Threat Reduction Programs: The 'Bottom-Up' Approach," in *Dismantling the Cold War: U.S. and NIS* [Newly Independent States] *Perspectives on the Nunn-Lugar Cooperative Threat Reduction Program*, eds. John M. Shields and William C. Potter, (London, MA: The MIT Press, 1997), 247 and 408 (appendix: CTR Funding by Country, 1 July 1996); and *Kazakhstan* (see chap. 2, note 5).

10. Initially, these other funding sources included Official Representation Funds (ORF), used primarily to support dignitary visits, and commander in chief (CINC) Initiative Funds (CIF), the latter now known as Combatant Commander Initiative Funds (CIF). CIF, authorized under Title 10 *United States Code* (*USC*) section 166a, had been used since at least January 1990 for bi-

lateral and multilateral activities with foreign military personnel, including joint exercises, military training and education, and bilateral and regional cooperation programs; USEUCOM used it extensively for its military contact programs during the early years of the program. DOD Directive 7250.13, *Official Representation Funds*, 17 February 2005, http://www.dtic.mil/whs/directives/corres/pdf/725013p.pdf; DOD Directive 7280.4, *Commander in Chief's (CINC's) Initiative Fund (CIF)*, 26 October 1993; and Smith, *Breaking Away*, 43 (see chap. 2, note 2).

11. For a history of the development of USEUCOM's military contact program, see Robert T. Cossaboom, *The Joint Contact Team Program: Contacts with the Former Soviet Republics and Warsaw Pact Nations, 1992–1994* (Washington, DC: Joint History Office, Office of the Chairman of the Joint Chiefs of Staff, 1997).

12. "U.S.–Kazakstan Agreement to Seal Up World's Largest Nuclear Test Tunnel Complex," *DOD News Release*. Reference number 536–95, 3 October 1995, http://www.fas.org/nuke/control/ctr/news/95-10-03.html

13. *National Security Strategy*, 20 (see chap. 2, note 1).

14. IMET provides military training and education to selected foreign military and defense-associated civilian personnel on a grant basis. Training is provided in the United States or overseas by US military or civilian personnel or contractors. In 1976 Congress separated military training from the Military Assistance Program by establishing the IMET program. The original intent was twofold: (1) to encourage effectively mutual beneficial relations and increased understanding between the United States and foreign countries in furtherance of goals of international peace and security; and (2) to improve the ability of participating foreign countries to utilize their own resources, including defense articles and services obtained from the United States, with maximum effectiveness, thereby contributing to greater self-reliance by such countries. IMET is not the only program through which foreign countries can receive US military training—it may also be purchased through the FMS program using national funds or FMF grant funds. John A. Cope, *International Military Education and Training: An Assessment*, McNair Paper 44 (Washington, DC: National Defense University, October 1995), 5–6; and *Management of Security Assistance* (Wright-Patterson AFB, OH: Defense Institute of Security Assistance Management, June 2001), 543–46, 808.

15. Cope, *International Military Education and Training*, 42 (see chap. 2, note 14).

16. Fiscal Year 1995 allocations were Belarus, $100 thousand; Estonia, $200 thousand; Georgia, $75 thousand; Kazakhstan, $100 thousand; Kyrgyzstan, $50 thousand; Latvia, $200 thousand; Lithuania, $200 thousand; Moldova, $50 thousand; Russia, $700 thousand; Turkmenistan, $50 thousand; Ukraine, $600 thousand; Uzbekistan, $50 thousand. *Congressional Presentation for Building Democracy, Fiscal Year 1995* (Washington, DC: Department of State, 1995), 27, 43–44.

17. Ibid., 89, 91, 124, 127, 136–37.

18. Ibid., 137; *Congressional Presentation, Foreign Operations: Fiscal Year 1996* (Washington, DC: Department of State, 1996), 199–200; and *Congres-*

sional Presentation for Foreign Operations, Fiscal Year 1997 (Washington, DC: Department of State, 1997), 155.

19. *History of the George C. Marshall Center*, http://www.marshallcenter .org/site-graphic/lang-en/page-mc-about-1/xdocs/mc/factsheets-history/ 01-center.htm (accessed 27 February 2006; and author with Graduate Support Office, Marshall Center, correspondence, 13 February 2006.

20. Ulrich, *Democratizing Communist Militaries*, 65 (see chap. 2, note 8); and *Program in Advanced Security Studies*, http://www.marshallcenter.org/ site-graphic/lang-en/page-coll-pass-1/xdocs/coll/pass/pass-overview.htm (accessed 27 February 2006). The Web site offers the following description of the program:

> The PASS is a 12-week advanced course of study for security affairs professionals. It consists of both a core curriculum, which all participants take, and a series of elective seminars, from which participants may select based on their professional needs and interests. Designed for military officers in the ranks of lieutenant through colonel, as well as Ministry of Defense civilians, diplomats, national law enforcement officers, and officials from all ministries that deal with domestic and international security matters, the PASS will be offered three times in 2006.
>
> The PASS, taught in English, German, and Russian, consists of core studies, electives, and field studies augmented by assigned readings, seminar discussions, debates, panels and role-playing exercises. Students must be proficient in one of the three languages . . . .
>
> The Executive Program in Advanced Security Studies (EPASS) is designed for men and women, over the age of 35, that serve [sic] as lieutenant colonels, colonels, senior diplomats, parliamentary staffers, or equivalent ranks in internal, national security or border control agencies. The Leaders Program in Advanced Security Studies (LPASS) provides a forum for younger men and women, ages 25–35, serving as lieutenants through majors, young diplomats, and civilian counterparts serving in government agencies responsible for security issues.

Chapter 3

Expansion

*The goal is to prepare in advance, so that if we are ever
called to do a mission like this, we are not meeting people
for the first time.*

—Brig Gen Martin R. Berndt
explaining the CENTRASBAT
exercise in September 1997

The period from 1996 though 1998 marked a steep increase
in US security-cooperation efforts in Central Asia. Although
funding for the denuclearization efforts began to decline, funding for the IMET program tripled, funding for new initiatives
such as the ICP and FMF was initiated, military contacts and
exchange visits expanded and deepened, and many of the security-
cooperation programs began to focus on a new unit, the
CENTRASBAT. By the end of this period, USCENTCOM had
assumed responsibility for military relationships in Central
Asia. Most of the increase in activities was with Kazakhstan
and Uzbekistan, and, to a lesser degree, Kyrgyzstan. Turkmenistan, with a foreign policy of positive neutrality, limited its
interaction with the US military; Tajikistan was still suffering
from its civil war.

Roots of Expansion

There are a number of factors that contributed to the dramatic expansion of the security-cooperation programs in Central Asia. Most importantly, by the end of 1995, the nuclear
weapons in Kazakhstan had been secured, eliminating what
had been the primary and most immediate concern for the
United States. The ballistic and cruise missile warheads were
returned to Russia by April 1995, and the last nuclear device
in Kazakhstan, in limbo at the Semipalatinsk Nuclear Test Site
since 1990, was destroyed in May. Although much more work
remained on the program (the SS-18 ICBMs were returned to
Russia in September 1996 and the missile silos destroyed in

September 1999), the initial concerns regarding the nuclear warheads had been resolved.[1] Both the United States and Kazakhstan viewed these initial denuclearization efforts as successes in military cooperation, and senior policy officials and military officers in both countries were ready to build on those achievements.

Additionally, US perspectives on the role of security cooperation had continued to evolve during the early years of the Clinton administration. Security-cooperation activities were now seen as valuable tools to support *engagement*, the process of assisting the political and economic transformations in Eurasia, and in doing so expanding the number of nations with democratic governments and open economic systems. Engagement, in short, would lead to *enlargement* of stable, secure, prosperous, and free states—as described in the 1995 *National Security Strategy of Engagement and Enlargement*.[2] This new perspective fundamentally altered the role of US military forces in peacetime. Armed forces were no longer simply preparing and training for the next war. Instead, they were a critical tool used to promote US foreign policy objectives:

> The U.S. military plays an essential role in building coalitions and shaping the international environment in ways that protect and promote U.S. interests. Through means such as the forward stationing or deployment of forces, defense cooperation and security assistance, and training and exercises with allies and friends, our armed forces help to promote regional stability, deter aggression and coercion, prevent and reduce conflicts and threats, and serve as role models for militaries in emerging democracies.[3]

In 1995 the United States still had hopes that the Central Asian states would continue the modest steps taken toward political and economic reforms, although in reality very little had been accomplished. But a new concern arose: potential Russian monopolization of the energy infrastructure in Central Asia. By this time, it was clear that the oil and natural gas deposits in Kazakhstan, Turkmenistan, and Uzbekistan could form a significant percentage of the world's energy resources, and Washington wanted to ensure Moscow did not control their exploitation and shipment to the West. At the time, all of the existing oil and gas pipelines from Central Asia transited Russia, giving Moscow a monopoly in the export and distribution process. Promoting new pipelines that did not transit Russia had both a practical and a political aspect: while it would help guarantee free access to these resources, Washington also saw the development of the oil and gas deposits as the platform for economic prosperity and political development in Central Asia.[4]

These factors drove the Clinton administration to adopt a more active foreign policy in Central Asia, but also to alter its foreign policy toward Russia with regard to Moscow's involvement in the Caucasian and Central Asian states and their energy resources. Washington had originally viewed a democratizing Russia as a source for stability and security in these southern areas. By the mid-1990s, however, US officials had concluded this approach had failed. Although Russia had strategically and militarily withdrawn from the region, except for the deployment of forces in Tajikistan, it continued to deal with the Central Asian states with a heavy hand. The United States sought to promote the independence and sovereignty of the Central Asian states as a means of decreasing Russian influence, and in doing so increase the potential of these nations to adopt political and economic reforms. This challenge toward Russian hegemony in Central Asia marked the beginning of a new rivalry.

Washington's approaches to Central Asia were not unwelcome. By the mid-1990s, Kazakhstan, Uzbekistan, and Kyrgyzstan were eager to develop new military ties with Western nations, particularly the United States. The defense structures of the Commonwealth of Independent States (CIS) had proved to be completely inadequate, and Russia had quickly established bilateral military agreements with each nation to provide structure and continuity to the relationships. The Central Asian states largely welcomed the support, but by the mid-1990s had recognized its limitations. The Russian military was collapsing— deployments in Moldova, Georgia, and Tajikistan and the strategic morass in Chechnya left little to offer. Almaty, Bishkek, and Tashkent began searching for additional security partners, particularly in the West. Kazakhstan and Kyrgyzstan sought to balance new relationships with their existing ties to Russia, but Uzbekistan sought a strategic shift, and ultimately saw the United States as its primary partner.[5]

An important element of the desire to seek outside partners was the state of development of the armed forces of these nations.

Through this period, Kazakhstan, Kyrgyzstan, Turkmenistan, and Uzbekistan continued to grow, stabilize, and mature their armed forces. All had established their own defense ministries, and most had created specific offices within them responsible for international military cooperation.[6] Kazakhstan's first defense attaché to the United States, Lt Col Muslim M. Altynbayev, the son of Defense Minister Col Gen Mukhtar Altynbayev, was accredited by the DOD in May 1997.[7] The establishment of these organizations and the growth of indigenous capabilities meant these forces were better poised to absorb the increased programs offered by the United States.

A bureaucratic constituency similarly began to develop within the Departments of Defense and State that could advocate for increased resources and attention. By 1995 defense attachés had been assigned to the embassies in Kazakhstan and Uzbekistan; attachés would be assigned to the other countries in 1997.[8] Desk officers within various offices in the Defense and State Departments were specifically assigned to manage these growing programs in Central Asia and, by extension, the relationships with these countries. Offices, organizations, and commands no longer viewed security cooperation with Central Asia as a adjunct to the programs in Eastern Europe and Russia, but strategically important in its own right.

By the mid-1990s, the conditions were set for the United States to increase its military cooperation activities in Central Asia. Additional resources were found, new programs were added, and new relationships were built. Through its security -cooperation programs, the United States sought to balance its relationship to Kazakhstan with a new one involving Uzbekistan. At the time, many observers saw Uzbekistan to be the key to regional stability and advocated that Tashkent should receive primacy in US foreign policy in the region. Frederick Starr, soon to be the director of the new Central Asia–Caucasus Institute at Johns Hopkins University, argued in an influential *Foreign Affairs* article in early 1996 that Uzbekistan was "uniquely positioned to anchor the security of the region."[9] His thoughts were echoed by Zbigniew Brzezinski and others, including Secretary of Defense William J. Perry, who praised Uzbekistan as "an island of stability."[10] Nonetheless, US policy sought a balance between Tashkent and Almaty in this period, and security assistance funding continued to favor Kazakhstan, if only by a small amount.[11]

The United States and Uzbekistan initiated this new relationship when, on 13 October 1995, Secretary Perry and Uzbekistani minister of defense Lt Gen Rustam Akmedov signed a "Memorandum of Understanding and Cooperation on Defense and Military Relations," similar to the framework document agreed to by Kazakhstan in early 1994.[12] Both of these agreements established bilateral working groups (BWG) between the United States and each country. These working groups would meet on an annual basis to negotiate the broad areas of cooperation the two countries would undertake during the following year. The results of the BWGs were captured in a Plan of Cooperation that was signed by the secretary of defense and the respective minister of defense. The United States conducted separate BWGs with Kazakhstan and Uzbekistan that outlined cooperative efforts for 1996, providing a certain measure of structure to the activities. Washington wanted to avoid favoring one over the other, so along with relatively equal levels of funding and comparative levels of interaction, it promoted multilateral initiatives such as CENTRASBAT to encourage regional cooperation and reduce Russian influence.

Denuclearization

Denuclearization and democratization continued to be important objectives for the expanded security-cooperation efforts, but they became increasingly disconnected. Although the denuclearization effort originally spawned the military contacts program, one of the original methods for promoting democratization, by the mid-1990s these activities were almost completely separate. Part of this was due to the elimination of nuclear weapons in Kazakhstan, which meant there was no longer a need to establish military ties designed specifically to defuse a potential nuclear crisis; instead, the defense ties established through the military contact programs primarily were used to promote other objectives. Additionally, the CTR program increasingly used US (and occasionally Kazakh or Russian) contractors to carry out the actual activities in Kazakhstan, thereby reducing the interaction between uniformed members of the two military forces. Bureaucratically, the denuclearization effort was executed by the OSD, the Defense Special Weapons Agency (DSWA),[13] and the OSIA, while the military contact programs generally were conducted by the combatant commands such as USEUCOM, USACOM, and USPACOM.[14] Likewise, the bureaucratic structures in the Central Asian states separated the two activities. In Kazakhstan, denuclearization and arms control activities were managed by the Kazakhstan Center for Monitoring Arms Reductions and Supporting Inspection Activities (established in 1992, but beginning actual operations in 1995), while other security cooperation programs were managed by the International Military Cooperation Department within the Ministry of Defense.[15] As DOD agencies (including those conducting the CTR Program) began to increase their attention on proliferation issues, they began to work more closely with nonmilitary organizations within Kazakhstan, such as the Customs Service and Border Guards. (Although frequent restructuring and reorganization of governments ministries within Kazakhstan meant these services were occasionally subordinated to the Ministry of Defense.) Finally, USEUCOM, which conducted a significant percentage of the military contact events during the early years, increasingly linked those activities with programs such as the Marshall Center to reinforce the concept of democratization.

Proliferation Prevention

The CTR program continued to eliminate the remaining vestiges of the nuclear weapons infrastructure in Kazakhstan, but the emphasis and funding slowly began to shift toward securing and eliminating biological and chemical weapons and toward preventing the proliferation of the materials, technology, and knowledge needed to develop any type of weapon of mass destruction (WMD).

Based on the personal relationships established through the denuclearization effort, US and Kazakh officials agreed in June 1996 to jointly eliminate a legacy of the vast Soviet biological weapons program, the anthrax production facilities at Stepnogorsk, (for which $5 million was specifically authorized by Congress). Other initiatives soon followed, including an agreement to eliminate partially constructed chemical weapons facilities at Pavlodar and the expansion of the CTR program to Uzbekistan. In 1997, under a temporary umbrella agreement with the Uzbekistani Ministry of Defense, DOD began a five-year program to eliminate the chemical weapons production facility at Nukus, and, in October 2001, started to demilitarize the biological weapons testing range at Vozrozhdeniye Island.[16] Securing and eliminating biological and chemical weapons formed the core of the CTR program's work in Central Asia for the next six to seven years (table A.6 and figure A.5, appendix A).

The CTR program also initiated proliferation prevention efforts in Central Asia, but these were soon shifted to other agencies. From its inception, the CTR program included the objective of improving export controls and border security in recipient nations in order to prevent the proliferation of nuclear materials. In Kazakhstan, this effort included assistance in drafting the necessary legislation to support the new State Border Service and Customs Service and building infrastructure, but it also included the first transfer of equipment to Kazakhstani security forces. Six patrol boats, including five 27-foot Boston Whalers and one 42-foot Sea Ark, were delivered in late 1995 and early 1996 to assist with enforcement capabilities on the Caspian Sea. Originally intended for the Kazakhstani Customs Service, a ministerial restructuring meant these boats were ultimately delivered to the new Kazakhstani Navy, which was given the responsibility of maritime security. (Another ministerial reorganization in 1999 shifted these patrol boats to the State Border Service.) In conjunction with the transfer of the patrol boats, the US Army Corps of Engineers conducted a Port Engineering Infrastructure Survey at Aktau and Bautino, Kazakhstan, in July 1996. At the time, the Kazakhstani Ministry of Defense planned to establish a naval headquarters and training institute at Aktau, and the port survey was intended to determine its suitability for military use.[17]

At the end of 1995, however, the export controls initiative was removed from the CTR Program and the Defense Department and transferred to the Department of State, becoming the EXBS Program.[18] In 1995 Congress mandated DOD and the Federal Bureau of Investigation (FBI) establish a joint program to "deter, interdict, and prevent the possible proliferation and

acquisition of weapons of mass destruction (WMD) by organized crime groups and individuals" within the former Soviet
Union, primarily through law enforcement training and the
provision of some equipment. Similarly, in 1997 DOD established a joint effort with the US Customs Service (USCS), now
part of the Department of Homeland Security (DHS), to improve
the counterproliferation capabilities of border services. While
this program included some training, it primarily focused on
providing equipment.[19] These two programs have been combined under the title of the ICP. Funding for the program has
been modest—just over $3 million was spent in Central Asia
from 1995 through 1999 (table A.4, appendix A).[20]

Kazakhstan and Uzbekistan were the first nations in Central
Asia to benefit from the ICP. Joint DOD-FBI teams traveled to
Almaty and Tashkent in late 1996 to explain the program and
conduct country assessments. Both countries were invited to
send delegations to the DOD-FBI-sponsored WMD Executive
Seminars held in Budapest, Hungary; the Kazakh representatives attended in June 1997 and the Uzbeks in August. Kyrgyzstan was also admitted to the program in August 1997 and
attended the seminar the following February. Soon the ICP program began executing events in Central Asia: ICP teams managed a colloquium on legal issues in Uzbekistan in April 1998
and conducted a series of training events in Druzbha, Aktau,
and Almaty in July. Kazakh, Kyrgyz, and Uzbek delegations also
attended training through the ICP at the Department of Energy's
Pacific Northwest National Laboratory Radiation Academy in
Washington State in October 1998.[21]

Democratization

Simultaneously, the efforts to promote democratization within
the military forces in Central Asia also began to narrow its focus toward more specific objectives, although this development
was slow, uneven, and generally applicable only to Kazakhstan. Two specific objectives were deliberately identified through
bilateral Plans of Cooperation—noncommissioned officer professional development and defense resource management—and
one emerged through opportunity rather than deliberate planning—civil-military relations in the context of disaster response.

Military Contacts Program

The military contacts program matured and expanded during this period, assisted by several new initiatives. In 1992, as USEUCOM solidified its JCTP as the military contact program with nations of East Europe and the European portion of the former Soviet Union, the National Guard Bureau in Washington, DC, proposed creating a parallel State Partnership Program (SPP) to link specific state National Guard organizations with these same nations. The SPP started in the Baltic region (largely because the withdrawal of Soviet forces left these new states with no military forces, institutions, or equipment) with agreements signed in early 1993 with Estonia, Latvia, and Lithuania, but soon grew to include most of the nations in the region.[22] Kazakhstan was partnered with Arizona in 1993, but events did not start until 1995; Kyrgyzstan, Turkmenistan, and Uzbekistan were partnered in 1996 (table 2). (Tajikistan was eventually partnered in 2002.)

The SPP offered many advantages: having the National Guard as a resource ensured the military contact programs were not unduly affected by the major reductions in the active duty force structure through the 1990s; the Guard's role as citizen-soldiers provided increased exposure to the concepts of civil-military relations, and the SPP included opportunities for broad governmental, academic, and commercial ties between these states and nations.[23] The National Guard units began to conduct an increasing number of the military contact events each year.

The second initiative started with NATO. In January 1994 at the Brussels Summit, NATO leaders established the Partnership for Peace (PfP) Program as a means of developing practical

Table 2. State Partnership Program (SPP) agreements

Country	Partner State	Date of Agreement
Kazakhstan	Arizona	31 August 1993
Kyrgyzstan	Montana	30 July 1996
Tajikistan	Virginia	20 October 2003
Turkmenistan	Nevada	30 July 1996
Uzbekistan	Louisiana	30 July 1996

(Reprinted from National Guard Bureau, International Affairs [J5-IA)] http://www.ngb.army.mil/ia/states/states_map%5B1%5D.htm.)

military ties with its former adversaries in the Warsaw Pact
that would lead to partnerships, and for some, membership.
These ties were bilateral between NATO and the partner nation,
but the structure and many of the specific events conducted
under this program fostered increased multilateral ties. A nation joined the PfP program by signing a Framework Document,
in which it commits:

> to preserve democratic societies; to maintain the principles of inter-
> national law; to fulfill obligations under the UN Charter, the Universal
> Declaration of Human Rights, the Helsinki Final Act and international
> disarmament and arms control agreements; to refrain from the threat
> or use of force against other states; to respect existing borders; and to
> settle disputes peacefully. . . . to promote transparency in national de-
> fense planning and budgeting to establish democratic control over
> armed forces, and to develop the capacity for joint action with NATO in
> peacekeeping and humanitarian operations . . . The Framework Docu-
> ment also enshrines a commitment by the Allies to consult with any
> Partner country that perceives a direct threat to its territorial integrity,
> political independence or security.[24]

The partner nation defines the areas in which it wishes to
cooperate through a presentation document and then develops,
in concert with NATO, an Individual Partnership Program (IPP)
describing specific events that will help it meet its goals. These
events could be conducted by a NATO organization or by a
NATO member state under the PfP program. Over time, this
process can ultimately lead some nations to a Membership Action Plan, which identifies the specific actions necessary to be
eligible for full membership within NATO (table 3).

Most nations in Central Asia joined PfP soon after it was announced but it took until mid-1996 for Kazakhstan, Kyrgyzstan,
and Uzbekistan to develop their first IPPs. NATO's interest and

Table 3. Partnership for Peace (PfP) program framework documents

Country	Date	Signatory
Kazakhstan	27 May 1994	Foreign Minister Saudabayev
Kyrgyzstan	1 June 1994	President Akayev
Tajikistan	20 February 2002	Ambassador Rahimov
Turkmenistan	10 May 1994	Foreign Minister Shikmuradov
Uzbekistan	13 July 1994	Foreign Minister Saidkasimov

(Reprinted from NATO Partnership for Peace Web site http://www.nato.int/pfp/sig-cntr.htm.)

involvement in Central Asia remained limited throughout the 1990s with only a limited number of multinational events such as personnel exchanges, exercises, seminars, and conferences, often conducted by the United States or Turkey. The Central Asian states have been reluctant participants in NATO activities, however, preferring bilateral relationships whenever possible, and in recent years a number of NATO nations have established bilateral security cooperation programs to complement those done via the NATO channels. Often specific NATO activities are conducted by a single lead country such as Turkey and are often portrayed or perceived in country as bilateral activities.[25] Until 2002 the focus of these efforts was largely on civil-military cooperation, defense reform, civil defense and emergency response, peacekeeping, and with a few scientific and educational exchanges. While many of these efforts have continued, much more effort is now given to counterterrorism and counter-drug trafficking initiatives. But the PfP program helped reinforce US objectives of denuclearization and democratization and offered additional tangible objectives for its security cooperation efforts—increasing the interoperability of the Central Asian military forces so they could participate in NATO-led peacekeeping and humanitarian operations.[26]

To encourage the development of the PfP program, in July 1994 at a NATO meeting in Warsaw, Poland, Pres. William J. Clinton announced his intent to ask Congress for up to $100 million in funding for a new Warsaw Initiative Fund (WIF).[27] These funds could be used to fund partner nation participation in exercises, seminars, conferences, and other events that were either part of the nation's PfP program or that were agreed to be "in the spirit of" the PfP objectives. WIF could also be used to fund interoperability programs, including equipment transfers (table 4).

Only a few of these WIF interoperability programs, including the environmental exchanges, defense planning seminars, and defense resource management studies (DRMS) were implemented in Central Asia, and Kazakhstan and Uzbekistan were the primary recipients. Some were more successful than others: the defense environmental assessments and exchanges later became an important element of the military contact program, but the resource management studies were ultimately

35

Table 4. Interoperability programs eligible for Warsaw Initiative Fund (WIF) funding

Command, control, communications, computers, intelligence studies	Regional airspace studies
Logistics exchanges	Navigation aids studies
Public affairs exchanges	Civil-military planning seminars
Legislative affairs exchanges	Infrastructure assessments
Environmental exchanges	Defense assessments and studies
Inspector general exchanges	Defense planning seminars
Comptroller exchanges	Defense resource management studies
Parliamentary exchanges	Partnership information management

(Reprinted from DOD Manual 5105.38-M, *Security Assistance Management Manual* [Washington, DC: Defense Security Cooperation Agency, March 2006], 514.)

cancelled in 1998–1999 because USCENTCOM planners believed the training was not effective and the Kazakhstanis and Uzbekistanis were not focused on the effort.[28]

Beyond promoting increasing interoperability and integration with NATO, the WIF program offered the practical benefit of offering an additional source of funding, beyond CTR and Combatant Commander's Initiative Fund (CIF), for the military contact programs. This funding became available in 1996, with $1.125 million allocated for events with Kazakhstan, $25 thousand for Kyrgyzstan, $25 thousand for Turkmenistan, and $1.375 million for Uzbekistan allocated for that year.

Another source of funding for military contact events, known as the traditional commander in chief (CINC) activities (TCA) program, was initiated in 1996 specifically to support the foreign military interactions by the unified commanders. With certain restrictions, TCA funds could be used for:

- Military liaison teams
- Traveling contact teams
- State Partnership Programs
- Regional conferences and seminars
- Personnel and information exchanges
- Unit exchanges

- Staff assistance/assessment visits
- Training program review and assessments
- Ship rider programs
- Joint/Combined exercise observers
- Combined exercises
- Humanitarian civic assistance projects
- Bilateral staff talks
- Host nation medical and dental support meetings
- Guard and Reserve participation in these types of programs
- Program administration[29]

CTR and WIF, however, remained the most common sources of funding for military contact programs, and USCENTCOM, after it took over responsibility for the military contact program in Central Asia in 1999, seldom used TCA, reserving it for use with nations in the Middle East that were not eligible to receive CTR and WIF funding.[30]

In 1995, for the first time, the DOD developed bilateral annual military contact plans with Kazakhstan and Uzbekistan that attempted to capture all of the contact events scheduled for the following year. The number of events for each country grew dramatically as well. The program with Kazakhstan, for example, had 19 scheduled events for 1996, 26 for 1997, and 41 for 1998; for Uzbekistan 14, 18, and 39, respectively (table 5).

Table 5. Military contact events planned with the Central Asian states, 1996–1999

	1996	1997	1998	1999
Kazakhstan	19	26	41	40
Kyrgyzstan			12	22
Turkmenistan			7	15
Uzbekistan	14	18	39	34

Adapted from Director of Strategy and Plans, US Joint Chiefs of Staff, *Bilateral Military Contact Plans, Planning Reference Book*, 2000 Joint Chiefs of Staff/Office of the Secretary of Defense Planning Conference for the NIS Peacetime Engagement, Washington, DC, June 1999.

Note: Although military contact events may have been conducted with Kyrgyzstan and Turkmenistan prior to 1998, formal plans were not developed until then.

The plans do not tell the entire story, as some events each year were cancelled while others were added, but the growth in the program is evident. In August 1998, the US defense attaché in Tashkent, for example, noted that while 17 events were actually conducted in 1995, 27 were conducted in 1996, and 54 events in 1998.[31] Unfortunately, few records were kept on the number, type, or details of the military contact events that were executed in these countries.

As these events were conducted by a variety of commands (USEUCOM, USPACOM, USACOM, USCENTCOM, and the national guards from the SPP states), there was little focus to the individual military contact plans. Kazakhstan, which had the largest quantity of military contact events from 1996 through 1999 (for which the planning was done in 1995 through 1998), also had the largest range of visits, covering 25 separate topics over the four year period. Many of these topics, including the counternarcotics, legal, military police, air traffic control, communications, chaplain, financial management, personnel management, public affairs, engineering, logistics, and transportation functional areas, had only a single information exchange visit, raising the question of how useful these visits were in practical terms of influencing the development of the Kazakhstani armed forces. However, three main themes for cooperation began to figure prominently in the military contact plans of these countries through this period: officer and noncommissioned officer professional development programs, civil-military cooperation in response to natural disasters, and military medical operations. These three themes accounted for over 40 percent of the military contact events conducted in Central Asia during this period.[32]

However, the military contacts program was not coming close to achieving its primary objective of democratizing the armed forces of the Central Asian states, and it is not clear that the US planners involved in developing the events recognized democratization as a goal. The Military Contacts Program is authorized under *United States Code* Title 10, Section 168, specifically states: "The Secretary of Defense may conduct military-to-military contacts and comparable activities that are designed to encourage a democratic orientation of defense establishments and military forces of other countries."[33] As described by Dr. Marybeth Peterson Ulrich, "the legal basis of the program clearly supports military democratization activities aimed at influencing the ideological orientation of the participant states." Yet only about 40 percent of the planned contact events during this period could be considered as promoting a democratic orientation in this region. Surprisingly, almost 80 percent of those planned for Turkmenistan fall in this category (primarily because of the emphasis on events relating to civil-military responses to disasters), while the statistics for the other countries fall off dramatically: 53 percent in Kyrgyzstan, 40 percent in Kazakhstan, and 30 percent in Uzbekistan.[34]

Education and Training Programs

Commensurate with the expansion in military contacts was a vast expansion of the training and education programs, including increased attendance at the Marshall Center (which, incidentally, was included on the military contact plans for each country). Whereas only 14 individuals from Central Asia attended courses at the Marshall Center in 1994, on average 26 attended each year between 1995 and 1997, and 46 in 1998. (Many others attended shorter conferences at the Marshall Center.) The Marshall Center also began sponsoring conferences within the region that focused on democratization; the first of which was in Tashkent in August 1996 on "Democratic Oversight, Civil-Military Relations, and Regional Stability and Security in Central Asia" and the second in Almaty in December 1997.

Significant increases in IMET funding began in 1996.[35] IMET funding for Kazakhstan, Kyrgyzstan, Turkmenistan, and Uzbekistan, which totaled $370 thousand in 1995, more than tripled to $1.125 million in 1996, and grew steadily for the next several years. The State and Defense Departments continued to advocate for the IMET funding by stressing its role in promoting democratic reform in the region, arguing that the training provided by these funds would help establish military forces supportive of the "democratic and economic transition and committed to a durable pattern of cooperation with the West." Initially most of this funding continued to be used primarily for English language training, both for student attending follow-on courses and for training English language instructors, but the increased funding allowed Central Asian military officers to also attend courses in maritime search and rescue, military justice, defense resource management, and infantry training.[36] Central Asian officials were eager to take advantage of this opportunity; even Turkmenistani president Niyazov allowed one of his lieutenants to attend infantry officer training in the United States.[37]

Another of the important aspects of the expansion of the IMET program was having sufficient funding to allow offering seats to Kazakhstan and Uzbekistan at US staff and war colleges.[38] Each of the US military services operates its own tiered educational system, known collectively as professional military education (PME), for the development of its officer corps, with specific schools and colleges for selected officers as they progress in rank. Initially, Kazakhstan and Uzbekistan were invited to attend the staff colleges for mid-grade officers (majors and lieutenant colonels, lieutenant commanders and commanders); the curriculum at these schools lasts a full academic year. The first Kazakhstani officers graduated from the Army Command and General Staff College (CGSC) at Fort Leavenworth, Kansas, and the College of Naval Command and Staff (CNSC) in Newport, Rhode Island, in 1997 and from the Air Command and Staff College (ACSC) at Maxwell AFB, Alabama, in 1998; the first Uzbekistani officers graduated from ACSC in 1997 and CNSC in 1998 (table B.4, appendix B). These courses, although among the most expensive offered through the IMET program, are the best methods for providing professional education, appreciation of US perspectives on democratic principles, and exposure to American life because of their length, exposure to American military counterparts, and opportunities to live in American communities.

Expanded IMET Program

The continuing emphasis on using security cooperation program to promote democratic reform was encouraged by a modification to the IMET Program mandated by Congress in 1991. Known as Expanded IMET (E-IMET), it had two significant implications. First, training could be provided to civilian personnel outside of the ministries of defense whose duties include defense or security-related issues, such as individuals in the legislative branch or members of a nongovernmental organization. Second, a percentage of each country's IMET allocation was required to be used for courses that emphasized themes that supported democratization:

- Respect for democracy and civilian rule of law, including the principle of civilian control of the military

- Respect for internationally recognized standards of human rights

- Military justice systems in democratic societies

- Responsible defense resource management[39]

Some countries with poor human rights records, such as Indonesia and Guatemala, were permitted to take only courses that qualified under the E-IMET program (this restriction was lifted from Indonesia in 2005). Initially the requirement to use a certain percentage of funding on E-IMET courses was politically sensitive in some countries, but as a condition of receiving aid it proved very effective. After a few years it was dropped as increasing numbers of courses had their curriculums modified to qualify as E-IMET and as countries requested valued courses, such as attendance at staff and war colleges (described below), that met the criteria. Currently, security assistance program managers simply seek to find a balance between E-IMET courses and technical training, and E-IMET courses have consistently made up a significant portion of the education and training courses offered to the Central Asian military forces under the IMET program. Appendix D provides a listing of courses that qualify under the E-IMET Program.

The Expanded IMET program spawned institutes which offered programs specifically designed to meet the goals of promoting military justice systems, defense resource management, and civil-military relations. The Defense Institute for International Legal Studies (DIILS), which originated as the International Training Detachment of the Navy Justice School at Newport, Rhode Island, began providing courses named Disciplined Military Operations and Military Justice in Kazakhstan and

Uzbekistan, respectively, in 1996, and to date has trained over 400 students from Central Asia (table B.5, appendix B). The Defense Resource Management Institute (DRMI) at the Naval Postgraduate School (NPS) in Monterey, California, received its first in-residence students from Kyrgyzstan and Uzbekistan in 1996, and subsequently trained a total of 87 students from the region through in-residence courses and mobile education teams (MET) (table B.6, appendix B). A third specialized institution, the Center for Civil-Military Relations (CCMR), also at the NPS, accepted its first students from Central Asia in 2003 (table B.7, appendix B).

Military Academies and Flight Training

Two other specialized training and education opportunities, not part of the IMET program, were also offered in Central Asia during this period: attendance at the military service academies and participation in flight training. In 1998 the United States invited Kazakhstan, Kyrgyzstan, and Uzbekistan to nominate promising young individuals to attend the US service academies: the US Military Academy at West Point, New York; the US Naval Academy at Annapolis, Maryland, and the US Air Force Academy at Colorado Springs, Colorado.[40] The nominees were required to meet the same stringent physical and educational application requirements as US applicants to be selected. (Frequently foreign nominees are academically deficient because of the differences in education systems or due to poor English language skills.) There are nearly 10 thousand applicants each year for each academy, and less than 20 foreign students are admitted to each one. Foreign students are fully integrated into every aspect of the academy program and upon graduation are awarded a bachelor's degree and are expected to be commissioned in the armed forces of their parent nation.

Kyrgyzstan was the first to have a nominee selected—Cadet Marat Davletshin entered West Point in 1998 and graduated with the Class of 2002—and has been the most successful, with a total of five individuals accepted at three academies. Kyrgyzstan currently has two students at West Point, both of whom will graduate in 2008 and, despite a lack of a navy or a significant air force, a student at the US Naval Academy and one at the US Air

Force Academy, both in the class of 2007. Kazakhstan has had two graduates from West Point (in 2004 and 2005), with another graduating in 2007 (table B.8, appendix B, and fig. 3).[41]

The second specialized training opportunity was the ALP, funded by the US Air Force through its normal operating budget. Established first in 1996, ALP offered a year of English language training followed by a year of flight training at Columbus AFB, Mississippi, in T-37 trainers, the same type of aircraft used by US Air Force pilots as they begin flight training. Upon graduation, the foreign officer is awarded US Air Force flight wings. Only 20 such invitations are extended to foreign air forces each year, and Uzbekistan was offered a slot in 1998. The ALP program was discontinued between 1999 and 2001 because the increased requirement for flight training quotas by the US Air Force left few available for optional security assistance programs, but when it resumed, invitations were offered to Kazakhstan, Kyrgyzstan, Turkmenistan, and Uzbekistan (table B.9, appendix B).

Including the Central Asian states in these specialized, long duration, training and education opportunities such as the service academies and the ALP program, while supporting the

Figure 3. Kazakhstani Cadet Elena Milyuk with US general Richard Myers, chairman of the Joint Chiefs of Staff, at the West Point graduation, June 2005 (Reprinted from the collection of Col Assylbek Mendygaliev, defense attaché of the Republic of Kazakhstan. Used with permission.)

objective of promoting democratization within the armed forces, had a secondary objective. These programs were considered to be long-term investments in the future military leadership of the armed forces of Central Asia. It was assumed that the US military education and training offered through the war colleges, academies, and flight training was so superior to other avenues that these young officers would quickly rise to positions of authority and influence as they progressed in their careers. In short, these programs specifically sought to groom future commanders of foreign militaries: "An ALP candidate should be a top graduate of the participating country's air force academy or other young officer with potential to achieve top leadership positions in their air force."[42] The experiences these foreign officers gained through their long study programs in the United States, side-by-side with young American military officers and cadets, would leave them with a fundamentally favorable perspective of the United States, and the personal friendships created through these two- and four-year programs would pay great benefits in future years when both the American and foreign officers reached higher positions.

Regional Cooperation

A key component of US policy in Central Asia in this period was reducing Russian influence and integrating Central Asia into Western economic and political structures, and the strategy used to achieve this goal was to increase the national sovereignty of the Central Asian states and promote regional cooperation among them. In this way, it was believed, each of the nations could individually and collectively oppose Russian pressures in political, economic, and security matters, while simultaneously advancing their own political and economic reforms. Regional cooperation became a new and important objective in US security cooperation programs.

US planners, searching for a means to put policy into action, turned to a new initiative—the Central Asian Battalion, or CENTRASBAT—a combined peacekeeping unit consisting of companies from Kazakhstan, Kyrgyzstan, and Uzbekistan. From the US perspective, CENTRASBAT would provide an alternative to Russian predominance in managing regional crises and would give the Central Asian states a means to respond on their own.[43] Soon this unit and its related annual exercise would come to dominate US security cooperation efforts in the region.

Central Asian Battalion

In December 1995, the Council of Defense Ministers of Kazakhstan, Kyrgyzstan, and Uzbekistan proposed the creation of a combined peacekeeping battalion that could operate in UN-sponsored missions. This proposal was approved by the presidents of the three nations, and the concept was expanded to include requesting NATO assistance in training and equipping CENTRASBAT under the PfP program.[44]

With a strength of approximately 500 men, CENTRASBAT was to consist of a headquarters staff, three motorized rifle companies (one from each nation), reconnaissance and medical detachments, mortar and air defense batteries, and grenade launcher and engineering platoons. All elements of the unit, including those from Uzbekistan and Kyrgyzstan, were to be garrisoned at Zhibek-Zholy in the Chimkent region of Kazakhstan, near the border with Uzbekistan. Kazakhstan and Uzbekistan each contributed 40 percent and Kyrgyzstan 20 percent to the estimated $2 million annual cost of maintaining the unit.[45]

NATO did not rush to assist in the creation of the unit, but US officials were eager to get involved. CENTRASBAT offered several benefits. First, it could serve as a visible and active method for promoting regional cooperation, and it would help distance these nations from Russia. From the US perspective, even President Nazarbayev appeared to agree with this approach when he stated in May 1996 that the unit was not meant to support territorial claims against another nation, "but we don't want other states to have territorial claims against us."[46] Second, it would help provide a nexus to focus the expanding elements of US security cooperation programs. Third, following its experiences in Somalia and the former Yugoslavia, the United States was eager to train other nations to take over peacekeeping duties in troubled spots around the world. USACOM, which had already hosted Kyrgyz and Uzbek detachments at Fort Polk, Louisiana, for Cooperative Nugget 95, a peacekeeping and refugee assistance exercise, stepped forward to lead the US participation.

USACOM conducted two major CENTRASBAT exercises. The first started in August 1997 with detachments from Kazakhstan, Kyrgyzstan, and Uzbekistan undergoing airborne refresher training at Fort Bragg, North Carolina. On 14 September, these 40 soldiers plus 500 members of the US 82d Airborne Division embarked on an 18-hour, 7,700 mile nonstop flight in six C-17 cargo aircraft from Pope AFB, North Carolina, to Chimkent, Kazakhstan, for the longest airborne drop in history. There they were joined by another 80 troops from Turkey and Russia, who also arrived directly from their home countries, and the 620 airborne troops, hit the landing zone within a short two-hour period. Marine Corps general John Sheehan, commander of USACOM, led the airborne drop as the first one out of the aircraft. On the ground, the forces practiced securing the Sairam airport against a simulated adversary. Joined by the remainder of the CENTRASBAT unit, they practiced peacekeeping skills such as controlling checkpoints, inspecting vehicles, providing humanitarian assistance, and maintaining separation zones. After two days of training, all but 120 of the US soldiers returned home, and the exercise shifted to Uzbekistan for the second stage, which consisted of additional peacekeeping training with Turkish, Russian, Latvian, and Georgian troops.[47]

CENTRABAT 97 served its purposes. First, it visibly demonstrated to Russia that the United States was engaging in a new, active role in promoting stability and security in Central Asia. General Sheehan emphasized both points when he remarked that the exercise indicates "the US interest that the Central Asian states live in stability," and the fact that "there is no nation on the face of the earth where we can't go."[48] These sentiments were not lost in Moscow. In less than a week, the Russian State Duma issued a statement condemning the exercise, claiming: "Under the guise of statements on the peacekeeping nature of such maneuvers, the US Armed Forces are intensively developing new potential theaters of military actions in the immediate vicinity of Russia's frontiers. It cannot be ruled out that in the course of such long-range troop landings, a possible landing of US Army units on Russian territory is also being developed."[49]

CENTRASBAT 97 also demonstrated to the Central Asian leaders that mutual cooperation can bring results. Sheehan laid the credit directly at their doors: "Three years ago, people said this type of operation was not possible. I say, look at what is happening today. It did happen, because the three presidents [of Kazakhstan, Uzbekistan, and Kyrgyzstan] wanted it to happen, and the three ministers [of defense] made it happen."[50]

But CENTRASBAT 97 also carried with it the seeds of its own demise. The exercise scenario was artificially constructed to include the first stage in Kazakhstan and the second in Uzbekistan to avoid slighting one of the two major participants. Seeking balance, or at least avoiding the appearance of favoritism, became a fundamental rule for US planners. The exercise also included elaborate opening and closing ceremonies which tended to overshadow the more mundane training aspects. In time, CENTRASBAT would become more of a showcase unit and exercise rather than one preparing for potential combat or peacekeeping operations. And while the Central Asians were generally enthusiastic participants, even to the point of painting their vehicles white with big blue UN markings, American observers were disappointed in their skills and concluded it would be years before CENTRASBAT became a viable unit. Retired US Army major general James Johnson, then serving as DOD's military representative to Central Asia, remarked: "As far as it went, the training conducted for this exercise was good, but it didn't teach proficiency. The 82d's training doctrine is to teach soldiers to crawl, walk, and run. Here, they are learning to crawl and beginning to walk, but they aren't learning to run. That's going to take a lot more time."[51] It is not clear, however, that this assessment was ever passed to the ministers of defense of the Central Asian states, and their frustration with the slow progress of the unit would soon become evident.

USACOM repeated the exercise in September 1998, this time with 259 soldiers from the 10th Mountain Division from Fort Drum, New York, and 272 members of CENTRASBAT. Another 200 soldiers from Turkey, Russia, Georgia, and Azerbaijan also participated in the peacekeeping and humanitarian assistance exercise. Again, the exercise was split, starting at the CENTRASBAT garrison in Zhibek-Zholy in Kazakhstan, moving to Chirchik in Uzbekistan for seminars, and then to Osh in Kyrgyzstan for field training (fig.4). Notably, the Kazakhs angered their Uzbek hosts by conducting their airborne drop ahead of schedule.[52]

Figure 4. Uzbekistani army contingent of CENTRASBAT, Chirchik, Uzbekistan, July 1998 (Reprinted from author's personal collection.)

Multilateral and Bilateral Exercises

CENTRASBAT was not the only exercise used to promote regional cooperation. The United States also invited these nations to a series of multilateral exercises it had been conducting under NATO's PfP program. As mentioned above, in August 1995, even before formal military cooperation programs had been established with Kyrgyzstan and Uzbekistan, platoons from those two countries were invited to Fort Polk, Louisiana, to participate in Cooperative Nugget 95, a peacekeeping and refugee assistance exercise. Along with being the first PfP exercise held in the United States, Cooperative Nugget 95 was the first time US and Central Asian troops had trained together in a combined exercise. The following year, a platoon from Kazakhstan's CENTRASBAT element joined them at Camp Lejeune, North Carolina, for a peacekeeping and amphibious assault exercise called Cooperative Osprey 96. These exercises, conducted by USACOM, soon became a routine part of the growing military cooperation program during this period, and the three nations generally sent elements of their CENTRASBAT unit to participate. All three nations returned to Fort Polk in June–July 1997 for Cooperative Nugget 97 and then again to Camp Lejeune in June 1998 for Cooperative Osprey 98. The Central Asian states also participated in NATO PfP exercises sponsored by USEUCOM; including the communications and information systems interoperability exercise Combined Endeavor 98 in Sembach, Germany. These exercises offered the Central Asian states opportunities to train with other NATO nations as well as work together in a relatively benign training environment. (Kazakhstan was to participate in the Combined Endeavor exercise each year thereafter.)[53]

Concurrent with these multilateral exercises, but not directly designed to promote regional cooperation, the United States also began a series of bilateral special operations forces exercises (SOFEX) with the special forces of Kazakhstan and Uzbekistan.[54] As Central Asia was not assigned to any of the regional unified commands, US Special Operations Command, Pacific (USSOCPAC) in Hawaii initiated the program, turning to its 1st Special Forces Group (SFG) at Fort Lewis, Washington, for the personnel. This was an unusual choice, as the 1st SFG's skills include Asian languages such as Korean, Chinese, or Japanese, rather than Russian, Uzbek, or Kazakh, but it reflects the challenge of establishing a new program and the multiple commands operating in the region during this period. Balance Kayak exercises were held in Kazakhstan in August 1996, June 1997, August 1998, and spring 1999, focusing primarily on combat medical training and civic action. Balance Ultra exercises were held in Uzbekistan in autumn 1996, June 1997, September 1998, and June 1999 in the Ferghana Valley, and focused on combat medical training and mountain training. In 1999 US forces planned to expand the program to Turkmenistan with a counter-drug exercise using personnel from the 5th SFG at Fort Bragg, North Carolina, subordinate to US Special Operations Command, Central (USSOCCENT), but it is not clear whether this exercise ever took place.[55]

Equipment Transfers

The emphasis on the CENTRASBAT unit, peacekeeping operations, and NATO interoperability through the PfP program also opened the door to the first set of military equipment transfers from the DOD to the armed forces of Central Asia.[56] Under certain conditions governed by the Foreign Assistance Act (FAA) of 1961, the Arms Export Control Act (AECA) of 1976, and the International Traffic in Arms Regulation (ITAR), foreign military forces are permitted to purchase defense goods from the United States via the FMS program. On 19 March 1997, President Clinton issued Presidential Determination 97-19 authorizing Kazakhstan, Kyrgyzstan, Turkmenistan, and Uzbekistan to use the FMS program—and, except for Tajikistan, the last of the post-Soviet states to gain this approval. As for all countries, however, this authorization was not a carte blanche—all requests for military equipment were carefully controlled by DOD and DOS, with significant Congressional oversight on major weapon sales. Simultaneous with the Presidential Determination, the State Department requested Congress authorize FMF grant funds in 1997 for Kazakhstan, Kyrgyzstan, Turkmenistan, and Uzbekistan to purchase US defense goods and services. The State Department justified this request by linking it with the missions of the CENTRASBAT unit: "to enhance . . . capability to operate jointly with NATO forces in peacekeeping, search and rescue, humanitarian and other operations," a rationale that stayed consistent for the next several years.[57]

In 1997 the first year FMF was authorized for Central Asia, Kazakhstan received $1.5 million; Kyrgyzstan, $800 thousand; Turkmenistan, $500 thousand; and Uzbekistan, $1 million. In 1998 these amounts increased by about 50 percent, and then stabilized for the next several years (table A.6 and fig. A.5, appendix A). In 1998 Kazakhstan, Kyrgyzstan, Turkmenistan, and Uzbekistan were also authorized to receive surplus US military equipment at no cost through the Euro-Atlantic Excess Defense Articles (EDA) program.[58] The provision of FMF and the authorization for EDA, however, did not lead to immediate deliveries. It would take several more years before US military equipment began arriving in Central Asia.

Reaching the Summit

From 1995 to 1998, US security cooperation objectives in Central Asia expanded; while some become more diffused, others became more focused. The major programs for denuclearization were completed in Kazakhstan and efforts to address proliferation and export control issues began. US efforts to promote democratization became somewhat more focused during this period, with military contact events and education programs starting to focus on defense resource management and officer and noncommissioned officer professional development, particularly in Kazakhstan. And only in Kazakhstan, however, was this objective formally stated in the planning documents. But the military contact program also became much more diffuse, with multiple commands executing events across a broad range of topic areas. And despite the fact that both the military contact program and the training and education programs were justified as promoting the democratization of the armed forces in Central Asia, there was little evidence that US security-cooperation planners saw themselves in that role and actively pursued that fairly vague objective, except in the case of defense resource management and officer and noncommissioned officer professional development. Likewise, US and Central Asian forces began to exercise together in both multilateral and bilateral forums, including in the hallmark annual CENTRASBAT event, and the United States initiated the FMF and EDA programs to offer military equipment to these nations. The rapid growth in security cooperation programs appeared to be having some impact, but the Central Asian states were still waiting for the true benefits to appear.

This growth, however, must be put into context. Central Asia remained strategically unimportant in US security cooperation planning, greatly overshadowed by larger and more complex programs conducted in other regions such as Eastern Europe. The US military planned approximately 100 military contact events with Kazakhstan from the beginning of the program through 1998, while it planned almost 700 events with the Czech Republic in essentially the same period.[59] The State Department provided just over $4 million in IMET funding from 1996 to 1998 to Kazakhstan, Kyrgyzstan, Turkmenistan, and Uzbekistan, a combined total of only 80 percent of what was provided to the three Baltic States during the same period. Likewise, FMF funding in the same period totaled $9.4 million for the four nations, roughly equivalent to what was offered to

Uganda. Despite the relative expansion of the programs compared to what had been conducted through 1995, Central Asia remained a backwater in US security cooperation efforts.

Notes

1. *Kazakhstan*, 63–64 (see chap. 2, note 3).

2. *A National Security Strategy*, 9–10 (see chap. 2, note 1).

3. *A National Security Strategy for a New Century* (Washington, DC: The White House, 1997), 8.

4. Stephen Blank, "The United States and Central Asia," in *Central Asian Security: The New International Context*, edited by Roy Allison and Lena Jonson (Washington, DC: Brookings Institution Press, 2001), 130–31.

5. Marina Pikulina, *Uzbekistan in the Mirror of Military Security: A Historical Preface to Current Events* (Surrey, United Kingdom: The Conflict Studies Research Centre), 1999, 1–3.

6. Kazakhstan established its Ministry of Defense in May 1992, Kyrgyzstan in August 1993, Tajikistan in December 1992, Turkmenistan in July 1992, and Uzbekistan in early 1992. Susan Clark, "The Central Asian States: Defining Security Priorities and Developing Military Forces," in *Central Asia and the World: Kazakhstan, Uzbekistan, Tajikistan, Kyrgyzstan, and Turkmenistan*, ed. Michael Mandelbaum, (New York: Council on Foreign Relations, 1994), 206.

7. Author with Defense Intelligence Agency (DIA), correspondence, February 2006.

8. The Defense Attaché Office in Almaty, Kazakhstan, was established in January 1994; in Tashkent, Uzbekistan, in November 1995; in Bishkek, Kyrgyzstan, in February 1997; in Ashgabat, Turkmenistan, in July 1997, and in Dushanbe, Tajikistan, in October 1997 (Although, the attaché for Tajikistan was normally based in Almaty and traveled to Tajikistan on an irregular basis with an armed escort.) Author with DIA, correspondence, April 2006.

9. Frederick Starr, "Making Eurasia Stable," *Foreign Affairs* 74, no. 1 (January/February 1996), 85.

10. Shahram Akbarzadeh, *Uzbekistan and the United States: Authoritarianism, Islamism, & Washington's Security Agenda* (New York: Zed Books, 2005), 62–65.

11. From 1995 to 1999, Kazakhstan received $1.844 million in IMET funds, $5.550 million in FMF, and four war college slots; Uzbekistan received $1.657 million in IMET, $4.200 million in FMF, and three war college slots. Only in one area did Uzbekistan receive more than Kazakhstan: Tashkent was offered an Aviation Leadership Program scholarship in 1998. See tables A.1–A.6, appendix A.

12. Turkmenistan would eventually sign a similar, although much shorter and vaguer, "Joint Statement on the Results of US–Turkmenistani Defense Consultations" in April 1998; the United States and Kyrgyzstan never established a framework agreement. Director of Strategy and Plans, US Joint

Chiefs of Staff, *Planning Reference Book*, 2000 Joint Chiefs of Staff/Office of the Secretary of Defense Planning Conference for the NIS [newly independent states] Peacetime Engagement, Washington, DC, June 1999.

13. Formerly the Defense Nuclear Agency.

14. Rueckert, *On-Site Inspection*, 170 (see chap. 2, note 2); and Harahan and Bennett, *Creating the Defense Threat Reduction Agency*, 10–12 (see chap. 2, note 2).

15. Rueckert, *On-Site Inspection*, 184 (see chap. 2, note 2); and Trip Report, Central Asia Orientation Visit, Maj Michael J. McCarthy, US Central Command (USCENTCOM) Directorate of Intelligence, 31 July 1998. Of note, Col Assylbek Mendygaliev, who was the director of the Kazakhstani Center for Arms Reduction in 1998 during the first official USCENTCOM visit to the region, is now the defense attaché of the Republic of Kazakhstan in Washington, DC.

16. Daughtry, "Forging Relationships," 330–33 (see chap. 2, note 4).

17. *Kazakhstan Port Engineering Infrastructure Survey*, (Stuttgart, Germany: US Army Corps of Engineers Transatlantic Programs Center, Europe, 1996), 1.

18. Cooperative threat reduction (CTR) funds continued to be used for these programs until 1997, at which time Congress appropriated separate funding accounts. "Interdicting Nuclear Smuggling: International Counterproliferation Program," Nuclear Threat Initiative, http://www.nti.org/e_research/cnwm/interdicting/index.asp; Daughtry, "Forging Relationships," 326–27 (see chap. 2, note 4); and "Cooperative Threat Reduction Assistance to Kazakhstan," (see chap. 2, note 12).

19. Office of the Coordinator of US Assistance to the NIS, *U.S. Government Assistance to and Cooperative Activities with the New Independent States of the Former Soviet Union, FY2000 Annual Report* (Washington, DC: Department of State, 2001), 239–40; and "Interdicting Nuclear Smuggling (see chap. 3, note 18).

20. Office of the Coordinator of US Assistance to the NIS, *U.S. Government Assistance To and Cooperative Activities with the New Independent States of the Former Soviet Union, FY2000 Annual Report* (Washington, DC: Department of State, 2001), 240, Appendix 1; Office of the Coordinator of US Assistance to the NIS, *U.S. Government Assistance To and Cooperative Activities with the New Independent States of the Former Soviet Union, FY2001 Annual Report* (Washington, DC: Department of State, 2002), 260, Appendix 1; Office of the Coordinator of US Assistance to the NIS, *U.S. Government Assistance To and Cooperative Activities with the New Independent States of the Former Soviet Union, FY2002 Annual Report* (Washington, DC: Department of State, 2003), Appendix 1; Office of the Coordinator of US Assistance to the NIS, *U. S. Government Assistance To and Cooperative Activities with the New Independent States of the Former Soviet Union, FY2003 Annual Report* (Washington, DC: Department of State, 2004), 240, Appendix 1; Office of the Coordinator of US Assistance to the NIS, *U.S. Government Assistance To and Cooperative Activities with the New Independent States of the Former Soviet Union, FY2004 Annual Report* (Washington, DC: Department of State, 2005), Appendix 1.

21. Author with Defense Threat Reduction Agency, correspondence, April 2006.

22. Of interest, USEUCOM also attempted to establish relationships using units from the Army Reserve, thereby increasing both the bilateral ties and the units available for military contact events. Kazakhstan was partnered with the 63d Army Reserve Command (63d ARCOM), which consisted of reserve combat service and combat service support units in California, Arizona, and Nevada. That relationship apparently never developed, as there is no indication that the 63d ARCOM played a role in the military contact events of the mid-to-late 1990s and is not part of the current program. Cossaboom, *The Joint Contact Team Program*, 19–20 (see chap. 2, note 11).

23. John R. Groves Jr., "PfP and the State Partnership Program: Fostering Engagement and Progress," *Parameters* XXIX, no. 1 (Spring 1999), 43–53.

24. *The Partnership for Peace*, NATO, http://www.nato.int/issues/pfp/index.html (accessed 22 March 2006).

25. Robin Bhatty and Rachel Bronson, "NATO's Mixed Signals in the Caucasus and Central Asia," *Survival* 42, no. 3 (Autumn 2000), 132–33.

26. Jennifer D. P. Moroney, "Building Security in Central Asia: A Multilateral Perspective," in *In the Tracks of Tamerlane: Central Asia's Path to the 21st Century*, ed. Daniel L. Burghart and Theresa Sabonis-Helf (Washington, DC: National Defense University Press, 2004), 348–49.

27. The total amount of $100 million for the Warsaw Initiative Fund (WIF) program in 1996 was split between the budgets of the Departments of State and Defense. In a bureaucratic slight-of-hand, the State Department recoded $60 million of FMF funds already designated for these nations as its contribution to WIF, so only the $40 million from the Defense Department were actually new funds. Director of Strategy and Plans, US Joint Chiefs of Staff, *Planning Reference Book*, 1999 Joint Chiefs of Staff Planning Conference for the NIS Peacetime Engagement, Washington, DC, May 1998; and Director of Strategy and Plans (see chap. 3, note 12).

28. Director of Strategy and Plans (see chap. 3, note 12); and author with the Office of the Secretary of Defense, correspondence, September 2005 and March 2006; and "DRMS Participants," *DRMS*, [Defense Resource Management Studies] http://drms.ida.org/drmsindex .htm (accessed 16 April 2006).

29. OSD, talking paper, traditional combatant commander activities (TCA) funding summary, 3 June 1999; Director of Strategy and Plans (see chap. 3, note 12).

30. The military contact programs use Combatant Commander's Initiative Fund less frequently through this period and not at all by 1998. Director of Strategy and Plans (see chap. 3, note 12).

31. Trip Report (see chap. 3, note 15).

32. Director of Strategy and Plans (see chap. 3, note 32).

33. *United States Code*, Title 10, Subtitle A, Part I, Chap. 6, Section 168. *Military-to-military contacts and comparable activities*, http://www.law.cornell .edu/uscode/html/uscode10/usc_sec_10_00000168----000-.html.

34. I am indebted to Dr. Marybeth Peterson Ulrich for this methodology, who used it with much greater skill and effect in her book *Democratizing Communist Militaries* (see chap. 2, note 8). Data derived from *Bilateral Military Contact Plans* (see chap. 3, note 31).

35. IMET funding had dropped dramatically in 1994 and 1995 for all countries; total funding for 1995 was only $26.350, million, a 43 percent reduction from the 1988–1993 median of $46.100 million. Cope, *International Military Education and Training*, 13–14 (see chap. 2, note 14).

36. *Congressional Presentation*, 320–25, 367–68, 373–74 (see chap. 2, note 18); *Congressional Presentation for Foreign Operations, Fiscal Year 1997* (Washington, DC: Department of State, 1997), 332–39, 350–51, 357–59; and *Congressional Presentation for Foreign Operations, Fiscal Year 1998* (Washington, DC: Department of State, 1998), 605–10, 620–22, 627–29.

37. "Turkmenistan: Military Officers to Receive Training in U.S.," *Moscow Interfax*, 10 February 1996; and author with Defense Language Institute English Language Center, correspondence, November 2005.

38. The US military professional military education (PME) system generally has three levels, one each for junior officers (captains), mid-grade officers (majors), and senior officers (lieutenant colonels and colonels), although this varies somewhat by service. In most cases, the institutions at each level are designated as colleges and are grouped into a single university for each service, with joint colleges grouped under the National Defense University at Fort McNair in Washington, DC. Although some Central Asian officers have attended the junior-level PME colleges (most often the US Air Force Squadron Officers College at Maxwell AFB, AL), this discussion focuses on Central Asian attendance at the mid-grade and senior-grade colleges. For ease of discussion, the term "war college" will be used throughout this paper.

39. Cope, *International Military Education and Training*, 6 (see chap. 2, note 14).

40. Attendance at the service academies cannot be funded using the IMET program, but generally DOD will waive the tuition costs given the economic conditions in these countries.

41. Author with Service Academy Exchange Program Coordinator, correspondence, US Military Academy, 16 February 2006; Author with Service Academy Exchange Program Coordinator, correspondence, US Naval Academy, 13 February 2006; and Author with Service Academy Exchange Program Coordinator, correspondence, US Air Force Academy, 13 February 2006.

42. Air Force Instruction 16-108, *Managing the Aviation Leadership Program*, 1 September 1995, 4.

43. Neil MacFarlane, *Western Engagement in the Caucasus and Central Asia* (London: Royal Institute of International Affairs, 1999), 53.

44. "CENTRASBAT," *GlobalSecurity.org*, http://www.globalsecurity.org/military/ops/centrasbat.htm (accessed 6 January 2006); and "Central Asian Military Unit Nears Birth," *The Jamestown Foundation Monitor* 2, Issue 89 (7 May 1996), http://www.jamestown.org/publications_details.php?volume_id=20&issue_id=1061&article_id=9869 (accessed 29 January 2006).

45. Pikulina, *Uzbekistan in the Mirror of Military Security*, 8 (see chap. 3, note 5); and "Central Asian Military Unit Nears Birth," (see chap. 3, note 45).

46. "Central Asian Military Unit Nears Birth," (see chap. 3, note 45).

47. "CENTRASBAT," (see chap. 3, note 45); Douglas J. Gillert, "After Jumping, Battalion Learns to Crawl," *American Forces Press Service News Articles*, 1 October 1997, http://www.defenselink.mil/news/newsarticle.aspx ?id=41525 (accessed 17 March 2006); Linda D. Kozaryn, "Parachutes Ready: Next Stop Kazakhstan," *American Forces Press Service News Articles*, 3 September 1997, http://www.defenselink.mil/news/newsarticle.aspx?id=41131 (accessed 17 March 2006); "Historic U.S.-Led Military Exercise Begins," *The Jamestown Foundation Monitor* 3, no. 172 (17 September 1997), http://www .jamestown.org/publications_details.php?volume_id=2&issue_id=234& article_id=2653 (accessed 10 February 2006); "Uzbekistan: Uzbek President Calls Military Exercise 'Historic Event'," *Moscow Interfax*, 19 September 1997; and "Uzbekistan: Military Exercises End, Defense Minister Comments," *Moscow ITAR-TASS*, 20 September 1997.

48. "Historic U.S.-Led Military Exercise Begins," (see chap. 3, note 48).

49. "Russia: Duma Criticizes Government Over US Exercises in CIS [Commonwealth of Independent States] States," *Moscow Interfax*, 26 September 1997.

50. Gillert, "After Jumping, Battalion Learns to Crawl," (see chap. 3, note 48).

51. Ibid.

52. "CENTRASBAT," *GlobalSecurity.org*, (see chap. 3, note 45); "Kazakhstan: Almaty Conference Prepares for NATO Peacekeeping Exercise," *Moscow Interfax*, 5 February 1998; and Lyle J. Goldstein, "Making the Most of Central Asian Partnerships," *Joint Forces Quarterly*, no. 31 (Summer 2002), 83.

53. Kenley Butler, "U.S. Military Cooperation with the Central Asian States," Center for Nonproliferation Studies, 17 September 2001, http://cns .miis.edu/search97cgi/s97_cgi?action=View&VdkVgwKey=..%2F..%2Fcnsweb %2Fhtdocs%2Fresearch%2Fwtc01%2Fuscamil.htm&queryzip=Kenley+Butler &Collection=CNS+Web+Site (accessed 17 February 2006); "Cooperative Nugget 95 Closing Ceremony," *Department of Defense News Release* no. 467-95, 24 August 1995, http://www.defenselink.mil/releases/release.aspx?release id=602 (accessed 12 February 2006); Memorandum For Correspondents 088-m, "Exercise Cooperative Nugget '97 Scheduled," 29 May 1997, http://www.defense link.mil/news/May1997/m052997_m088-97.html (accessed 12 February 2006); and "CIS: Central Asian Battalion to Participate in NATO Exercises," *Moscow Interfax*, 7 August 1996.

54. Some sources identify the Balance Kayak and Balance Ultra exercises as part of the joint combined exchange training (JCET) program, but they were not. These events, and others conducted in the region during this period, were special operations forces exercises (SOFEX), which were conducted by the special operations component command within the theater (first US Special Operations Command, Pacific, and later US Special Operations Command Central), and in the case of Central Asia, were funded through the CTR program. (Although in more recent years counternarcotics funding has been used.) On the other hand, the JCET program, established in 1991, was de-

signed to provide an opportunity for US special forces units to hone their own skills in a foreign environment similar to one in which they may conduct future operations. JCET events (which are technically not exercises) have the additional but secondary benefit of providing training to the host nation. Details on JCETs are usually classified, so it is impossible to assemble a complete picture of the program in Central Asia. Other special operations units, such as the US Air Force's 6th Special Operations Squadron, may have also conducted SOFEXs or JCETs in Central Asia during this period. Author interviews at USCENTCOM, September 2005; author with the Office of the Secretary of Defense, correspondence, April 2006; and author with USCENTCOM, correspondence, April 2006.

55. Col Shamil' Gareyev, "Military Cooperation: Uzbekistan and the U.S.A." *Asia-Pacific Defense Forum* (Winter 1997), http://www.pacom.mil/forum/winter_97/UZBEK_r.html (accessed 10 February 2006); Col S. A. Zhasuzakov, "JCET Balance Kayak 97—Kazakhstan and the U.S.: Training Together," *Asia-Pacific Defense Forum* (Summer 1998), http://www.pacom.mil/forum/Summer_98/KAYAK_r.html (accessed 10 February 2006); "Uzbekistan: U.S. General Expected in Tashkent Today," *Moscow Interfax*, 6 June 1997; Director of Strategy and Plans (see chap. 3, note 12); and Director of Strategy and Plans (see chap. 3, note 28).

56. The provision of the patrol boats to the Kazakhstani Customs Service in 1995–1996 under the CTR program did not fall under the FMS program as the Boston Whalers and Sea Arc were considered commercially-available civilian equipment rather than military equipment, and therefore not subject to the International Traffic in Arms Regulations. Directorate of Defense Trade Controls, US Department of State, *International Traffic in Arms Regulations (ITAR)*, http://www.pmddtc.state.gov/itar_index.htm.

57. Identical language is used in the FMF justifications for Kyrgyzstan, Turkmenistan, and Uzbekistan. *Congressional Presentation for Foreign Operations, Fiscal Year 1997* (Washington, DC: Department of State, 1996), 334, 338, 351, 359.

58. Author with the Office of the Coordinator of US Assistance for Europe and Eurasia, US Department of State, correspondence, March 2006; and *Congressional Presentation for Foreign Operations, Fiscal Year 1999* (Washington, DC: Department of State, 1998), 1006.

59. Ulrich, *Democratizing Communist Militaries*, 189–203 (see chap. 2, note 8).

Chapter 4

Reassessment

The goal of U.S. policy in Central Asia would be not to dominate the region, but to make it free of other powers' domination, thus making it possible for the five Central Asian states to become stable and peaceful. In other words, instead of dominating Central Asia, the United States would be satisfied to see it as a no-man's land.

—Dr. Eugene B. Rumer, National
Defense University, Washington, DC

By 1999, the dramatic increase in security-cooperation programs reached a plateau. The foundations of US security-cooperation efforts with Kazakhstan, Kyrgyzstan, Uzbekistan, and Turkmenistan had been established, and the programs proceeded for the next few years without significant changes. The contact programs had reached a sustainable level of interaction between the partner militaries, although coordinating the events was beginning to tax the resources of the US defense attachés in the region. US special operations forces were routinely conducting small but focused training exercises with their counterparts. The four nations were receiving modest levels of IMET and FMF funding for training and equipment. Improving the capabilities of the CENTRASBAT unit provided the focus for many of the programs, and its annual exercise served as the centerpiece of the US security-cooperation efforts. In the words of Kyrgyz defense minister Lt Gen Esen Topoyev, meeting with US Marine Corps general Anthony Zinni, commander of USCENTCOM, in the spring of 2000, the relationship "had acquired a continual and steady nature."[1] In total, these programs were very modest compared to US efforts in other regions, but seemed sufficient for the limited interests Washington had in the region. But other geopolitical currents began to unsettle the ties that had been built; all participants were beginning to reexamine the newer, stronger, relationships and reevaluate whether these linkages were meeting their objectives.

59

Roots of Reassessment

This period of reassessment was most evident in US–Uzbekistani relations, and it derived from Washington's increasing concerns over Pres. Islam Abdughanievich Karimov's growing authoritarianism. Since Uzbekistan's independence in 1991, the Karimov regime has been noted for its systematic abuse of human rights in attempts to eliminate opposition and maintain political stability. Both the Clinton administration and Congress were becoming increasingly frustrated with the lack of progress on political and economic reform and the abysmal state of human rights. But, by the late 1990s, the persecution of the relatively moderate opposition groups and increasing instances of "harassment, arrests, beatings, and attempted assassinations," fostered the creation of more radical groups.[2]

In February 1999 Tashkent was rocked by a series of explosions set off by the Islamic Movement of Uzbekistan (IMU), a militant Islamic group that sought to establish a caliphate based in the Ferghana Valley. The Uzbekistani government reacted strongly to the bombings, seeing them both as an attempt to assassinate Karimov (who was traveling by car nearby) and to overthrow the government. The bombings were followed by an IMU invasion of the Batken Valley in Kyrgyzstan in 1999, and a second invasion in 2000. Along with military operations coordinated with Kazakhstan, Kyrgyzstan, and Tajikistan, Uzbekistan stepped up its internal repressive measures and human rights abuses.[3]

The United States reacted with mixed signals. At USCENTCOM (which had recently assumed responsibility for the region), General Zinni sought to increase military engagement programs in order to try to influence the Karimov regime, but the Clinton administration and State Department were unwilling to expand the security-cooperation activities for fear of being seen as rewarding repressive regimes.[4] Visiting officials routinely lectured Karimov on the importance of respecting human rights, but took little other action.[5] Trying to balance the competing aims of security and promoting human rights, Washington neither expanded the cooperation programs nor reduced them; instead, it maintained them at a level that ensured it could not accomplish any of its strategic objectives. It also demonstrated to

Karimov that he could safely ignore American pressures to improve Uzbekistan's internal political situation and that he could not rely on the United States to satisfy his fundamental security concerns.

The IMU invasions in 1999 and 2000 also undermined US efforts to promote regional security cooperation. While Uzbekistan, Kazakhstan, Kyrgyzstan, and Tajikistan made some attempts to coordinate their military response to the incursions, the first three did not use the joint CENTRASBAT unit to counter the threat, and instead used other national forces. The states then began a series of mutual recriminations, blaming each other for conditions that permitted the attacks. Uzbekistan also established minefields along its border with Kyrgyzstan to prevent future attacks through that country, which dramatically reduced cross-border trade and resulted in several deaths. Both Kazakhstan and Kyrgyzstan had been concerned about the growth in Uzbekistan's military capabilities, and now both began to see Tashkent as a possible future threat. US efforts to promote regional cooperation through programs began to meet with resistance, as the fundamental distrust between Kazakhstan, Kyrgyzstan, and Uzbekistan began to overshadow the modest attempts at collaboration.[6]

Washington was also reassessing its relationship with Almaty. Kazakhstan may have adopted some of the trappings of democracy, but had never implemented them in practice. The Organization for Security and Cooperation in Europe (OSCE) considered the March 1994 parliamentary elections neither "free nor fair," and by the middle of 1995 Nazarbayev had dissolved the parliament, instituted presidential rule, and adopted a new constitution which gave him far-reaching powers. But, until the late 1990s the Clinton administration still hoped that these trends could be reversed. The January 1999 presidential elections and the October 1999 parliamentary elections, both of which were orchestrated by Nazarbayev to ensure favorable results, were seen as final death blows to any efforts toward democratic reform. Instead of offering congratulations, Clinton's post-election letter to Nazarbayev recommended that "a deeper commitment by Kazakhstan to democracy and market reform" would be "very important" for both Kazakhstan and bilateral relations.[7] Nazarbayev rejected the recommendation because he considered it inap-

61

propriate and threatening to his hold on power. In April 2000 at the Eurasian Economic Summit, he declared "We in Central Asia are not going to blindly run for [all] our worth after the United States in the issues of democratizing our countries."[8]

In Washington's view, Kazakhstan appeared to be backsliding on cooperation in security issues as well. In March 1999 senior Kazakh defense officials, including Minister of Defense Altynbayev, were implicated in a scheme to smuggle MiG-21 fighter aircraft to North Korea. Altynbayev was removed from office, but in November 1999 a similar episode led to the dismissal of his successor, acting Minister of Defense Bakhytzhan Ertaev, and head of the National Security Council Nurtai Abukaev. Although Almaty removed the offending leaders, they were not severely punished (and Altynbayev returned later as Minister of Defense). Both sides recognized these events severely strained US–Kazakhstani relations. Foreign Minister Kaymzhomart Tokaev remarked: "We used to be very good partners. Big damage has been brought to our cooperation. I as Foreign Minister understand the seriousness of the situation. We are ready to do our part."[9] Washington curtailed many of its security-assistance programs, and some military aid packages were completely cancelled.

Washington was also concerned about the continual backsliding on democratic reform in Kyrgyzstan. Pres. Askar Akayev, the darling of Western observers, in the early 1990s when he instituted a broad set of political and economic reform initiatives, had slowly increased his personal control over the Kyrgyz government, reduced the role of civil society, and clamped down on his political opposition. In 1998, presidential pressure convinced the constitutional court that Akayev was eligible to run for president for a third time in 2000, sidestepping the constitutional clause that permits only two terms by claiming the first, which started before independence, did not count. Parliamentary elections in 2000 fell short of international standards, and the presidential elections the same year were worse. Kyrgyzstan was clearly backsliding on democratic reform.[10]

Struggling with the competing interests of influencing these regimes through military cooperation, while trying to punish them for violating human rights, the Clinton administration tried to walk a fine line in the 1999 National Security Strategy: "With countries that are neither staunch friends nor known foes, military cooperation can serve as a positive means of building security relationships today that will contribute to improved relations tomorrow. At the same time, we will remain firmly committed to ensure that we do not train or assist known human rights violators."[11]

Denuclearization and Proliferation Prevention

Despite the leveling off of security-cooperation programs and setbacks caused by political events, two organizational changes brought new structure, focus, and objectives to the US security-cooperation efforts in Central Asia: the establishment of the DTRA and the assignment of the Central Asian states under the Unified Command Plan to USCENTCOM. Additionally, the creation of the Central Asia Border Security Initiative (CASI) in April 2000 marked the first attempt to synchronize security-cooperation programs across departments within the federal government.

A series of terrorist attacks in 1995, including the Aum Shinrikyo use of sarin gas in the Tokyo subway system in March and the Oklahoma City bombing in April, deeply influenced Senator William S. Cohen's thinking on the nature of future threats against the United States. When he became secretary of defense in 1997, Cohen argued that proliferation of weapons of mass destruction and their potential use by terrorists was the most important security challenge faced by America. In a major reorganization that took affect in October 1998, he combined the OSIA, DSWA, Defense Technology Security Administration (DTSA), CTR, and chemical/biological defense programs previously executed by OSD into a new organization, the DTRA.[12] The reorganization placed greater emphasis on proliferation prevention, by ensuring that chemical, biological, and nuclear materials and technology did not get passed from the former Soviet Union to states or terrorist organizations that might use them against the United States, linking (but not integrating) the biological and chemical weapons elimination programs conducted under CTR and the border security programs under the International Counterproliferation Program (ICP).

The merging of these organizations did not have an immediate effect on the execution of the proliferation prevention programs in Central Asia, which, like the other security-cooperation efforts, experienced a general slowdown during this period. DTRA continued slow but steady efforts via the CTR program to eliminate nuclear weapons infrastructure in Kazakhstan and the biological and chemical weapons facilities in Kazakhstan and Uzbekistan. DTRA officials managing ICP attempted to expand the program into Tajikistan and Turkmenistan with no success; delegations from both countries attended a WMD executive seminar in May 2001 but otherwise shunned the program. There were no ICP activities in Kyrgyzstan, and those in Kazakhstan and Uzbekistan stalled. Funding dipped in 2000 and only 12 training events occurred between 1999–2001, compared to 19 between 1996–1998.[13] Despite these setbacks, the proliferation prevention programs began to show some modest results. In early 2000, a shipment of 10 lead-lined boxes containing radioactive material was stopped by Uzbekistani officials at the border with Kazakhstan using a $1,200 detection device provided by the ICP, and the following year Kazakhstani officials who had received ICP training in 1998 seized another illegal shipment.[14]

The ICP was one of several programs executed in Central Asia by the United States that were designed to improve border security capabilities in these countries. For most of the 1990s, these programs had been relatively small and independently managed. The IMU invasions in 1999, however, prompted Clinton administration officials to try to link these programs together to better meet this regional threat. In April 2000, during a tour of Central Asia, Secretary of State Madeline Albright announced the new CASI that encompassed six assistance programs, including EXBS, ICP, and other counterterrorism, counternarcotics (CN), law enforcement, and customs reform efforts, that had been designed to improve border security operations. ICP was the only DOD program under CASI, and it is unclear whether the subsequent funding increases in later years was as a result of this connection. But, CASI marked the first real attempt to harmonize these programs across federal agencies.[15]

Democratization

As with the consolidation of denuclearization and proliferation prevention programs under DTRA, changes in the unified command structure centralized the programs that promoted military democratization and regional cooperation. As previously indicated, Central Asia had remained a responsibility of the Joint Staff, and a number of commands were conducting military cooperation activities in the region. USCENTCOM began to take a more active role in the region starting in early 1997 and was ready to assume control of the security-cooperation efforts when the decision was publicly announced in February 1998.[16] In fact, in July 1998 General Zinni, who became the commander of USCENTCOM in August 1997, hosted General Altynbayev, minister of defense of Kazakhstan, the first senior military officer from Central Asia to visit CENTCOM in Tampa, Florida.[17] General Zinni was a strong proponent of increased engagement with Central Asia, advocating that the region's energy resources and potential instability from terrorism, drug trafficking, and corruption (largely stemming from Taliban-controlled Afghanistan) made these countries "front line states."[18] General Zinni made his first trip to Central Asia in September 1998, a year before USCENTCOM officially assumed full responsibility for the region, and made a total of five trips before his retirement in the summer of 2000.[19]

USCENTCOM's assumption of responsibility for the region brought greater structure to the security-cooperation programs. Secretary of Defense William Cohen had directed each regional commander to create theater engagement plans, outlining how they intended to create positive and constructive relationships with the friendly military forces in their respective areas of responsibility. General Zinni leveraged this effort to create the first US military strategy for Central Asia. He recognized that USCENTCOM was institutionally focused on the continual confrontation with Iraq, and any remaining attention was devoted to planning for a potential conflict with Iran. To avoid other important but less critical efforts being overlooked, General Zinni divided Central Command's area of responsibility into four separate subregions: East Africa, Persian Gulf, Egypt and Jordan, and South and Central Asia (the latter of which included Afghanistan and Pakistan). Although there were many issues that crossed boundaries, each subregion had unique challenges and required specific strategies. General Zinni understood the long-term imperative of building security relationships in Central Asia, as reflected in his strategy: "the importance of the South and Central Asian subregion will continue to grow as the economies of these countries and access to the subregion's natural resources develop."[20] General Zinni also assigned each subregion to one of his subordinate commanders; USSOCCENT was tasked to act as the lead agency for building relationships with South and Central Asia.[21]

Military Contact Program and Education and Training Programs

Despite the new strategy, there was little immediate change in the military contact or training and education programs. USCENTCOM exercised influence over the development of the 1999 plan and had complete authority over the development of the 2000 plan. USACOM, USPACOM, and USEUCOM (with the exception of the Marshall Center) withdrew from participating in military contact events in Central Asia. Nonetheless, the military contact programs continued to emphasize largely the same functional areas as before, including officer and noncommissioned officer professional development, medical information exchanges, and civil-military responses to environmental disasters. The notable exception was an increase in senior-leader and staff-exchange visits to Central Asia, a reflection of USCENTCOM's efforts to become more familiar with the region. But the military planners also started to propose, plan, and execute events that built on the experiences of previous events, rather than simply repeat an exchange or offer an event on a completely new topic. This trend is particularly evident in officer and noncommissioned officer development, civil-military responses to environmental disasters, defense resource management, and defense planning. Additionally, in 1999 and 2000 USCENTCOM planned 21 events with the CENTRASBAT elements of Kazakhstan, Kyrgyzstan, and Uzbekistan on peacekeeping and search and rescue as a means to help prepare these detachments for the annual CENTRASBAT exercise.[22]

IMET funding was advocated by the State Department generally using the same arguments, although regional stability and cooperation began to gain equal billing with democratization. IMET funding and the number of students trained remained consistent through this period, with a slight dip for Kazakhstan in 1999 due to the MiG-21 incident.[23] Given the amount of available resources, there were few alternatives, so USCENTCOM continued with the modest programs it had inherited. However, increasing numbers of military students attended combat training courses as opposed to English language instructor courses, professional courses such as defense resource management, or war colleges. This trend toward increasing combat skills is addressed in more detail below.

Regional Cooperation

USCENTCOM inherited the CENTRASBAT program when it assumed responsibility for the region, and it conducted the May 1999 exercise as a peacekeeping and humanitarian assistance seminar in a hotel in downtown Tampa, just outside of its headquarters at MacDill AFB. The seminar format allowed the USCENTCOM staff to become more familiar with the needs and perspectives of the Central Asian states and also gave the delegations from Central Asia an opportunity to become familiar with USCENTCOM's perspective on the region. For the first time, Turkmenistan participated as an observer.[24]

The Demise of CENTRASBAT

But by late 1998, US efforts to encourage regional cooperation through CENTRASBAT were faltering. Originally conceived as a combined battalion with a company from each of the three participating nations and rotating command structure, it never achieved this goal. Despite the original plan, each company was garrisoned in its own country and the battalion came together only for the annual exercises.[25] The command and control structure, with rotating commanders and geographically dispersed elements, were too challenging to overcome. The battalion was never used in an operational mission, despite opportunities in post-civil war Tajikistan and against the IMU incursions in 1999 and 2000.[26] CENTRASBAT may have been overly ambitious—Kazakhstan, Kyrgyzstan, and Uzbekistan were new nations still attempting to establish their own sovereignty and develop indigenous armed forces, and the establishment of a joint rapid reaction/peacekeeping force detracted from both objectives. In the end it proved to be counterproductive. Although the concept originated with the three participating nations, the United States assumed ownership of the effort when it began funding and orchestrating the annual exercises. In time, CENTRASBAT came to be seen as an "American project," and the Central Asian states lost a sense of ownership. Kyrgyzstani Defense Minister Topoyev captured this sense in a July 2004 interview:

> This was a good example of how any international program should *primarily* meet the interests of the country where it is being carried out. It is necessary to take into account the interests and positions of the region's countries on regional security issues. The degree to which they [the interests] coincide with foreign programs' goals should be taken into consideration as well. *The peacekeeping battalion created in Central Asia did not prove relevant exactly for these reasons* [emphasis added].[27]

By 1999, General Zinni recognized Kazakhstan, Kyrgyzstan, and Uzbekistan were discouraged with the program. He had observed the 1998 exercise in Central Asia and participated in the 1999 seminar, so he recognized the limitations of the program. The apparent irrelevance of CENTRASBAT in the face of the IMU incursions brought the issue to a head, particularly when one Kazakh observer noted: "The question arises of what the real significance of the CENTRASBAT exercises is for strengthening security."[28] General Zinni and other US officials abandoned the concept of a joint CENTRASBAT unit as a means for promoting regional cooperation and encouraged each of the three nations to form separate battalions which could operate independently, collectively, or with other international peacekeeping forces.[29] The multinational unit was disbanded at the end of 1999, although the CENTRASBAT name continued to be used for exercises for a few years. Planning for the September 2000 exercise was based on each country providing an entire battalion, and it ultimately became the largest in the series

68

with approximately 1,400 participants. But the IMU incursions in the summer of 2000 forced Uzbekistan and Kyrgyzstan to withdraw from the exercise in August, only to reconsider and rejoin prior to the opening ceremonies. In response to the new threats to the region, last minute changes to the scenario allowed the exercise to focus more on border security and counterinsurgency rather than on peacekeeping operations. In 2001, the exercise was renamed Regional Cooperation and was executed as a small command post drill at the US training facilities at Ramstein Air Base, Germany.[30] The United States cancelled the exercise in 2002 because of ongoing combat operations in Afghanistan, the one for 2003 remained on the books for a while but was also cancelled because of the invasion of Iraq.[31] While CENTRASBAT was the centerpiece of the US security-cooperation programs with Central Asia in the late 1990s, few officers at USCENTCOM today even know what it was.[32]

Disaster Response and Environmental Security

But the demise of CENTRASBAT did not end US efforts to promote regional cooperation. General Zinni saw new opportunities with a theme that had started with the expansion of the military contact program in the mid-1990s—disaster response and environmental security. The National Guard had always played an important role in responding to natural disasters in the United States, primarily in its responsibility to the state governor, so the Arizona and Louisiana National Guards included a small number of disaster response events in their proposals for the military contact plans with Kazakhstan and Uzbekistan. The 1996 plans, for example, included a proposal for a Kazakhstani delegation to observe a disaster response exercise at the Palo Verde Nuclear Generating Station in Arizona, in which the Arizona National Guard would participate. Two proposals for Uzbekistan were made to observe the Louisiana National Guard in a disaster response command and control exercise in New Orleans, and to have an Uzbek platoon participate in a Combat Engineer disaster response exercise with the 225th Engineering Group in Pineville, Louisiana.

Kazakhstan and Uzbekistan quickly appreciated the value of these events. Central Asia is subject to devastating natural disasters such as seasonal flooding, landslides, and earthquakes; the latter of which have completely destroyed Almaty, Ashgabat, and Tashkent at various times over the last century. In both countries, the military would be called upon to respond to a disaster, whatever the source. These military contact events helped them formulate plans and requirements. From General Zinni's perspective, these events also fostered democratization of the military as they demonstrated in a very practical manner the civil-military coordination needed to address these catastrophes: "We decided to hold conferences on disaster assistance in some of these countries. They brought their fire, police, emergency service units, and military; we brought experts from the U.S., who showed them how to intermix the civilian and military and cooperate with each other; and we did all this in the name of the U.S. ambassador."[33]

General Zinni also used the growing set of disaster response activities to promote regional cooperation. In 1999 the military contact plans included a three-phase International Workshop on Earthquake Response (IWER), later renamed International Workshop on Emergency Response. IWER was hosted by the Arizona National Guard and conducted in both Phoenix, Arizona, and Almaty, Kazakhstan. IWER included large delegations from Kazakhstan, Kyrgyzstan, Turkmenistan, and Uzbekistan, and represented the first US-sponsored regional exercise beyond CENTRASBAT. The Arizona National Guard sponsored a second exercise on flood management in 2000, and the IWER exercises became a significant pillar of US security-cooperation efforts in the region. The Montana National Guard and Kyrgyzstan hosted IWER 2002 in Bishkek, again with an earthquake scenario, and the Louisiana National Guard and Uzbekistan hosted IWER 2003, focusing on petrochemical disasters, in Baton Rouge.

Concurrent with these efforts were military contact events, including assessments and information exchanges, which focused on environmental security. In the second half of the 1990s, these were primarily conducted with Kazakhstan, which suffers from the effects of over 470 nuclear explosions at the Semipalatinsk test site during the Soviet era. At least one event was also executed in Uzbekistan. General Zinni built on these early bilateral efforts on environmental security to support his objective of regional cooperation. In April 2000, USCENTCOM sponsored an environmental security conference in Oman that included delegations from the Central Asian states. Subsequent conferences in 2001 and 2002 were hosted by the Marshall Center. Kazakhstan hosted the conference in 2003, and the following year it was combined with the IWER exercise in Tashkent.[34]

Military Capabilities

Although it was becoming more apparent that CENTRASBAT would be unsuccessful in its role of promoting regional cooperation, US planners still saw value in developing the peacekeeping capabilities of Kazakhstan, Kyrgyzstan, and Uzbekistan. Additionally, as the Central Asian military leaders became more discouraged at the lack of US response to the IMU incursions, US security-cooperation officials saw the need to focus more attention on building indigenous military capabilities for each country. Developing military capabilities through exercises, training courses, and equipment deliveries began to develop as a distinct objective for US security-cooperation programs.

Equipment Deliveries

The United States continued to provide funding (FMF) for equipment purchases in small amounts to Kazakhstan, Kyrgyzstan, Turkmenistan, and Uzbekistan through this period. The total amount provided to these nations each year, on average, was $5.7 million; not much more than the total provided in 1998. This aid was again justified as supporting CENTRASBAT, NATO interoperability, and the development of capabilities for peacekeeping, search and rescue, and humanitarian operations. The only new proposal was the request for FMF for Turkmenistan, where the State Department indicated Ashgabat was considering a project that would provide "Western-standard, day/night, all-weather approach capability for a Turkmen airfield that will be open to US Air Force aircraft." Unfortunately, this initiative, which could have directly supported future US military operations, was later cancelled. Despite the concerns in

Central Asia over the IMU incursions, there was no mention in the 2000 or 2001 FMF justifications of using the aid to develop counterinsurgency capabilities in these countries.[35]

Ironically, just as CENTRASBAT was collapsing, the military equipment purchased for it under the FMS program began to arrive in Central Asia. Despite having first received FMF in 1997, the Central Asian states did not begin to receive equipment deliveries under the FMS program until 1999, and the first deliveries were so inconsequential as to almost be insulting. When the new security assistance officer arrived in Almaty in May 2001, he found that of the $7 million in FMF allocated for Kazakhstan since 1997, only $29 thousand worth of flight suits had actually been delivered.[36] USCENTCOM officials began to understand Central Asian frustrations with the FMS program on the first official visit to the region in the summer of 1998. In Tashkent, Minister of Defense Gen Hikmetulla Tursunov pleaded for USCENTCOM assistance in receiving the 16 high mobility multipurpose wheeled vehicles (HMMWV) Uzbekistan had ordered, wanting to receive them prior to the CENTRASBAT exercise in September. Those vehicles would not arrive until February 2000 (fig. 5). In Turkmenistan, Gen Danatar Kopekov, the minister of defense, castigated American officials, stating he had been unable to use the approximately $1 million in FMF funds promised to date: "We don't owe you, and you don't owe us, but if you make a promise we would like an answer. I am fed up with promises and I have seen no results."[37] In fact, Turkmenistan was not to come to an agreement with the United States on equipment sales until 2002, and the first deliveries did not occur until 2003.[38]

Some equipment did start to slowly trickle into Central Asia, with most of it going to Uzbekistan and Kyrgyzstan. In February 2000, Tashkent finally received its HMMWVs, a delivery many observers, not fully appreciating the slowness of the FMS system, claimed was a US response to the IMU incursions the previous year. Uzbekistan also started to receive several English language laboratories and Kyrgyzstan received uniforms, mountaineering equipment, and radios. Kazakhstan, dismayed at the lack of responsiveness to its requests, cancelled its open FMS agreements, and directed all available funds be used to refurbish the barracks at the Atyrau Naval Base on the Caspian

Figure 5. US ambassador Joseph Pressel delivering first high mobility multipurpose wheeled vehicle (HMMWV) provided under the foreign military sales (FMS) program, Tashkent, Uzbekistan, February 2000 (Reprinted from US Embassy, Tashkent. Used with permission.)

Sea, a project that would take four years to complete. Fortunately, by December 2001, $2.500 million worth of radios and communications gear and $850 thousand worth of web belts, rucksacks, and body armor arrived. These were the first deliveries for the Kazakh element of CENTRASBAT, over five years after military aid under the FMF program was first proposed.[39]

Likewise, some of the Central Asian states began to receive US equipment under the EDA program. This equipment, no longer deemed useful by the US military, is offered on an "as is, where is," and usually on a "first-come, first-serve" basis. In 1998, Kazakhstan, Kyrgyzstan, Turkmenistan, and Uzbekistan were first authorized to receive grant EDA.[40] The State Department initially advocated approval by arguing that it would provide radios and other communications equipment for the CENTRASBAT unit (and for Turkmenistan, which was not a part of

CENTRASBAT). But, it was unlikely that NATO-interoperable communications equipment would be available through EDA.

It was not until 2000 that equipment under this program was first delivered, and most of the EDA provided to the Central Asian states was miscellaneous office or kitchen equipment, tools, or uniform items. The primary exception was the 82-foot patrol boat, *Point Jackson*, delivered to Turkmenistan for maritime security on the Caspian Sea. Given the type of equipment and timing, it is possible that some of it was surplus materials left behind after the CENTRASBAT 2000 exercise. Of note, Kazakhstan was slated to receive the USCGC *Mariposa* (WLB-397), a Basswood-class 180-foot buoy tender originally built in 1944, through the EDA program. However, due to the disruption in the security-cooperation programs caused by the MiG-21 sale to North Korea, the deal was cancelled in 1999 (table 6).[41]

Table 6. Excess defense articles (EDA) deliveries to Central Asia

Recipient	Delivery Date	Equipment	Acquisition Value	Delivery Value
Kazakhstan	2000	Office furniture and computer equipment	$159,283	$55,749
Kazakhstan	2004	2 UH-1 helicopters	$922,704	$185,440
Turkmenistan	2000	*Point Jackson* patrol boat	$575,000	$230,000
Uzbekistan	2000	Hand tools	$113,783	$0
Uzbekistan	2000	Clothing and individual equipment	$113,783	$105,777
Uzbekistan	2000	Textiles	$113,783	$52,817
Uzbekistan	2000	Miscellaneous kitchen equipment	$113,783	$0
Uzbekistan	2000	Rope, cable, chain, and fittings	$113,783	$0
Uzbekistan	2000	Mountaineering equipment	$113,783	$50,575

(Reprinted from *Congressional Budget Justification for Foreign Operations, Fiscal Year 2002* [Washington, DC: Department of State, 2001], 511; and Defense Security Cooperation Agency EDA Database http://www.dsca.mil/programs/eda/search.asp.)

Note: Given the identical acquisition values reported for all equipment transferred to Uzbekistan in 2000, this data likely has been incorrectly reported. Additionally, the total delivery value of these items reflected in the EDA Database, at $209 thousand, differs slightly from the value of $239 thousand which was reported to Congress in 2001.

Not all US offers to help build necessary military capabilities met with success. On a visit to Ashgabat in 2000, General Zinni proposed assisting the Turkmen government in addressing pipeline security issues. The Turkmen minister of defense brushed aside this offer, stating "Well, this will be addressed as soon as the pipeline is arranged."[42] Ashgabat had limits on the type of military aid it would accept from the United States, and clearly assistance in securing the pipelines was outside of those limits.

Training Courses

As previously mentioned, during the three-year period 1999–2001 there was a shift in the type of training courses provided through the IMET program. Previously, the IMET program in Central Asia had focused primarily on English-language courses to build a cadre of in-country English-language instructors, and later on professional courses that would advance military democratization and defense reform. As late as 1998, less than 32 percent of the students from Central Asia attending IMET courses in the United States were gaining combat skills in such courses as infantry, armor, or field artillery officer training.[43] Additionally, almost 320 students attended Disciplined Military Operations, Military Justice, Peace Operations, and Defense Resource Management courses taught by DIILS and DRMI METs in Central Asia.[44]

From 1999 to 2001, almost 55 percent of the IMET courses were focused on combat skills. Central Asian military personnel came to the United States for Ranger training, Special Forces operations qualification, Special Forces sergeants course, airborne training, winter mountain leader course, and infantry, armor, and field artillery officer courses.[45] Attendance at the war colleges dropped by a third, and only a single MET visited the region, training only 16 Uzbekistani students. The emphasis on CENTRASBAT had finally caught up with the IMET program, as most of the personnel attending these courses were assigned to that unit. But it is clear that the IMET program had started shifting away from promoting military democratization and defense reform toward providing combat skills. This trend was partially offset by a 50 percent increase in the number of students attending the Marshall Center, which is not funded through IMET. What is not clear is whether this shift was deliberate or simply a function of the emphasis on CENTRASBAT.

75

Exercises

Officers and enlisted personnel from Kazakhstan, Kyrgyzstan, and Uzbekistan continued to participate in NATO PfP exercises such as Cooperative Nugget, Cooperative Osprey, Combined Endeavor, and others more often in Europe than in the United States. The US- and NATO-funded Central Asian participation was funded with WIF and matching PfP funds. US officials encouraged Central Asian military leaders to take part in as many exercises as possible, believing that increasing the linkages to Western institutions such as NATO would help reform Central Asian military establishments. These exercises became a routine but important element of the security-cooperation program.

While the NATO exercises continued unchanged, the rest of the exercise schedule underwent a transformation. The most important change to the exercise program stemmed from General Zinni's decision to task USSOCCENT, his special operations component command, to act as the lead agency for building relationships in Central Asia. In a 1999 interview, US Army Brig Gen Frank J. Toney Jr., then USSOCCENT's commanding general, outlined his new mission: "We've just been given responsibility for Kazakhstan, Kyrgyzstan, Tajikistan, Turkmenistan, and Uzbekistan. General Zinni has made us the operational lead, and he wants to use SOF [special operations forces] with our military-to-military peacetime engagement techniques to open up those particular countries for training with US forces."[46] General Toney ramped up the SOFEX and JCET programs to meet this need and he turned to the subordinate 5th Special Forces Group (5 SFG) at Fort Campbell, Kentucky, for the A-Teams.

Each of the seven SFGs in the US Army specializes in operating in a particular area of the world, and the 5 SFG's region was the Middle East and Southwest Asia. Some members spoke Russian, Uzbek, Tajik, or another of the indigenous languages of Central Asia. With approximately 54 A-Teams, each with 12 personnel, available for missions, the 5 SFG began conducting month-long exercises up to four times a year in Kazakhstan, Kyrgyzstan, and Uzbekistan. Those in Kyrgyzstan were known as Balance Knight and Balance Knife exercises. Balance Umbra was held in April 2000 with Uzbekistani special forces in Chirchik and focused on counterinsurgency operations in mountain environments; Balance Empire was held in June 2001 and focused on desert operations. Some sources suggest exercises were also conducted in Tajikistan and Turkmenistan during this period. The training in these exercises focused on combat skills: patrolling, small arms training, and explosives handling.[47]

The 5 SFG was not the only special operations unit to exercise in Central Asia. The Air Force's 6th Special Operations Squadron (6 SOS), specializing in training foreign aviation units in internal defense, deployed operational detachments to Central Asia several times during this period. Two members of the unit were in Uzbekistan for language training in September 2001 and played a minor role in coordinating basing rights at Karshi-Khanabad. And on at least one occasion, US Navy sea-air-land teams (SEAL) passed through the region.[48]

One of these events was expanded to meet a specific Kazakh desire for bilateral field training. In late 1998, as Kazakh military leaders debated the future of CENTRASBAT, they wanted to continue field exercises with the US military in order to train their peacekeeping company as it expanded to a battalion. They invited the United States to participate in a bilateral exercise in the summer of 1999 called Zhardem. Linked to the Balance exercises, it is often referred to as Balance-Zhardem. From 14 July–10 August, 54 Americans and over 150 Kazakhs from the peacekeeping unit conducted a crisis response, humanitarian assistance, and refugee management exercise that included combat drills such as mountain training, artillery raids, and defending against combined arms assaults. Zhardem was a success and became a permanent element of the exercise schedule, with evolutions in March 2002 and March 2005.[49]

Following the IMU incursions in the summer of 1999, these special operations training exercises took on a new significance as the most responsive and effective means of providing US support to the Central Asian military forces. Other elements of the security-cooperation toolset were not flexible enough to meet this new need. Training courses available through the IMET program took too long to schedule and generally provided only basic skills. The bureaucracy of the FMS program meant that it could take years before new equipment could be delivered. (The HMMWVs delivered to Uzbekistan in February 2000 had been on order since 1998.) The CENTRASBAT exercise program, concerned with peacekeeping and humanitarian operations, was focused on the wrong skill sets. But the special operations exercises provided a means to quickly and effectively train counterinsurgency forces in Kazakhstan, Kyrgyzstan, and Uzbekistan.

On the Eve

In the final months of 2001, few expected many major changes to the security-cooperation efforts in Central Asia. Funding levels and programs had generally reached a plateau and political developments in the region appeared to have placed a cap on what Washington was willing to provide. Central Asian political and military leaders began to appreciate the limits to which the United States was willing to assist in their security. As it would turn out, they had expected more funding, more equipment, more training, and more security guarantees than they actually received. Some programs generated more frustrations than others. The slowness of the equipment deliveries and the increasing irrelevance of the CENTRASBAT unit made it clear that US aid would not fundamentally transform the capabilities of these military forces. And the struggle to find additional resources made it clear to US officials that they had few available means to influence political and military developments in the region.

When USCENTCOM assumed responsibility for Central Asia in 1999, few in the headquarters thought that the relationships they needed to build through security-cooperation programs would so quickly be put to the test. Most probably assumed the programs would continue in the long, slow process common to these efforts. Perhaps a few dreamed of small improvements such as those being gained through the JCETs and special operations exercise programs. On the eve of 10 September, most US officials engaged in the security-cooperation programs in the region expected another year of modest advancements. The terrorist attacks on 11 September 2001, would change those perspectives overnight, and the security-cooperation programs in Central Asia would see growth on a scale never before seen.

Notes

1. Dana Priest, *The Mission: Waging War and Keeping Peace with America's Military* (New York: W. W. Norton & Company, 2003), 115.

2. Leila Kazemi, "Domestic Sources of Uzbekistan's Foreign Policy, 1991 to the Present," *Journal of International Affairs* 56, no. 2 (Spring 2003), 210–11.

3. Ibid., 210–13.

4. Priest, *The Mission*, 100–101 (see chap. 4, note 1).

5. Kazemi, "Domestic Sources of Uzbekistan's Foreign Policy," 212 (see chap. 4, note 2).

6. Annette Bohr, "Regionalism in Central Asia: New Geopolitics, Old Regional Order," *International Affairs* 80, no. 3 (May 2004), 487, 495.

7. Robert Legvold, "U.S. Policy Toward Kazakhstan," in *Thinking Strategically: The Major Powers, Kazakhstan, and the Central Asian Nexus*, ed. Robert Legvold (Cambridge, MA: MIT Press, 2003), 92–93.

8. Ibid., 93–94.

9. Ibid., 94.

10. Martha Brill Olcott, *Central Asia's Second Chance* (Washington, DC: Carnegie Endowment for International Peace, 2005), 43.

11. *A National Security Strategy*, 11 (see chap. 3, note 3).

12. Joseph P. Harahan and Capt Robert J. Bennett, *Creating the Defense Threat Reduction Agency* (Washington, DC: Defense Threat Reduction Agency, 2002), 2–20.

13. Defense Threat Reduction Agency correspondence (see chap. 3, note 21).

14. Defense Threat Reduction Agency, "Success Stories: Impact of the ICP [International Counterproliferation Program] on Proliferation," http://www.dtra.mil/Toolbox/Directorates/OSI/Programs/icp/success.cfm (accessed 28 April 2006); Bruce B. Auster, "Nation & World, Speed-Reading the Book of Life; The Cigarette Spies; Stopping 'Dirty' Bombs; Selling Hate Online; How They Got Here," *U.S. News and World Report*, 17 April 2000, http://www.usnews.com/usnews/culture/articles/000417/archive_018014.htm (accessed 28 April 2006); Harahan and Bennett, *Creating the Defense Threat Reduction Agency*, 38 (see chap. 4, note 12); and Office of the Coordinator of US Assistance to Europe and Eurasia, *U.S. Government Assistance to and Cooperative Activities with Eurasia, FY 2001 Annual Report* (Washington, DC: Department of State, 2002), 260.

15. Director of Strategy and Plans, US Joint Chiefs of Staff, "Central Asia Border Security Initiative (CASI) Background Paper," undated, in *Addendum to the Peacetime Engagement Planning Reference Book*, 2001 Joint Chiefs of Staff/Office of the Secretary of Defense Russia-Eurasia Policy and Strategy Conference, Washington, DC, 2–6 April 2001.

16. Ronald H. Cole, Walter S. Poole, James F. Schnabel, Robert J. Watson, and Willard J. Webb, *The History of the Unified Command Plan, 1946–1999* (Washington, DC: Joint History Office, Office of the Chairman of the Joint Chiefs of Staff, 2003), 109. USCENTCOM, which had conducted Operation Desert Storm against Iraq, also received responsibility for contingency plan-

ning and executing military operations in the region, a point which was not lost on Russia. This responsibility became critical after 11 September 2001, when USCENTCOM staged out of Central Asia to conduct operations in Afghanistan.

17. Tom Clancy, Gen Tony Zinni (retired), and Tony Koltz, *Battle Ready* (New York: G. P. Putnam's Sons, 2004), 338.

18. Priest, *The Mission*, 104 (see chap. 4, note 1).

19. Clancy, Zinni, and Koltz, *Battle Ready*, 342–43 (see chap. 4, note 17); and Priest, *The Mission*, 103 (see chap. 4, note 1).

20. Bhatty and Bronson, "NATO's Mixed Signals," 134 (see chap. 3, note 25).

21. Clancy, Zinni, and Koltz, *Battle Ready*, 311–34 (see chap. 4, note 17).

22. Director of Strategy and Plans, US Joint Chiefs of Staff, *Peacetime Engagement Planning Reference Book*, 2001 Joint Chiefs of Staff/Office of the Secretary of Defense Russia-Eurasia Policy and Strategy Conference, Washington, DC, 2–6 April 2001.

23. *Congressional Presentation for Foreign Operations, Fiscal Year 1999* (Washington, DC: Department of State, 1998), 680–86, 696–98, 702–704; *Congressional Presentation for Foreign Operations, Fiscal Year 2000* (Washington, DC: Department of State, 1999), 660–68, 684–87, 693–97; *Congressional Presentation for Foreign Operations, Fiscal Year 2001* (Washington, DC: Department of State, 2000), 491–95, 504–06, 510–12; *Congressional Presentation for Foreign Operations, Fiscal Year 2002* (Washington, DC: Department of State, 2001), 363–67, 373–75, 379–80.

24. Author's personal experience as a participant, May 1999, Tampa, FL.

25. Trip Report (see chap. 3, note 15).

26. Martin C. Spechler, "Regional Non-Cooperation in Central Asia: A Pathology," *Economic Developments and Reforms in Cooperation Partner Countries: The Interrelationship Between Regional Economic Cooperation, Security, and Stability*; NATO Economic Colloquium, Bucharest, Romania, 2–4 May 2001, 269.

27. "Kyrgyzstani Defense Minister Says NATO Cooperation Crucial for Military Policy," *Moscow Interfax*, 5 July 2004.

28. Lyle J. Goldstein, "Beyond the Steppe: Projecting Power into the New Central Asia," *Journal of Slavic Military Studies* 17, no. 2 (April–June 2004), 194.

29. Embassy of the United States, Tashkent, Uzbekistan, Press Release, "Head of US Central Command Visits Uzbekistan," 16 May 2000, http://www.usembassy.uz/home/index.aspx?&mid=216&lid=1&overview=623 (accessed 8 March 2006); and Sherman W. Garnett, Alexander Rahr, and Koji Watanabe, *The New Central Asia: In Search of Stability—A Report to the Trilateral Commission*, (New York: The Trilateral Commission, 2000), 28.

30. "CENTRASBAT," (see chap. 3, note 45); and Lt Col James DeTemple, "Central Asia," *The NIS Observed: An Analytical View* 5, no. 14 (17 September 2000), http://www.bu.edu/iscip/digest/vol5/ed0514.html#centasia (accessed 12 March 2006); Butler, "U.S. Military Cooperation" (see chap. 3, note 54); Elizabeth Sherwood-Randall, "Building Cooperative Security Ties in Central Asia," *Stanford Journal of International Relations* 3, no. 2 (Fall/Winter 2002), http://www.stanford.edu/group/sjir/3.2.06_sherwoodrandall.html (accessed

17 February 2006); and "Uzbeks, Kyrgyz 'disappointed' at NATO inaction over militants – Kazakh paper," *Eurasianet.org*, 22 September 2000, http://www .eurasianet.org/resource/kazakhstan/hypermail/200009/0051.html (accessed 17 February 2006).

31. Robert Karniol, "Antiterror Needs Cancel CENTRASBAT Exercise," *Janes Defense Weekly* 37, no. 4, 23 January 2002.

32. USCENTCOM personnel, interviewed by author, 27–29 September 2005.

33. Clancy, Zinni, and Koltz, *Battle Ready*, 320 (see chap. 4, note 17).

34. Edward L. Hughes, Ken H. Butts, Bernard F. Griffard, and Arthur L. Bradshaw Jr., eds., *Responding to Environmental Challenges in Central Asia and the Caspian Basin*, USCENTCOM Central Asia States Environmental Security Conference, 6–8 March 2001, Garmisch-Partenkirchen, Germany, Report (Carlisle, PA: US Army War College Center for Strategic Leadership, 2001), 11, http://stinet.dtic.mil/cgi-bin/GetTRDoc?AD=ADA423651& Location=U2&doc=GetTRDoc.pdf; and Bernard F. Griffard, "Enhancing Regional Stability and Security in Central Asia: Implementing the U.S. Central Command Disaster Preparedness Program," *Center for Strategic Leadership Issue Paper*, vol. 10-04 (Carlisle, PA: US Army War College Center for Strategic Leadership, November 2004), 2, http://www.carlisle.army.mil/usacsl/ publications/ 10-04.pdf (accessed 23 January 2006).

35. *Congressional Presentation for Foreign Operations*, (see chap. 4, note 23).

36. Lt Col William Lahue, USA, "Security Assistance in Kazakhstan: Building a Partnership for the Future," *The DISAM Journal of International Security Assistance Management* 25, no. 1 (Fall 2002/Winter 2003), 10.

37. Trip Report (see chap. 3, note 15).

38. *Foreign Military Sales, Foreign Military Construction Sales, and Military Assistance Facts* (Washington, DC: Defense Security Cooperation Agency, 2004), 13, 28–29.

39. Embassy of the United States, Tashkent, Uzbekistan, Press Release, "U.S. Government Delivers Military Transport Vehicles to Uzbekistan," 14 February2000, http://www.usembassy.uz/home/index.aspx?&mid=216&lid =1&overview=646 (accessed 8 March 2006); Defense Language Institute English Language Center (DLIELC) correspondence (see chap. 3, note 38); Lahue, "Security Assistance in Kazakhstan," 10 (see chap. 4, note 36); and "Fiscal Year 2002 U.S. Government Assistance to and Cooperative Activities with Eurasia" (Washington, DC: Department of State, January 2003), http://www .state.gov/p/eur/rls/rpt/c10251.htm (accessed 8 March 2006).

40. Office of the Coordinator of US Assistance for Europe and Eurasia, US Department of State, *Congressional Presentation for Foreign Operations, Fiscal Year 1999* (Washington, DC: Department of State, 1998), 1006.

41. Marat Kenzhetaev, "Kazakhstan's Military-Technical Cooperation with Foreign States: Current Status, Structure and Prospects," http://mdb.cast .ru (accessed 6 March 2006).

42. Priest, *The Mission*, 116–17 (see chap. 4, note 1).

43. Director of Strategy and Plans (see chapter 3, note 28).

44. Author with Defense Institute for International Legal Studies, and Defense Resource Management Institute, correspondence, January 2006.

45. Director of Strategy and Plans (see chap. 3, note 28); Director of Strategy and Plans (see chap. 4, note 22); *Foreign Military Training and DOD Engagement Activities of Interest*, vol. 1, FY 1999 and 2000 (Washington, DC: Department of State, 2000), http://www.state.gov/www/global/arms/fmtrain/toc .html; and *Foreign Military Training and DOD Engagement Activities of Interest*, vol. 1, FY 2000 and 2001 (Washington, DC: Department of State, 2001), http://www.state.gov/www/global/arms/fmtrain/toc.html.

46. Glenn W. Goodman Jr., "Low-Key Spadework By Green Berets Reaps Valuable Benefits For War In Afghanistan," *Armed Forces Journal International*, January 2002, 60.

47. Ibid.; Chivers, "Long Before War" (see chap. 1, note 2); "U.S., Uzbekistan military hold joint training," *United Press International*, 22 June 2001; "To Which Extent is Realistic the Threat of Armed Incursion into the Southern Border of Uzbekistan?" *Uzbekistan Local Press Digest, Eurasia.org* (undated) http://www.eurasianet.org/resource/uzbekistan/press_digest/digest 4_1.shtml; Office of the Coordinator of US Assistance to Europe and Eurasia, *US Government Assistance to and Cooperative Activities With Eurasia, Fiscal Year 2001 Annual Report* (Washington, DC: Department of State, 2002), 98; and Director of Strategy and Plans (see chap. 4, note 22).

48. Chivers, "Long Before War" (see chap. 1, note 2); Lt Gen Michael W. Wooley, "America's Quiet Professionals: Specialized Airpower—Yesterday, Today, and Tomorrow," *Air and Space Power Journal* 19, no. 1 (Spring 2005), 59; and Robert Burns, "Commandos Specialize in Secret Missions," *Associated Press*, 29 November 2002.

49. "U.S.–Kazakhstani Military Exercises Previewed," *Moscow Rossiyskaya Gazeta*, 27 June 1999, 7; "Plan, Goals for Zhardem Exercises Assessed," *Moscow Obshchaya Gazeta*, 15–21 July 1999, no. 28, 7; and "Solemn Closing Ceremony of the Kazakhstani–American Combined Exercise 'Balans-Zhardem' with Participation," Kazakhstani Ministry of Defense Public Affairs Office, August 1999, http://www.mod.kz (accessed 18 April 2006).

Chapter 5

Rewards and Rebalance

Can we count on overflight rights for the duration? And where do we stage? Where do we base? . . . In the north, maybe we can strike a deal with President Karimov in Uzbekistan. Maybe even with the Turkmenbashi . . . Uzbekistan, of course, will be vital to the operation. . . . But President Karimov is sitting on the fence. But we've got to convince him we'll stay the course once we go in. . . . I think we can work out our issues with Tajikistan and Kyrgyzstan.

—Gen Tommy Franks, US Central Command
speaking to his staff on 12 September 2001

In the weeks following the terrorist attacks on 11 September 2001, the Central Asian region, which had for so long been underappreciated by strategic planners in Washington, gained new value. Deputy Assistant Secretary of State B. Lynn Pascoe asserted in testimony before Congress that "it was critical to the national interests of the United States that we greatly enhance our relations with the five Central Asian countries" to prevent them from becoming harbors for terrorism.[1] US military forces deployed to bases in Central Asia to conduct offensive operations against the Taliban and al-Qaeda in Afghanistan. All five of the Central Asian states granted the US and coalition forces overflight privileges and most offered basing rights. US forces were established primarily at Karshi-Khanabad in Uzbekistan and Manas in Kyrgyzstan, but were also permitted to use, with certain restrictions, facilities in Kazakhstan, Tajikistan, and Turkmenistan.

Army general Tommy Franks, the successor to General Zinni as USCENTCOM commander, knew the overflight and basing rights came at a price.[2] Although these nations were reimbursed for costs associated with using the facilities,[3] General Franks wanted to do as much as possible to ensure rapport with the civilian and military leaders in these countries so he could maintain access into Afghanistan. General Franks sought every opportunity to increase the existing security-cooperation programs and develop new ones as a means of rewarding the Central Asian nations for their support in Operation Enduring Freedom. He told his staff he wanted to bring "goodies" each time he traveled to the region, making four trips by January 2002.[4]

High Watermark

From September 2001 to August 2002 marked the high watermark of US security-cooperation efforts in Central Asia. Instead of being viewed as the backwater in Washington's and USCENTCOM's security-cooperation calculus, Central Asia moved to the forefront. Resources were redirected and new programs were established. Among the first steps in this expansion was establishing a security-cooperation relationship with Tajikistan.

For the previous decade, Tajikistan had been left out of most US security-cooperation initiatives. Until 1997 the civil war and resulting turmoil provided few opportunities for security-cooperation activities, and concern over human rights and the integration of the opposition forces meant Washington kept Dushanbe at arms length. Tajikistan was not eligible for WIF funds as it had not joined NATO's PfP, and with no nuclear, chemical, or biological weapons facilities, there was little justification for including Tajikistan in the CTR program.[5] The only program Tajikistan participated in was attending the Marshall Center, and by the end of 2000 some 42 Tajik officers and civilians had graduated.[6] By 2001, however, US policy makers believed the country had stabilized enough to allow for a few tentative links, and in January, Deputy Assistant Secretary of Defense Jeffrey Starr visited Dushanbe to initiate discussions.[7] General Franks followed with a visit in May 2001 during which he conveyed Pres. George W. Bush's message that Tajikistan was considered to be a "strategically significant country" for stability and security in Central Asia and offered to initiate specific security-cooperation programs.[8] Little of substance had been accomplished by September, but Tajikistan was soon to benefit from its willingness to host US forces. When Tajikistan joined the NATO PfP program in November 2001, it became eligible for WIF funding and began participating in related military contact events and exercises.

The United States also formalized and expanded its security relationships with the other countries in the region, most notably Uzbekistan. On 12 March 2002, US Secretary of State Colin Powell and Uzbekistani foreign minister Adulaziz Kamilov signed a Strategic Partnership and Cooperation Framework which offered the strongest statement Washington had ever issued regarding security in Central Asia: "The U.S. affirms that it would regard with grave concern any external threat to the security and territorial integrity of the Republic of Uzbekistan."[9] It was much less than President Karimov wanted, but it marked a significant, if only temporary, step in the relationship between the two countries. Likewise, USCENTCOM sought to reinvigorate its relationship with Turkmenistan, particularly by way of the SPP with the Nevada National Guard which had been dormant for several years.[10]

With a supplemental authorization from Congress, over $55.650 million in FMF funds were provided to the Central Asian states in 2002—almost twice as much as had been provided for the entire region from 1997 through 2001. The overwhelming majority, $36.207 million, was given to Uzbekistan, but Kyrgyzstan received $11 million and Kazakhstan $4.750 million. Tajikistan received $3.700 million, almost as much as longtime partner Kazakhstan. Although all four nations were willing to host US forces, the increase in FMF was clearly directed to those countries chosen by the United States for its basing needs. Fortunately, over $8.462 million in equipment previously ordered also began to arrive in Central Asia, more than twice as much as had been delivered to that point, and much of that went to Kazakhstan (the radios and individual equipment for KAZBAT identified in the previous chapter). Training and education programs also saw an increase: IMET funding almost doubled to over $3 million, and war college quotas doubled.

New programs were initiated as well. The Regional Defense Counterterrorism Fellowship, established in March 2002, supplemented IMET by providing Defense Department (as opposed to State Department) funds for attendance in nonlethal counterterrorism training and education courses. Kazakhstan, Kyrgyzstan, Tajikistan, and Uzbekistan began to receive funds in 2003 (table A.9, appendix A). In most cases, this funding was used to attend courses that would have normally been funded through IMET, such as Air Command and Staff College, Signal Officers Basic Course, and the International Defense Management Course.

However, in some cases, the Regional Defense Counterterrorism Fellowship (RDCTF) program was used to fund attendance at new courses specifically focused on counterterrorism, such as Combating Terrorism in a Democratic Society and Civil-Military Responses to Terrorism offered primarily at the same institutions that had previously seen students from Central Asia, such as the Center for Civil-Military Relations at NPS and the DIILS.[11]

Similarly, in June 2002, Uzbekistan, while considering using its FMF to purchase radios and other communications gear, requested an assessment of its communications systems and networks. USCENTCOM tasked the US Air Force's Electronic Systems Center to conduct a command, control, communications, computers (C4) study under the Regional Airspace Initiative Program, one of the interoperability programs eligible for WIF funding. This study was completed in September 2003.[12]

Not all programs showed such a dramatic increase. Because of ongoing combat operations in Afghanistan, the special operations exercise program had to be scaled back and some military contact events were cancelled due to the lack of available US forces to participate. In Uzbekistan, for example, three of eight special operations exchanges and 14 of 37 military contact events scheduled for 2002 were cancelled.[13] Fortunately, some critical events continued: for example, the 6 SOS was still able to deploy to Uzbekistan and Kyrgyzstan in 2002, and the 10 SFG from Fort Carson, Colorado, sent a twelve-man team to train Kazakhstani forces in counterterrorism operations in February and March, 2002.[14] The Regional Cooperation exercises for 2002 and 2003, which had supplanted CENTRASBAT, were also cancelled. To make up for these cancellations, the Central Asian states, particularly Uzbekistan, were invited to participate in many more multilateral NATO PfP exercises, hosted by USEUCOM and US Joint Forces Command (USJFCOM). Uzbekistan, for example, participated in Cooperative Endeavor 02, Cooperative Nugget 02, Cooperative Safeguard 02, Cooperative Zenith 02, and Strong Resolve 02.[15]

The Central Asian states reciprocated to Washington's overtures by sending liaison officers to USCENTCOM headquarters in Tampa. Five Uzbek officers arrived in December 2001, five from Kyrgyzstan arrived in May 2002, and three from Kazakhstan in June 2002.[16] Although the purpose of assigning these officers to USCENTCOM was to facilitate the coordination of support for Operation Enduring Freedom in Afghanistan and, in the case of Kazakhstan, Operation Iraqi Freedom, their presence at the headquarters marked a major step in the bilateral relationships and occasionally assisted in planning and executing security-cooperation activities. Likewise, as a reflection of the new relationship between Uzbekistan and the United States, in June 2002, Tashkent sent Lt Col Ilkhomjon Bekmirzaev, who was serving as a liaison officer at USCENTCOM, to Washington to serve as its defense attaché, the first new attaché since 1997.[17]

New Equilibrium

As quickly as the programs increased in the fall of 2001, they began to decrease a year later. FMF allocations, which exceeded $55 million in 2002, dropped to just over $16 million in 2003 and then below $10 million in 2004. The downward trend continued through 2006 and the projections for 2007. IMET funding continued to increase for a year, but then returned to its 2002 level of approximately $3 million per year. Part of this decrease is a reflection of the end of combat actions in Afghanistan and the perceived decreasing need to reward the Central Asian states for their support, but there were other factors that led to a rebalance of the security-cooperation programs in the region. Increasing concern over human rights abuses led to a slow but steady decline in US relations with most of the Central Asian states, culminating in an almost complete severing of the security-cooperation relationship with Uzbekistan following the Andijon incident in May 2005 and the subsequent eviction of US forces from Karshi-Khanabad. Simultaneously, the increasing pressures of the war in Iraq led to additional tensions and distractions.

Human Rights and the Colored Revolutions

Some Central Asian leaders saw the new relationship with the United States in the war on terrorism as an opportunity to eliminate any remaining opposition to their rule. US officials continued to advocate that human rights considerations would continue to factor heavily in US policy toward the region, but Central Asian elites, particularly in Tashkent and Bishkek, believed their cooperation with the United States would inoculate them against US disapproval for their repressive actions and quickly labeled any opposition group as terrorist. Within months, both the US State Department and international political activists were noting that the human rights situation had demonstrably worsened since the US involvement started. In March 2002, US assistant secretary of state Lorne Craner admitted the Uzbekistani government was using the war on terrorism as a pretext for cracking down on domestic political opponents, but argued that more US involvement, rather than less, would eventually influence President Karimov to permit greater freedoms.[18] By December 2003, US secretary of state Powell declined to certify Uzbekistan as having made progress in respecting human rights an act which put a freeze on most security-cooperation activities between the two countries. Military contact events could continue, but Uzbekistan would not be granted any additional IMET or FMF funding.

Uzbekistan was not the only Central Asian state with a worsening human rights record during this period. An assassination attempt against President Niyazov on 25 November 2002, led to harsh repressive measures against opposition groups in Turkmenistan. While Niyazov has never been afraid of using force to maintain his hold on power, the aftermath of the attack brought particularly egregious abuses, including arresting family members of the accused conspirators, an unauthorized search of the Uzbekistani embassy, and the expulsion of the Uzbekistani ambassador. The United States, instead of backing Niyazov as he expected, called for an investigation into human rights abuses and condemned Turkmenistan for violating international conventions protecting diplomats. The relationship between the United States and Turkmenistan cooled as Niyazov turned to Russia for support.[19]

In November 2003, following what many believed to be rigged parliamentary elections, popular opposition overthrew the government of Pres. Eduard Shevardnadze in Georgia in what came to be known as the "Rose Revolution." Central Asian leaders were quick to note that Georgia had sided with the United States in the war on terrorism and hosted US forces under the Georgia Train and Equip Program (GTEP). The following autumn, a similar political upheaval—the "Orange Revolution"—in

Ukraine after fraudulent presidential elections once again drew an apparent linkage between military cooperation with the United States and internal instability and an overturning of the existing political order.

Soon the colored revolutions would come to Central Asia. In March 2005, demonstrators chased Pres. Askar Akayev from power. Although the US forces at Manas were not involved, President Karimov in Uzbekistan began to believe that the US military presence at Karshi-Khanabad, rather than serving as a force against insurgents such as the IMU, offered no protection to his regime and may in fact be a source of instability. When the United States called for an independent investigation of the deaths of hundreds of civilians at Andijon in May 2005, Karimov began to distance his government from the United States. Restrictions were placed in US operations from Karshi-Khanabad and on 29 July 2005, Karimov exercised a provision in the original basing agreement and gave US forces six months to leave.[20] By the spring of 2006, US Army major Paul Schmitt, the US SAO in Tashkent, characterized his work as "trying to conduct security cooperation in a hostile environment."[21]

The War in Iraq

Washington was increasingly concerned over the human rights situation in Central Asia becoming increasingly sensitive to charges that its security-cooperation efforts with these authoritarian leaders were exacerbating the abuses. But other factors were also impinging on Central Asia's primacy in security-cooperation affairs. Within USCENTCOM, the effort required to plan for the invasion of Iraq began to divert attention away from Central Asia. President Bush began seriously considering options against Iraq as early as November 2001, and planners at USCENTCOM immediately began updating and modifying existing war plans. When the original war plans proved inadequate, they developed a new concept of operations which General Franks briefed to President Bush on 5 August 2002. The president approved the concept and the following day General Franks issued orders to his subordinate commanders to start detailed planning actions.[22] Two weeks later he left Tampa on what was to be his last trip to Central Asia as the USCENTCOM

89

commander. When he returned, his attention and that of the USCENTCOM senior leadership and staff was focused increasingly on the coming conflict with Iraq. Despite the continuing operations in Afghanistan and continuing deployment of US units to the region, Central Asia again became a secondary consideration. Without the constant attention and influence of the senior leaders, the security-cooperation efforts in Central Asia began to lose momentum.[23]

The Iraq war had a negative impact on relations throughout most of Central Asia. With the exception of President Karimov (at least initially), Central Asian leaders were opposed to US operations against Saddam Hussein. Almaty was concerned that a successful US invasion would lead to a drop in oil prices and reduced investment in Kazakhstan's growing oil industry. Most of the leaders were also concerned that the war in Iraq would bring a resurgence in Islamic radicalism and terrorism throughout Central Asia. Soon, however, they began to understand the implications of the US efforts to overthrow the despotic regime of Saddam Hussein for their own futures—if Washington was willing to invade Iraq to install a new regime, what would it be willing to do against Turkmenistan and Uzbekistan?[24] The Iraq war both decreased US attention and increased Central Asian concerns.

Planning and Organizational Changes

Since the establishment of the JCTP program by USEUCOM in 1989, there had always been a distinction between *security-assistance* activities and *military-engagement* activities. This bifurcation was perpetuated by the military organizations that conduct each type of activity. Training and equipping programs were (and are) largely conducted by the military services (Army, Navy, Air Force, and Marine Corps) within their respective systems of training and acquisition organizations—often referred to as the *institutional* element of the service—as part of the military services' organize, train, and equip responsibilities under Title 10 of the *US Code*. Security-assistance training and education programs conducted by the Air Force, for example, are executed by Air Education and Training Command (AETC) as an embedded subset of the larger training and education programs for the US

Air Force. Likewise, the Air Force Materiel Command (AFMC) is responsible for executing foreign military sales within the processes used to acquire weapon systems and military equipment.

However, engagement activities such as military contact events and exercises are usually conducted by the combatant commanders and their subordinate component commands. USCENTCOM, is responsible for military contact programs and joint exercises, and relies on its subordinate commands—US Army Central Command (USARCENT); US Central Command Air Forces (USCENTAF); US Naval Forces, Central Command (USNAVCENT); US Marine Component, Central Command (USMARFORCENT); and USSOCCENT—to execute these activities. Although security-assistance programs and engagement activities could be directed toward the same goal, as they were for CENTRASBAT, they were viewed as independent and distinct activities governed by separate regulations and bureaucracies.

The publication of the *Quadrennial Defense Review* in late September 2001 for the first time drew together these separate activities and organizations under a new term, *security-cooperation*.[25] Security cooperation encompassed virtually all of the activities conducted by the US military during peacetime with the military forces of other nations, including the activities outlined in table 1. The process of integrating these activities and improving the long-term planning process for security-cooperation programs was significantly advanced in 2003 with the publication of the first DOD Security Cooperation Guidance. Defense Secretary Donald Rumsfeld wanted to bring more structure and integration to the various security-cooperation programs and initiatives the United States was conducting around the world, and he wanted to have those programs linked to specific goals and objectives for each region and country rather than the broad "show the flag" engagement activities of the 1990s. The 2003 Security Cooperation Guidance (a classified document not available to the public) provides that focus, and each regional command was tasked to revise its Theater Security Cooperation Plans (now called Theater Security Cooperation Strategies) to match this guidance.[26]

These two structural changes, along with the massive increase in security-assistance funding in 2002, forced USCENTCOM to reevaluate how it was organized to execute security cooperation within the command. Within the region, security-cooperation programs had largely been executed by the US defense attachés assigned to the US embassies as an additional responsibility. With the expansion of the programs in the late 1990s, it became clear that additional personnel were required. Permanent billets had been authorized as early as 1998, but were never filled. Instead, Army officers (usually captains and majors) undergoing training to become foreign area officers (FAO) at the Marshall Center were detailed to the embassies on three- or six-month rotations.[27] While this eased the workload of the defense attachés, the constant rotation of officers undermined continuity and the ability to develop and execute long-term programs. The first full-time security assistance officer (SAO), US Army lieutenant colonel William Lahue, arrived in Almaty in May 2001. USCENTCOM assigned full-time SAOs to Bishkek and Tashkent soon thereafter and in Tajikistan a full-time officer was assigned in the summer of 2004.[28] In Turkmenistan, the relatively small security-cooperation program is still managed by the US defense attaché.[29]

By mid-2002, it was clear to the security-cooperation planners in Tampa that simply pushing assistance to the region was counterproductive and they searched for ways to integrate the programs and build long-range plans. Within USCENTCOM, there traditionally had been little synchronization between the IMET and FMF programs, which resided in the logistics directorate, and the military contact program in the plans and policy directorate. In the spring of 2001, even before the new *Quadrennial Defense Review* introduced the concept of "security cooperation," General Franks reorganized his headquarters staff to combine these programs into a single, expanded "engagement" office to facilitate integration. Still, change came slowly. The normal rotation of staff officers brought in new personnel who were more receptive to the merger of the offices. With his attention more focused on Iraq, General Franks made his last trip to Central Asia in August 2002. After that, there was less pressure on the USCENTCOM staff to find "deliverables" and more time to develop long-term integrated programs. Staff members began developing strategies to harmonize the various programs, including those executed by DTRA that were previously seen as unrelated to security cooperation, as well as some outside of DOD's purview, such as the State Department's EXBS program.[30]

Similarly, the newly established SAOs in the region began to tie together the various programs within their areas of responsibilities. Lieutenant Colonel Lahue in Almaty worked with his counterparts in the Kazakhstani Ministry of Defense to establish a five-year plan of military cooperation. First, he invited a MET from the DISAM at Wright-Patterson AFB to help explain the intricacies of the IMET and FMS programs to the appropriate officials within the Ministry of Defense. This instruction helped ensure the plan would be developed on a realistic understanding of what the United States could provide, how the programs actually worked, and how the MOD could manage those resources within its own national defense budget.[31]

Following this MET, the SAO and the MOD jointly produced the five-year plan based on an understanding of common US and Kazakhstani security interests in the region. This plan was intended to "integrate and focus all available assets . . . in a targeted force development effort that meets both U.S. and Kazakhstani strategic objectives." The plan also cemented the primacy of the development of military capabilities over other considerations: "Support for systemic reform will be focused on those reforms required to meet the force development objectives."[32] The new plan, signed in September 2003, included the following goals:

- Force development
  - • Develop a NATO-interoperable peacekeeping force
  - • Develop a ground, maritime, and air-defense force in the Caspian Sea region
  - • Develop rapid-reaction and special-operations forces
- Systemic Reform
  - • Officer/NCO personnel management
  - • Professional noncommissioned officer corps
  - • Vehicle and equipment maintenance systems
  - • English-language training system[33]

Similar efforts occurred in the other Central Asian states. In 2002 Lt Col Jon Chicky, the USCENTCOM desk officer for Uzbekistan, developed a security-assistance strategy for Tashkent that meshed FMF, EXBS, and IMET over a five-year period in such a way that the armed forces of Uzbekistan, including troops from the Ministries of Internal Affairs and Emergency Situations, Committee for Protection of State Borders, and National Security Service, would be "transformed from legacy Soviet mechanized/motorized force to a professional, lighter, and mobile force eventually interoperable with U.S./NATO and able to defend the nation from external and certain internal threats." His plan, which was approved by USCENTCOM and the Uzbekistani Ministry of Defense, focused on six critical efforts:

- Expanding and equipping Uzbekistani special forces

- Improving communications interoperability within the Uzbekistani armed forces and with US and NATO

- Enhanced training/planning by creating a modeling and simulation capability

- Creating a professional officer corps and officer personnel management system

- Creating a professional noncommissioned officer corps

- Improving infrastructure and capabilities to secure borders[34]

By April 2004, Lieutenant Colonel Chicky's strategy had been turned into a five-year security-cooperation plan. The Ministry of Defense, which had participated in the development of the plan and in principle approved it, declined to sign it in order "to maintain flexibility;" although the SAO and MOD planners referred to it when coordinating security-assistance activities. Eventually the disruption in relations after Andijon made the document irrelevant.[35]

Similarly, in November 2003, the Marshall Center hosted a conference in Dushanbe to help the Tajikistani army build an unclassified military strategy which was used by the SAO to help coordinate assistance. This conference helped the SAO and Tajikistani MOD create a five-year bilateral plan, but this document was never signed and eventually was abandoned by the United States because of lack of follow-through by the Tajikistani MOD.[36] By the end of 2004, a five-year bilateral plan had been established with Kyrgyzstan.[37] These plans were useful for focusing security-cooperation efforts, but they often had the unintended consequence of being perceived by the MODs as promises rather than intentions, despite the caveats by the SAOs that executing the programs was dependent on annual FMF and IMET funding.

These organizational and planning changes further increased the integration of the military contact events and the security-assistance programs, particularly FMS, and USCENTCOM began planning and executing additional activities to be mutually supporting. For example, in 2004 the Montana National Guard hosted a series of military contact events on developing non-commissioned officer training syllabi to support the establishment of the NCO Academy in Koi Tash, built using FMF funds. Likewise, the Air Force sponsored a series of visits to C-130 bases in Arkansas and Kentucky to highlight the capabilities of the C-130 Hercules transport aircraft. The Kazakhstani air force was interested in acquiring several through the EDA program.[38] However, there was no apparent integration with other programs such as those conducted by DTRA. The organizational and planning adjustments also served to focus US security-cooperation activities on concrete aspects of building military capabilities rather than on less tangibles.

Military Capabilities

The *2001 Quadrennial Defense Review* first used the term *security cooperation* and also marked the shift in emphasis for security-cooperation programs. Unlike the perspectives of the 1990s, there was no discussion about the utility of security-cooperation tools to promote less tangible objectives such as military democratization. Published just weeks after the terrorist attacks on New York and Washington, the new focus was on building military capabilities (or *partner capacity*, as it was later to be called) in allied and partner nations to deter aggressors and prosecute the war on terrorism:

> A primary objective of U.S. security cooperation will be to help allies and friends create favorable balances of military power in critical areas of

95

the world to deter aggression or coercion. Security cooperation serves as an important means for linking DOD's strategic direction with those of U.S. allies and friends. . . . It requires that U.S. forces train and operate with allies and friends in peacetime as they would operate in war. This includes enhancing interoperability and peacetime preparations for coalition operations, as well as increasing allied participation in activities such as joint and combined training and experimentation. . . . A particular aim of DOD's security cooperation efforts will be to ensure access, interoperability, and intelligence cooperation, while expanding the range of pre-conflict options available to counter coercive threats, deter aggression, or favorably prosecute war on U.S. terms.[39]

President Bush's *2002 National Security Strategy* further emphasized countering terrorism as the primary role of security cooperation, and the *2006 Quadrennial Defense Review* reaffirmed this approach. State Department justifications for FMF became specific in requesting funds to build military capabilities, primarily counterterrorism and border security forces, in Central Asia. The 2005 request for Kazakhstan, for example, stated additional funding:

> will continue to enhance Kazakhstan's capability to combat terrorism in the region through security enhancements and counterterrorism support . . . will continue to provide assistance to the Peacekeeping Battalion and help support development of a rapid reaction brigade near the Caspian oil field in Atyrau . . . will enhance Kazakhstan's capability to respond to major terrorist threats to oil platforms or borders, while also enhancing its interoperability with NATO, U.S., and Coalition forces . . . will support the purchase of interoperable communications equipment, basic individual soldier equipment, vehicles, and power generator systems.[40]

Despite this shift, however, funding for FMF continued to drop, from $16.090 million in 2003 to an estimated $5.500 million in 2007. Much of this drop is attributable to the elimination of FMF funding for Uzbekistan, but the funding for Kyrgyzstan, Tajikistan, and Turkmenistan also slowed, totaling together only $2 million in 2007. Only for Kazakhstan did the funding remain steady. FMF to Almaty averaged $3.500 million each year from 2003 to 2007.

As a result of the large FMF allocations the previous year, deliveries reached a new peak in 2003, with over $42 million worth of equipment delivered and construction completed. Uzbekistan was the primary recipient, with almost $34 million worth of communications gear and other items provided. Tajikistan and Turkmenistan received deliveries under the FMS system for the first time in 2003. Ashgabat first received FMF in

1997, but, other than funding the transportation of the patrol boat provided under the EDA program in 2000, chose not to use it until 2002. Much of Kazakhstan's FMF was used to build barracks at Atyrau, which opened in July 2004, but it also received five HMMWVs in August 2004, supplementing the two it received in December 2001.[41] Almaty also advanced another step when it requested, and received, two UH-1 Huey helicopters through the EDA program, with refurbishment to the HUEY-II configuration provided through FMF. Likewise, Ministry of Defense officials initiated serious discussions on the possibilities of acquiring used C-130 Hercules transport aircraft, which would represent the first ever transfer of fixed-wing military aircraft to a post-Soviet state. Although the aircraft would be provided through the EDA program, Kazakhstan would be expected to absorb all costs for refurbishment, sustainment, and training through its national funds, another first for Central Asia. The HMMWVs, helicopters, and transport aircraft are intended to improve Kazakhstan's capabilities to rapidly respond to threats in any part of its vast territory, and, if completed, would dramatically improve the capabilities of its mobile forces.

Likewise, approximately a third of the military contact events also continued to emphasize the development of military capabilities, but they expanded in scope to include interaction with a wider variety of military and nonmilitary units on an increasingly large set of specialties. An increasing number of these events (anywhere from 10 to 40 percent of the number planned) focused on counterinsurgency, border security, counternarcotics, and aviation capabilities rather than on the previous specialties of peacekeeping and search and rescue. They began to more frequently include visits and contacts with nonmilitary units such as the Ministry of the Environment and Emergency Situations, Border Guards, Ministry of the Interior, and the National (presidential) Guard.[42] Even the Marshall Center adjusted to this new environment, adding a course named Program on Terrorism and Security Studies to match the previous course that addressed national security issues in democratic states. In 2004 and 2005 nine students from Central Asia attended.[43]

As combat operations in Afghanistan began to wind down, US special operations forces were once again available to participate in bilateral exercises and training events in Central Asia. In some cases, the units came directly from Afghanistan to attend. The third special operations exercise in Kyrgyzstan since September 2001 began in January 2003 and was known as Balance Knight. Lasting a month, it then transitioned to Balance Knife, which included the 6th Special Operations Squadron. Balance Knife focused on mountain warfare, navigation and communication, and medical training, the latter was provided by the South Korean medical contingent at Manas. US forces also provided a C-130 aircraft from Manas for airborne training. Five SOFEXs were planned for Uzbekistan in 2003, although some were later postponed or cancelled.[44]

Proliferation Prevention

The changes in the proliferation prevention efforts in Central Asia must also be seen in the context of increasing the capabilities of the indigenous forces. While activities designed to destroy nuclear-, chemical-, and biological-weapons infrastructure continued, the real focus of these programs almost completely shifted toward improving the ability of these nations to secure and control their own borders. There was less of a focus on eliminating facilities and more emphasis on providing equipment and training to border forces. The war in Afghanistan brought attention to the porous borders in Central Asia, but it took a year for this to manifest in additional resources for the proliferation prevention programs. Funding for the ICP, which had been bumped up to $1.200 million in 2002, more than doubled to $2.890 million in 2003, with roughly equal amounts going to projects in Kazakhstan and Uzbekistan. Fourteen training events were held in 2002 and another 12 in 2003. In Uzbekistan this training culminated in an integrated exercise held in Chirchik in October and November 2004. Soon thereafter, the disruption in Uzbekistani-American relations impacted the program and Tashkent cancelled the remaining scheduled courses. In 2005 and 2006 the focus of the ICP shifted toward Kazakhstan and new, more successful, efforts were initiated in Tajikistan.

DTRA also initiated a new proliferation prevention program through CTR in 2003. The Weapons of Mass Destruction Proliferation Prevention Initiative (WMD-PPI) appears to have many of the same objectives as ICP, EXBS, and other efforts designed to improve border security throughout the former Soviet Union. Reminiscent of the export control efforts executed by the CTR program in the early 1990s, WMD-PPI goals in Central Asia include improving Uzbekistan's ability to detect radiological materials at key border crossing points and providing surveillance radars, communications equipment, and small vessels to Kazakhstan to improve its ability to monitor the Caspian Sea.[45]

Central Asian border security was becoming more important for another reason as well. The growing recognition that the drug trade in Afghanistan was undermining the security and economic stability in the Central Asian states led to additional funding under DOD's CN program to improve border security, interdiction capabilities, and special operations forces in the region. Managed from the office of the Assistant Secretary of Defense for Special Operations and Low Intensity Conflict, this funding had actually started on a small scale in 2001 in Uzbekistan, with $230 thousand provided for programs that year and a similar amount was offered in 2002. The massive explosion in the drug trade coming from Afghanistan, however, drove DOD planners to funnel over $6.500 million to Uzbekistan for counternarcotics programs in 2003, with an additional $500 thousand to Tajikistan and $351 thousand for regional programs within Central Asia. Funding dropped in 2004, but spiked again in 2005 to over $20 million, with large amounts offered to Tajikistan, Turkmenistan, and Kyrgyzstan. By this time political events in Uzbekistan had caught up with the counternarcotics program, and only $47 thousand had been spent before the United States temporarily halted the program.

In 2006 DOD requested over $55 million in CN funding to support a wide range of border security improvements throughout Central Asia, including the construction of facilities, provision of equipment, and training and conferences. In Kazakhstan, CN funding would provide the border security forces with three rigid-hull inflatable boats (RHIB) and improve the port facilities at Bautino. In Kyrgyzstan, it would be used to improve three border crossings, renovate garrisons for the Panther and Scorpion Special Forces units, and provide a small amount of customs equipment and a variety of training courses and conferences. In Tajikistan, which used CN funding in 2005 to initiate a communications upgrade and establish a border crossing at the Nizhn-Pianj Bridge. Additional funding would be used to complete the communications project, establish two additional border crossings, and refurbish several border outposts. In Turkmenistan, two-border crossing points, one on the Turkmen-Iran border and another on the Turkmen-Afghan border, were established in 2005; funding in 2006 would complete an interagency communications equipment project, establish three more border crossings, and provide training through a combined exercise with the Nevada National Guard. Should additional funding be granted for Uzbekistan, it would be used to provide RHIBs and border sensors.[46]

With a proposed 2006 budget of $55 million, counternarcotics activities are now the single largest element of the US security-cooperation program in Central Asia. In fact, border security—whether those efforts are to prevent narcotics WMD smuggling, human trafficking, or terrorist movement—has become the single most important objective of US security-cooperation efforts in Central Asia. It is not clear whether the establishment of this priority resulted from a deliberate policy decision or simply reflects of the relative strength of the various bureaucracies in the US national security establishment. Border security programs are being planned and executed by various offices, but they appear to lack the integration and synchronization necessary to be most effective. Yet these programs appear to be largely discrete and conducted by various organizations within DOD (such as DTRA, OSD, and USCENTCOM). Border security also requires integration.

Regional Cooperation

Promoting regional cooperation continued to be important, if less emphasized. Disaster response and environmental management activities and exercises maintained the contacts established between Kazakhstan, Kyrgyzstan, Tajikistan, and Uzbekistan. The Marshall Center courses and conferences continued to promote collaborative solutions to regional issues such as disaster preparedness, narcotics trafficking, and Caspian Sea security.

Two new exercises, however, were also established to support this goal. Along with its regular Combined Endeavor exercise, which has included participants from Central Asia since 1999, USEUCOM had been conducting RESCUER/MEDCUER exercises for several years "in the spirit of" the NATO PfP program. The scenario was based on a mass casualty situation, RESCUER addressed brigade-level responses to a humanitarian disaster while MEDCUER provided field training for medical personnel. Beginning in 2005, USEUCOM invited some of the Central Asian states to participate. Kazakhstan and Kyrgyzstan sent delegations (Uzbekistan declined), in September 2005, to Vaziani in the Republic of Georgia for the event. Kazakhstan, Kyrgyzstan, and Tajikistan are expected to participate in RESCUER 06, scheduled for August 2006 in Yerevan, Armenia.

The more significant initiative was the reestablishment of the Regional Cooperation exercises in 2004. The last one occurred in 2001 and is often referred to as CENTRASBAT 01. It had been held as a command post exercise at the US training facilities in Einsiedlerhof, Germany. Regional Cooperation 04 followed that model with a battalion-level command-post exercise with a disaster-response scenario in early September 2004. At the same facilities. Kazakhstan, Kyrgyzstan, Tajikistan, and Pakistan participated while Turkmenistan sent observers. Uzbekistan declined to participate because of the presence of Pakistani delegates.

US exercise coordinators noted there was little interaction between the Central Asian delegations during the first planning conference held in January 2004. Each delegation attempted to work directly and exclusively with the US coordinators and all questioned the presence of the Pakistanis. The Pakistani delegation even questioned their own participation in what they saw as a "Central Asian" exercise. The US coordinators were surprised but pleased when the environment changed dramatically but inexplicably during the March 2004 planning conference—all of the delegations were enthusiastic about working with each other, and the exercise proceeded in September with apparent collaboration between the participating delegations.[47]

The 2004 exercise highlighted the need for increased cross-border coordination through a regional coordination center (RCC), which was established for the 2005 exercise. Kazakhstan, Kyrgyzstan, Tajikistan, and Pakistan participated, while

Turkmenistan, Russia, and the United Arab Emirates were invited to send observers. Held at the Joint Warfighting Center in Suffolk, Virginia, in July 2005, Regional Cooperation addressed operational-level tasks and relationships, as opposed to the tactical focus of the previous exercise, in a scenario that emphasized border security, illegal migration, narcotics trafficking, and consequence management. The need for the RCC was validated as was the need to establish formal diplomatic agreements between the nations in the region to permit the exchange of information in the event of an emergency (fig.6).

Figure 6. Central Asian participants in the Regional Cooperation 05 exercise, Suffolk, Virginia, July 2005 (Reprinted from US Central Command. Used with permission.)

The 2006 exercise, planned for July in Bishkek, Kyrgyzstan, will build on these lessons and will be open to Afghanistan, Uzbekistan, and Gulf states such as Saudi Arabia, Kuwait, Oman, Qatar, and Bahrain.[48] Based on the experiences in the Regional Cooperation exercises, in March 2006 USCENTCOM announced its intention to establish a regional disaster preparedness center in Central Asia, likely in Kazakhstan, in the next few years.[49]

Democratization

Democratization ceased to be a stated primary objective for the security-cooperation programs in Central Asia, but, legacy efforts in several countries ensured it remained an important element. Over 20 percent of the military contact events were dedicated to officer and noncommissioned officer professional development. A significant portion of those events, however, consisted of exchange visits by military academy cadets. There is probably some long-term value in having junior officer candidates from Kazakhstan or Kyrgyzstan visit the United States to experience, if only for a brief period, the opportunities available to their American counterparts. On the other hand, little linkage to the US security-cooperation objectives is seen in having US cadets visit Central Asia. Further, there is not now an established way to measure and evaluate the success of this kind of program. The majority of the military contact events for officer and noncommissioned officer professional development, however, addresses the more appropriate issues of establishing professional forces in these nations. The importance of these programs vary by country. While a quarter to a third of the events in Kazakhstan, Kyrgyzstan, and Uzbekistan were dedicated to professional development topics, only three such events were planned for Tajikistan out of the 48 total events planned for 2004–2005. In Kyrgyzstan, noncommissioned officer professional development also resulted in Bishkek's first use of FMF for construction: over $5.700 million was dedicated to upgrade facilities at Koi Tash for use as a joint brigade and professional development training centers.[50]

Likewise, approximately 15 percent of the military contact events supported disaster management, environmental security, or medical issues, which support democratization objectives by promoting appropriate civil-military relationships. More recently, the military contact plans for Kazakhstan and Kyrgyzstan have included exchanges on public affairs in the military, which promote US objectives of defense transparency.[51]

Similarly, the increase in IMET funds beginning in 2002 continued for the next two years. Over $10 million in IMET was authorized in these three years, more than had been provided to the region between 1993 and 2001. This massive increase in funding brought a corresponding increase in the number of Central Asian defense personnel attending US military courses—over 650, more than twice as many as had attended US courses previously. Eighty-four students, including 54 from Kazakhstan, attended English-language training at DLIELC in 2004. In an impressive use of its security-assistance funding, Kazakhstan requires its personnel to attend intensive training at its own Military Institute of Foreign Languages, established in part with US security-assistance funding, to achieve basic English-language proficiency before traveling to the United States. This has reduced the duration of each student's overseas tour and has permitted sending twice as many students to DLIELC.[52]

Other training and education programs showed a similar increase through 2003 and 2004. Attendance at the Marshall Center jumped to 104 in 2004, twice as many as had attended each year from 1998 to 2002. The Central Asian states continued to receive quotas at the mid-level US war colleges. In 2003, for the first time, Kazakhstan was offered a quota at the Industrial College of the Armed Forces (ICAF), a prestigious senior-level war college under the National Defense University. Almaty chose Col Muslim Altynbayev, the first Kazakhstani defense attaché in Washington, to attend the course. The following year, Kazakhstan received an invitation to send an officer to the National War College (NWC). Lt Col Merey Bisenov, who had previously attended Air Command and Staff College in 1997–1998, graduated from the NWC in the summer of 2005. Only two previous ALP scholarships had been offered in Central Asia, to Uzbekistan in 1998 and 2002. In 2003, as a result of Central Asian support for US operations in Afghanistan, ALP invitations were offered to Kazakhstan, Turkmenistan (which declined), and Uzbekistan. A similar number of invitations were offered in 2004 to Kazakhstan, Kyrgyzstan (which declined), and Uzbekistan.

Current Status

The United States need for bases and relationships in Central Asia brought an immediate spike in many aspects of security cooperation, but the needed resources were not long sustained. Within a year, IMET- and FMF-funding levels began to drop, and they have now reached a new, lower equilibrium. But the funding for the counternarcotics program rose dramatically in 2005 and now constitutes the single largest funding source for security-cooperation programs in Central Asia. The objective for most programs is now to improve the security of the borders in Central Asia, for counternarcotics, counterproliferation, or counterinsurgency and counterterrorism operations (fig. 7).

At the beginning of 2006, US efforts in the region range from working in a "hostile environment" in Uzbekistan to a steady, relatively integrated approach to Kazakhstan. An assessment of the challenges these programs face in planning and execution follows.

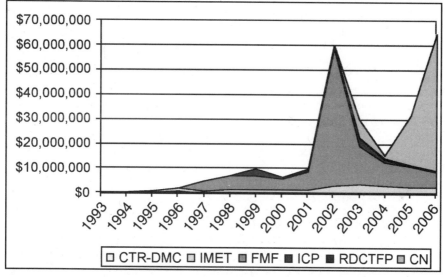

Figure 7. Selected US security-cooperation funding in Central Asia, 1993–2006 (adapted from data found in appendix A.)

Note: This chart reflects a compilation of relevant data included in the funding charts contained in appendix A except CTR funding, which largely focused on WMD elimination. It does not include all US security funding that has been spent in Central Asia, as many programs do not break out budget lines by country or region. However, it captures most of the spending and therefore portrays a fairly accurate historical perspective of US outlays in the region.

Notes

1. Jim Nichol, *Central Asia: Regional Developments and Implications for U.S. Interests*, CRS Issue Brief for Congress (Washington, DC: Congressional Research Service, Library of Congress, 2004), 3.

2. General Franks also understood that the price had just gone up. Prior to September 2001, he had initiated general discussions with Uzbekistani

president Karimov on the potential use of Karshi-Khanabad. General Franks was aware that Karimov knew the value of the airbase had gone up dramatically. Gen Tommy Franks with Malcolm McConnell, *American Soldier* (New York: Regan Books, 2004), 256.

3. Payment for the use of the airfields was handled in different ways. As Manas was a civilian airfield, Kyrgyzstan receives both a rental payment, approximately $2 million per year, and a payment for each takeoff and landing. Some sources estimate this at $5–$7 thousand per event. As the air bases in Tajikistan and Uzbekistan were primarily military facilities, Dushanbe and Tashkent received payments through the Coalition Support Fund (CSF), intended to offset costs that would otherwise have not been incurred had the country not been supporting US operations in the war on terrorism. In 2002 Tajikistan received $2.399 million which was used to repair the runway at Dushanbe ostensibly damaged by US aircraft, and Uzbekistan received $15.747 million which was used to upgrade facilities at Karshi-Khanabad and purchase other equipment through the FMS system. In 2005 Uzbekistan received an additional payment of $22.985 million which was the subject of much controversy. Although the proposal was developed and approved before the Andijon incident, it was paid afterwards. Many outside of the Bush administration advocated that the payment should be withheld to ensure Tashkent was not rewarded for the situation. The positions of the Defense and State Departments were that the US government should always pay its bills as a matter of principle. Author with the Office of the Secretary of Defense, March 2006; Bruce Pannier, "Kyrgyzstan: Bishkek Presents New Air-Base Terms to U.S.-Led Coalition," *Radio Free Europe/Radio Liberty*, 25 January 2006, http://www.rferl.org/features/features_Article.aspx?m=01&y =2006&id=E377D17F-622A-41E0-B9EA-1C9D4698B453 (accessed 26 January 2006); and Goldstein, "Beyond the Steppe" (chap.4, note 28).

4. Author with former US Central Command (USCENTCOM) staff members, correspondence, March 2006; and "Uzbekistan: Russian Agency Reports on US General's Meetings with Top Leaders," *Moscow ITAR-TASS*, 23 January 2002.

5. *Foreign Military Training and DOD Engagement Activities of Interest*, vol. 1, FY 1999 and 2000 (Washington, DC: Department of State, 2000), http://www.state.gov/www/global/arms/fmtrain/toc.html (accessed 8 March 2006).

6. The Marshall Center also hosted two conferences regarding Tajikistan prior to 2001. In August 1999, in support of the first post-civil-war national elections, it hosted Building Political Parties in Tajikistan: Cooperation and Competition, the only forum that included all of the opposition-party leaders, and in April 2000, in support of post-civil-war economic development, it hosted Building Institutional and Economic Foundations in Tajikistan. Author with George C. Marshall European Center for Security Studies, correspondence, February 2006.

7. Goldstein, "Making the Most" 85 (chap. 3, note 52),

8. Ahmed Rashid, "Western Powers Bolster Tajikistan as it Faces Renewed Threats to Stability and Security," *Central Asia—Caucasus Analyst*, 23 May

2001, http://www.cacianalyst.org/view_article.php?articleid=102 (accessed 23 March 2006).

9. "United States–Uzbekistan Declaration on the Strategic Partnership and Cooperation Framework," Embassy of the United States, Tashkent, Uzbekistan, 12 March 2002, http://www.usembassy.uz/home/index.aspx?&=&mid=218&overview=457 (accessed 8 March 2006).

10. "Nevada National Guard State Partnership Program in Turkmenistan," *The National Guard Bureau Office of International Affairs*, http://www.ngb.army.mil/ia/states/states/nv_turkmenistan%5B1%5D.htm (accessed 8 March 2006).

11. *Foreign Military Training and DOD Engagement Activities of Interest*, vol. 1, FY 2002 and 2003 (Washington, DC: Department of State, 2003), http://www.state.gov/t/pm/rls/rpt/fmtrpt/2003/ (accessed 8 March 2006).

12. Sara Bette Franken, "Regional Defense Counterterrorism Fellows Program," *The DISAM Journal of International Security Assistance Management* 26, no. 1 (Fall 2003), 12; Office of the Secretary of Defense correspondence (see chap. 5, note 3); Office of the Air Force Deputy Chief of Staff, Operations correspondence, March and April 2006; and author with the Air Force Electronic Systems Center, correspondence, February and March 2006.

13. USCENTCOM correspondence (see chap. 5, note 4).

14. "6th Special Operations Squadron Factsheet," 1st Special Operations Wing Public Affairs Office, http://www2.hurlburt.af.mil/library/factsheets/factsheet.asp?id=3492 (accessed 8 March 2006); and James Doran, "Americans Covertly Training Kazakh Troops," *Times of London*, 30 March 2002.

15. Bureau of European and Eurasian Affairs, *U.S. Assistance to and Cooperative Activities with Eurasia, FY 2002* (Washington, DC: Department of State, 2003), http://www.state.gov/p/eur/rls/rpt/c10251.htm (accessed 14 March 2006).

16. Elizabeth Wishnick, *Strategic Consequences of the Iraq War: U.S. Security Interests in Central Asia Reassessed* (Carlisle, PA: US Army War College Strategic Studies Institute, 2004), 2–4.

17. Defense Intelligence Agency, correspondence (see chap. 3, note 7).

18. Jeffrey Donovan, "U.S.: State Department Releases Human Rights Report Criticizing New Allies," *Radio Free Europe/Radio Liberty*, 5 March 2002, http://www.rferl.org/features/2002/03/05032002084601.asp (accessed 28 April 2006).

19. Ata Khaitov, "A New Role for Russia: Niazov's Best Friend," *The Jamestown Foundation Russia and Eurasia Review* 2, no. 3 (4 February 2003), 1–2.

20. Adam Ward, ed., "Uzbekistan Casts Out America: Setback or Opportunity for Washington?" *IISS Strategic Comments* 11, no. 6 (August 2005), 1–2.

21. Lt Col Dan Groeschen, Chief, Central and South Asia Branch, USCENTCOM, interviewed by the author, March 2006.

22. Bob Woodward, *Plan of Attack* (New York: Simon & Schuster, 2004), 30–153.

23. Author with former USCENTCOM personnel, correspondence, April 2006.

24. Ata Khaitov, "Central Asian Responses to the Iraq Crisis: Hope and Fears," *The Jamestown Foundation Russia and Eurasia Review* 2, no. 5 (4 March 2003); and Wishnick, *Strategic Consequences*, 14–17 (see chap 5, note 16).

25. *Quadrennial Defense Review Report* (Washington, DC: Department of Defense, 2001), 11.

26. Thomas S. Szayna, Adam Grissom, Jefferson P. Marquis, Thomas-Durell Young, Brian Rosen, and Yuna Huh Wong, *US Army Security Cooperation: Toward Improved Planning and Management* (Santa Monica, CA: RAND, 2004), 17.

27. Trip Report (see chap. 3, note 15).

28. Lahue, "Security Assistance in Kazakhstan," 10 (see chap. 4, note 36).

29. Groeschen interview (see chap. 5, note 21).

30. Author with former USCENTCOM staff members, correspondence, September 2005 and March 2006; and Priest, *The Mission*, 73 (see chap. 4, note 1).

31. Lahue, "Security Assistance in Kazakhstan" (see chap. 4, note 36); Craig M. Brandt, and Mark T. Ahles, "Defense Institute of Security Assistance Management Mobile Education Team Travels to Kazakhstan," *DISAM Journal of International Security Assistance Management* 25, no. 1 (Fall 2002/Winter 2003), 19.

32. Lahue, "Security Assistance in Kazakhstan," 13 (see chap. 4, note 36).

33. Ibid., 13–14; and "Kazakhstan to Purchase Military Hardware in US," *Moscow ITAR-TASS*, 20 February 2004.

34. CCJ5-E [USCENTCOM Joint Staff Office-5-E, Security Cooperation Division], Issue Paper, "Uzbekistan's Five-Year Security Assistance Plan," undated.

35. Author with the US Security Assistance Office, Tashkent, Uzbekistan, correspondence, April 2006.

36. Author with the Marshall Center, correspondence, April 2006.

37. "High-Level Kyrgyzstan–US Defense Talks Outline Military Cooperation to 2010," *Bishkek Kabar News Agency*, 5 October 2004.

38. Groeschen interview, March 2006 (see chap. 5, note 21).

39. *Quadrennial Defense Review*, 11 (see chap. 5, note 25).

40. *Congressional Budget Justification for Foreign Operations, Fiscal Year 2005* (Washington, DC: Department of State, 2004), 371.

41. "U.S. Government Aid Helps Defense Ministry Build Barracks in Atyrau," Embassy of the United States, Almaty, Kazakhstan, 23 July 2004, http://www.usembassy-kazakhstan.freenet.kz (accessed 8 March 2006); "U.S. Government Donates Five Humvee Ambulances to Kazakhstan's Peacekeeping Battalion," Embassy of the United States, Almaty, Kazakhstan, 17 August 2004, http://www.usembassy-kazakhstan.freenet.kz (accessed 8 March 2006).

42. USCENTCOM correspondence (see chap. 5, note 30).

43. "Program on Terrorism and Security Studies," George C. Marshall European Center for Security Studies, http://www.marshallcenter.org/site-graphic/lang-en/static/xdocs/coll/static/ptss/ptss-overview-en.pdf (accessed 28 April 2006).

44. "Bishkek Hosts US–Kyrgyzstani Military Exercises," *Moscow Interfax*, 17 March 2003; "US–Kyrgyz Military Exercises Underway in Bishkek," *News Agency Prima*, 19 March 2003; Roger M. McDermott, *Countering Global Terrorism: Developing the Antiterrorist Capabilities of the Central Asian Militaries* (Carlisle, PA: US Army War College Strategic Studies Institute, 2004), 22.

45. Senate, Testimony of Ms. Lisa Bronson, Deputy Under Secretary of Defense for Technology Security Policy and Counterproliferation, Before the Senate Committee on Armed Services Subcommittee on Emerging Threats and Capabilities, 108th Congress, 2d sess., 10 March 2004, http://armed-services.senate.gov/testimony.cfm?wit_id=3024&id=1077 (accessed 28 April 2006).

46. Office of the Secretary of Defense correspondence (see chap. 3, note 55).

47. Lt Col Dan Groeschen, chief, Central and South Asia Branch, US-CENTCOM, interviewed by author, September 2005; and USCENTCOM correspondence (see chap. 3, note 55).

48. Ibid.

49. Joshua Kucera, "CENTCOM Sets up Disaster Management Centre," *Janes' Defense Weekly*, 1 March 2006.

50. USCENTCOM correspondence (see chap. 5, note 30).

51. Ibid.

52. Author with DLIELC, correspondence, January 2006; and "Kazakhstan's Defense Ministry to Set up Language Institute," *Almaty Interfax-Kazakhstan*, 20 July 2004.

Chapter 6

Constraints and Limitations

*The system is badly broken. . . . We use chewing gum
and bailing wire to keep it together.*

—Gen Anthony Zinni
Commander,
US Central Command

Security cooperation is an inherently complex and difficult undertaking. Regardless of the countries involved, security-cooperation programs require years of effort and vast amounts of resources to have an impact, whether that be improved relationships or enhanced military capabilities. Often these programs must overcome significant cultural and language differences between the two armed forces, and those undertaken by the US military must accommodate the overwhelming differences between the size, capabilities, and available resources of the two forces. Beyond the general limitations of time and cost, each of the various security-cooperation activities has specific strengths and weaknesses that must be taken into account when building programs. And with little or no effort to measure and clinically analyze the results, it is difficult to best allocate resources (including canceling efforts that do not measure up) or adjust programs to maximize results. These challenges are inherent in all security-assistance programs, and have been part of all such efforts since Lend-Lease began in 1940.

There are other limitations, however, that are unique to US security-cooperation programs in Central Asia. Some of these are a function of the Central Asian environment and exist largely as a result of the history and development of these nations over the past fifteen years. Others are a function of US policies toward the region and the manner in which those policies have been executed through security-cooperation programs. These constraints and limitations—environmental, bureaucratic and policy, and programmatic—as well as thoughts on how to minimize or eliminate them, are addressed in this chapter.

Environmental Constraints

Despite the promise of the early 1990s, the Central Asian states have not made significant progress on political and economic reform, which directly and indirectly limits security-cooperation efforts. The population in all five states enjoys considerably fewer political freedoms than they did as Soviet citizens during the last few years of the Union of Soviet Socialist Republics' existence. Of course, there are degrees of control: Turkmenistan and Uzbekistan are the most authoritarian states in the region, followed closely by Tajikistan, while Kazakhstan and Kyrgyzstan are the least repressed.[1]

Lack of Political and Economic Reform

The lack of progress on political reform also creates a direct tension between the US objectives of promoting human rights and improving military capabilities. US policy has been consistent in pressing for greater political and economic freedoms while providing support on security issues. In theory, these two objectives are mutually reinforcing and security-cooperation programs can help achieve both. But critics have charged that US security cooperation in the region may have the unintended consequence of delaying political reform, particularly in the most autocratic countries. Human rights activists have three concerns over the increased US presence and programs since 11 September 2001:

> "Antiterrorism" can serve as a convenient blanket excuse for those governments to act aggressively even against opponents who have little or nothing to do with terrorism; incoming resources can artificially extend the life of governments that had been close to failure; and the US government, with troops on the ground and bases and other resources to protect, could oppose political change that could jeopardize its investment.[2]

While the first concern has been validated by the increasingly repressive tactics in Turkmenistan and Uzbekistan over the past few years, it is unclear whether US assistance has been indirectly propping up the most repressive governments. However, it is clear that the third concern has not panned out. The US forces in Kyrgyzstan played no role in the 2005 Tulip Revolution and US policy was to support a peaceful resolution of the unrest in a legal manner consistent with the desires of the Kyrgyz people. The status of the base at Manas apparently did not play a significant role in US efforts to find a solution. Furthermore, the United States was willing to risk eviction from Uzbekistan rather than to excuse Karimov's repression against the demonstrators in Andijon.

Beyond the tension between human rights and security as-sistance, the lack of political reform undermines the ability to use security cooperation to promote military reform that is nec-essary to create an environment that fundamentally accepts the values promoted by the United States. These include civil-ian control of the military and respect for human rights. Politi-cal systems are the determinants of the structure of civil-military relations in a society and authoritarian and democratic political systems produce different forms of civil-ian control and military professionalism.[3] Most studies on military reform in post-communist societies assume the de-sire for political reform is a necessary precondition. Experi-ences in Eastern Europe are mixed, however. In Bulgaria mili-tary reform largely stalled until 1997 when the pro-reform Union of Democratic Forces led by Ivan Kostov assumed power. Conversely, some observers suggest Ukrainian military reform proceeded without corresponding political progress.[4] Most ana-lysts would probably agree that reform must proceed on all fronts. Reform in only one arena (political, economic, or mili-tary) is unlikely to last or have significant impact without cor-responding reform in the others. Despite adopting some of the trappings of military professionalism, such as the elimination of conscription, institution of civilian oversight, and the estab-lishment of a senior noncommissioned officer corps, these countries will not fully achieve democratic military profession-alism unless there is concomitant political reform.

The slowness of political reform has also tended to perpetu-ate the legacy of Soviet suspicion toward Westerners. Often Central Asian officers, particularly those trained in Soviet or Russian military institutions, are still hesitant to work with Western officers, particularly when they know their own counter-intelligence services are monitoring their activities. This suspi-cion pervades the bureaucracy as well. As previously mentioned the defense ministries in Central Asia—adopting the practice of most countries—had established specific departments for handling external relations with foreign defense attachés. These departments, however, were tightly controlled by counterintelligence and saw their role as controlling or limiting contact. The officers assigned to these departments tended to treat security-cooperation activities as protocol matters requiring formal written requests for information, meetings, or contact events. These requests were translated into Russian or the local language and sent through the bureaucracy to the appropriate staff organization or unit, and when the response returned it was translated back into English. Setting up meetings could take weeks or months, and often attempts to adjust the dates of a military contact event would usually result in a cancellation. In Kazakhstan this issue was only resolved in 2003 with the establishment of an international cooperation center with full authority to work directly with foreign officials on security-assistance matters.[5]

In Uzbekistan, however, the authoritarian rule of Pres. Islam Karimov severely restricts the interaction between government officials and their US counterparts. In the words of one senior Uzbek official: "We don't know from one day to the next what the president is going to order us to do in changing foreign or domestic policy. Yesterday's enemies are today's friends, and there is little coherent advice we can give when we are not asked, and policy changes without reason or justification."[6] USCENTCOM security-cooperation planners state they have a good relationship with their counterparts, who they describe as cordial, hospitable, and friendly—but also note that in meetings, the Uzbekistanis are guarded and hesitant to discuss certain issues for fear of "getting on the wrong topic."[7]

The more authoritarian regimes in Turkmenistan, Tajikistan, and Uzbekistan have established strict controls over US security-cooperation programs. All are cautious about allowing impressionable junior officers to have too much contact with the United States through security-cooperation programs. Pres. Sapamurat Niyazov closely regulates opportunities for military officers to attend training programs, contact events, and exercises outside of Turkmenistan. Officers in the MOD have stated Niyazov personally approves each request, a process that requires excessive staffing and often results in disapprovals. Many invitations are never forwarded to the presidential office but are either ignored or politely declined by lower-level officials.[8] This restriction is not unique to military-cooperation programs—Niyazov has banned the teaching of foreign languages, including English, in public schools and has prevented students from accepting scholarships to foreign universities.[9]

The same is true in Tajikistan, where Pres. Emomali Rahmonov must personally approve the absence of any officer from the country. Over the past five years, several Uzbekistani students attending English-language training in San Antonio have deserted, some claiming political asylum in the United States. As a result, President Karimov has also imposed overt controls on his military officers, refusing to permit any to attend academic programs in the United States and significantly restricting the quantity and type of military contact events with the United States. Since 2005, President Karimov has eliminated all military contact events for young officers conducted outside Uzbekistan to ensure they will not be influenced by Western ideals.[10]

The political and economic situation in these countries, particularly in Kyrgyzstan and Tajikistan, is evident in the low pay and poor funding for military units and personnel. These factors foster pervasive corruption in these countries, including corruption within the military forces, which negatively impacts security-cooperation efforts both directly and indirectly. Power cables for the computers in the US-provided language labs in Kyrgyzstan were cut to make extension cords for other equipment. Some US-provided equipment is simply stolen by the personnel in the units and sold on the black market. Officers in Kyrgyzstan, for example, have loaded US uniforms in the back of their cars and sold them in the markets in Osh. The US SAO in Dushanbe considered a program to provide uniforms to a Tajikistani Army unit a success when she returned to the unit months later and saw the soldiers still wearing them. US efforts to build a noncommissioned officer professional development program in Kyrgyzstan suffered a setback when almost an entire class of students were recalled to their units well before the training had been completed. The commanders of these units use the soldiers as contract labor, and the length of the course was undermining their profits.[11] The indirect impact arises when the US military presence is seen to be fostering corruption. The US contracts for fuel deliveries to Manas in

Kyrgyzstan, for example, are reportedly controlled by family members of Pres. Kurmanbek Bakiyev, and the frozen food deliveries in Uzbekistan were managed by a member of President Karimov's family. [12]

Russian Influence

Every country in Central Asia retains very strong political, economic, and military ties to Russia. Even after 15 years of independence, the Central Asian states still conduct 40 to 50 percent of their trade with Russia.[13] Most of these relationships are bilateral, but all except Turkmenistan have security and defense ties with multilateral forums that are dominated by Russia. In parallel to the development of the CIS structures in early 1992, Russia established bilateral military relationships with each state in Central Asia. Russia signed agreements on friendship, cooperation, and mutual assistance with Kazakhstan on 25 May, Uzbekistan on 30 May, and Kyrgyzstan on 30 June, an agreement on friendship and cooperation with Turkmenistan on 8 June, and a series of military agreements with Tajikistan on 25 May 1993.[14] It is these bilateral military agreements, and the many that have been signed since, that continue to ensure Moscow's continuing strong influence in the security affairs of the Central Asian states.

This influence suffered some reduction in importance through the mid-1990s as each state worked to develop its own military forces from their inheritances from the Soviet Union. The desire for increased autonomy, sovereignty, and the use of the military as a socializing mechanism for these new states decreased the dependence they had on Russia. Likewise, internal economic difficulties in Russia meant that equipment deliveries to the Central Asian states dropped dramatically in the early 1990s. This reliance varied by state, as well. Tajikistan was almost totally dependent on Russia, while Uzbekistan made the most progress in its goal of limiting interaction with Moscow.

All of these agreements, and many others that have since been signed, include provisions for Russian equipment and training for the Central Asian states. Russia's recent windfall profits from oil and gas industries have permitted an even greater role in Central Asia, and Moscow is actively courting these governments with military aid. By the summer of 2003, for example, over 1,500 Kazakhstani personnel had graduated from Russian military educational institutions, and another 800 were enrolled at 43 separate military schools and war colleges. Since 2001, Kazakhstan has not had to pay tuition for its students; instead, those costs were deducted from Russian payments for leasing military facilities within Kazakhstan.[15]

Likewise, Kyrgyzstan has sent many of its military personnel to Russia for training. By November 1998 some 269 had graduated from Russian military schools. That number rose to more than 1,000 by September 2005. Similar patterns are found in the other Central Asian states to a greater or lesser degree. Turkmenistan resumed sending personnel to Russia for military training in 1996 and Uzbekistan in 2000. After Tajikistan's civil war ended in 1997, 72 Russian military advisors joined the staff of the Tajikistan Ministry of Defense to help create the unified armed forces. At least 10 remain at the Tajikistani State Border Troops training center and 10 more at the MOD Military Institute as of 2005, but it is likely that a large number of advisors remain throughout the Tajikistani military structure. Since 1993, about 100 Tajiks were admitted each year to Russian military schools and academies, and as of April 2005 some 400 Tajik cadets were attending Russian military schools and "tens of officers" were in advanced training. As of 2005, Russia was offering free military training to members of the Commonwealth Security Treaty Organization (CSTO).[16]

The Soviet military equipment inherited by all of the Central Asian states continues to form the vast majority of each nation's arsenal. Russian deliveries of spare parts and end items decreased in the early and mid-1990s as the defense industry underwent a dramatic reduction and reorganization, but transfers started to increase in the late 1990s. Kazakhstan currently receives military equipment from Russia at no charge as part of the leasing agreement, including up to $20 million worth of weapons and supplies in 2001. Russian support to the Kyrgyzstani military expanded after the 1999 IMU invasions, when Moscow delivered more than $1 million in uniforms, weapons, and ammunition. Since 2003, Russia has provided up to $3 million worth of equipment each year to Kyrgyzstan, including small arms, trucks, and helicopters. In 2001, Turkmenistan brokered a deal to pay for armaments, including coastal patrol boats, with shipments of natural gas. To reinforce its status as a major weapons supplier to Central Asia, Russia has also established repair facilities in Uzbekistan and Tajikistan.[17]

Russian influence in Central Asia is reinforced not only through bilateral ties and the multilateral forums, but also via bilateral military relations that the Central Asian nations maintain with other post-Soviet states. Ukraine, Belarus, Georgia, Azerbaijan, and Armenia all also rely on Soviet and Russian training, doctrine, and equipment to a great extent. Azerbaijan, for example, has opened its military schools to cadets from Kyrgyzstan and Turkmenistan. Belarus provides air defense training for many officers from all of the Central Asian states using Russian equipment and techniques, and Minsk recently announced reserved quotas in six military academies and universities for members of the CSTO. Ukraine provides training and a wide variety of military equipment, including patrol boats, radars and electronic equipment, aircraft, and ammunition to Kazakhstan, Turkmenistan, and Uzbekistan. Granted there have been some national modifications to the equipment and training, but much is based on Soviet and Russian design and doctrine. (Which doctrine is taught using the Russian language, thereby indirectly reinforcing Russian influence.)[18]

Russia's security-assistance programs are not without problems, however. Kazakhstani military personnel complained to US officials about the difficulties in obtaining spare parts for legacy Soviet aircraft, and Moscow's promises to provide equipment are not always fulfilled.[19] In September 2005, one Tajikistani official criticized a Russian protocol that had been signed the previous year, "the Russian side promised to supply us with two helicopters, but we have not yet received them . . . so far the Russian side has not supplied one piece of military equipment."[20] However, the legacy of Soviet equipment, training, and doctrine; and the absolute volume in Russian support still overwhelms US assistance efforts. In 2005, for example, approximately 70 Tajikistani officers were attending advance training and war colleges within Russia. In the same year, six attended courses in the United States—all at the DLIELC. The continued provision of training and equipment reinforces the use of Soviet and Russian doctrine, tactics, procedures, planning processes, and organizational structures throughout these military forces, which decreases the impact of US-supplied equipment and training.

Bureaucratic and Policy Constraints

While US security-cooperation programs are limited by Russian influence in the region, they are also constrained by policies of limited US defense commitment to Central Asia. Since the mid-1990s, US policy sought to exclude Russia from having a significant influence in security issues in Central Asia, but failed to offer replacements for the Soviet legacy and Russian support. Efforts to promote the Partnership for Peace program led to a very modest increase in NATO involvement in Central Asia, but it did not (and was not intended to) bring NATO security guarantees. Unlike the bilateral and multilateral security-cooperation programs conducted by NATO and the United States in Eastern Europe throughout the 1990s, which were largely driven by the ultimate goal of NATO membership, US and NATO security-cooperation programs were simply means to advance defense reform and democratization, improve indigenous military capabilities, and, to a limited extent, promote regional cooperation. The limits of US defense support became evident in 1999 and 2000, when Washington offered little additional support to Uzbekistan and Kyrgyzstan in response to the IMU incursions, which were the most serious and direct military threat these countries had faced.

Restrained Commitment

Likewise, the United States has emphasized an intention not to have a permanent or long-term military presence in the region. American military officials discounted Uzbekistan's first offers to allow US military bases on its territory in the mid-1990s, and this disinclination to offer long-term security assurances continued after September 2001. President Karimov sought such guarantees as payment for using Uzbek facilities for operations against the Taliban and al-Qaeda—his first requests were for immediate membership in NATO and a bilateral mutual defense treaty with the United States, neither of which he received.[21] Placated with promises of a strategic partnership and increased aid, Karimov ultimately agreed. Similarly, Kyrgyzstan wanted the United States to sign a 99-year lease on using Manas Air Base, but US officials declined. Instead, US officials were quick to make public announcements that the deployments to Uzbekistan and Kyrgyzstan in 2001 were temporary, lasting only until the terrorist threat in Afghanistan was defeated.[22]

The effect of these policies has been to reinforce to the Central Asian leadership that there is a limit to US interest, involvement, and presence in the region and that the United States should not be considered a reliable security partner. This undermines the efforts of the United States to reform and transform the defense establishments of these nations.

Short-Term Perspectives

As the history of US efforts in Central Asia demonstrate, security-cooperation programs often take years to achieve meaningful results, and even then, the results are not confirmed in a measurable way. US programs must first overcome the challenge of the federal budget cycle which can necessitate forecasting requirements two to three years in advance of obtaining funding. Most FMS programs must then meet the requirements of the normal military acquisition process, which can result in several more years between the initial request and the actual delivery of equipment. For example, in 1996 the State Department first advocated for FMF for Uzbekistan, and in 1997 provided the first allocation. However, Tashkent received its first equipment deliveries only in 2000—16 HMMWV.[23] But, the delivery of a weapon system or the provision of a training course does not mean the country has acquired the needed military capability. Depending on the complexity of the system or nature of the trained skills, it can take several more months or even years until the individual or unit is fully mission ready and the desired capability has been achieved.

However, US security-cooperation efforts are constrained by bureaucratic imperatives within the US government that force a short-term perspective in developing and executing programs.

Security-cooperation planners at all levels are focused on executing the current-year programs and forecasting for the following year, leaving little time to address longer-term goals and objectives. Much of this is driven by the budget cycle. Congress authorizes funding for most programs on an annual basis, and the final amounts can vary widely from year to year. Long-term plans can easily be undermined when expected levels of funding do not materialize. For example, the program to provide Kazakhstan with six UH-1 Huey II helicopters has been broken into multiple smaller programs, each with only two helicopters, to match the expected FMF authorizations for several years. A significant decrease in authorized funding could mean that fewer aircraft are procured or critical support elements, such as training and spare parts, are not provided, thereby undermining the success of the entire program.[24] Likewise, USCENTCOM planners develop bilateral military contact programs with each country in advance of knowing the funding levels that will be available, often resulting in having to cancel or postpone events that later cannot be supported. USCENTCOM's military contact plan for 2004 was budgeted at over $9 million, but less than $4 million was actually authorized, thus eliminating over half of the proposed events.[25]

The relatively frequent turnover of personnel and the lack of readily-available historical data also contribute to a short-term perspective. Lessons from previous activities are lost—by 2005, few planners at USCENTCOM remembered the existence of CENTRASBAT, much less the reasons for its demise. Except for the most recent years, the bilateral military contact plans, after-action reports, and annual expenditures of funds are generally unavailable, therefore planners for the military contact programs are unable to track trends or assess progress over time. Incomplete data suggests identical contact events have been conducted multiple times over the years. While occasional repetitions may be reinforcing, recurring visits could be perceived as "military tourism" rather than as meaningful contributions to building relationships and capabilities.

Insufficient Resources

Security-cooperation programs can also be very expensive, particularly when purchasing advanced weapon systems. Although US military equipment is generally more capable and reliable, it also tends to be relatively more expensive than that from other major suppliers. Transportation costs also can have a long-term impact on the costs of sustainment programs—the shipment of spare parts and travel of support personnel can easily become a significant portion of overall program costs. This is particularly true for security-cooperation programs with Central Asia, which must account for the underdeveloped transportation links with the West. Military contact event planners usually budget $10 thousand per person, per visit, in travel and related costs when using commercial transportation methods. Fortunately, since 2000, and perhaps earlier, Congress has authorized the use of DOD funds to offset the transportation of certain types of defense items to the Central Asian states.[26]

The low level of funding for security-cooperation programs in Central Asia is a significant external constraint. Allocations for FMF provide a useful benchmark. In 2004, for example, Congress authorized $4.633 billion in FMF for security-assistance programs around the world. Of that, however, $3.530 billion was earmarked for Israel, Egypt, and Afghanistan—the remaining funds, less than 17 percent of the total authorization, were divided up among the other qualifying nations. None of the Central Asian states were in the list of the top 20 recipients. Whereas Ecuador received $6.950 million and Bosnia-Herzegovina $14.900 million, Kazakhstan received a paltry $2.980 million.[27] Total FMF funding for the entire Central Asia region from 1997 to 2005 was just over $115 million, more than half of which was provided in 2002. The small sums allocated for Central Asia each year meant that, for the most part, equipment transfers are limited to relatively small amounts of supplemental gear, such as uniforms, radios, and medical equipment, rather than major end items.

The restraints of the funding programs diffuse the impact of US security-cooperation efforts in Central Asia. Generally, neither the OSD nor USCENTCOM have the ability to easily transfer funds from the various accounts to meet more pressing concerns in another area—monies allocated for counternarcotics efforts must be spent in that fashion, even if the requirement to improve counterinsurgency capabilities is more important. While new funding sources such as the RDCTF program have been created since 2001, they often duplicate other existing programs, such as IMET, but with narrow restrictions on their use. This complicates the planning efforts of security-cooperation practitioners.

Limited funding also tends to create sustainment issues. Defense Security Cooperation Agency (DSCA) mandates a "Total Package Approach" for sales of major weapon systems under the FMS program, whether they are funded by FMF, EDA, or national funds. The recipient military force is strongly encouraged to plan for and obtain all the necessary support needed to operationally and effectively utilize and sustain the weapon system, including training, technical assistance, spare parts, and technical manuals. Training programs, for example, address not only how to properly use the equipment, but also demonstrate the steps to build an appropriate training program within the armed forces of the recipient nation (known as "train the trainer"). But, funding constraints often result in subsequent long-term logistics and training shortfalls as sustainment programs get cut in favor of new equipment purchases.

This is not to suggest the United States should completely fund the equipment modernization programs of the Central Asian military forces. However, these nations, like many others in the former Soviet Union and Eastern Europe, tend to compartmentalize the assistance received from the United States. If the initial equipment item, such as a patrol boat, was provided at no charge through the EDA program and the initial training and support was funded through IMET and FMF, the patrol boat becomes an "American program." Despite the constant advice and recommendations by the SAOs, the defense ministry assumes all future support will continue to be provided by the United States.

The small programs in Central Asia face an other challenge—the security-assistance bureaucracy. As one of the most visible and politically-sensitive tools of US foreign policy, security assistance has become one of the most highly regulated and inspected programs in the federal government. US security-assistance organizations are often criticized as being overly bureaucratic, wasteful, unresponsive, and unwieldy. This paper is not the place to review those criticisms, and personal experience suggests most security-assistance programs are well managed and executed by professionals seeking to do their best. However, personal experience also suggests that large programs with major allies get visibility and attention, while the smaller programs with lesser-known nations risk getting lost in the shuffle. A set of computers for a command center in the Kyrgyz MOD, for example, was shipped to Bishkek with the wrong power cords. A simple solution would be for the US SAO at the embassy to procure the cords locally. Security-assistance regulations, however, mandate FMF funds can only be used to purchase goods from American-owned businesses, so a local purchase is not permitted. But the simple matter of the new cords has gotten lost in the bureaucracy, still unresolved, while the computers sit quiet and unused in the ministry, a reflection of the perceived unresponsiveness of US security-assistance support.[28]

Insufficient resources include the availability of units for military contact events and exercises. US military operational commitments can also limit the ability to meet security-cooperation objectives. Special operations forces, which have always had a very high operations tempo, have become even more operationally stressed with ongoing operations in Afghanistan, Iraq, the Philippines, and other locations. This has reduced the availability of these units to conduct SOFEX and JCET worldwide, including with the partner militaries in Central Asia.

Training programs will also suffer from reduced resources. Over the next few years the US Army's Training and Doctrine Command will lose 1,900 military instructor positions, shifting these billets to operational units. This restructuring will impact the availability of training courses that can be offered to the Central Asian militaries—fewer courses, offered less frequently, and for shorter durations. Many courses will be taught by DOD civilians or by contractors. While the content of the courses may not substantially change, the interaction with uniformed US military personnel and the opportunities for building military relationships will decrease. To the extent the DOD considers interaction between foreign and US military personnel a desirable end, a contributing factor to many other aspects of the success of security cooperation, every decrease in interaction must be taken very seriously.

The situation becomes more complicated when viewing the internal Central Asian dynamics. Each country has a variety of security services, and US security-cooperation activities attempt to interact with most, but not all, of them. For example, US policy restricts interaction with internal security agencies and prohibits interaction with organizations complicit in human rights violations. In Kyrgyzstan, the limited security-cooperation efforts are spread across the MOD, State Border Service, Ministry of Emergency Services, Ministry of the Interior, and the National Guard.[29] This approach is justified by asserting it permits US influence in all of the relevant security services. Often the political leadership in the country prefers this approach so as to balance the strengths and external ties of each of the security services and avoid creating a possible threat to their authority. But, attempting to engage with each security service in a nation diffuses the programs and limits their effectiveness.

Programmatic Constraints

Military contact events, by themselves, are the least effective method of achieving specific security-cooperation goals and objectives. The period of interaction for a single event is usually about a week, which is much too short to develop a meaningful relationship. Likewise, the depth of the information exchange is limited to familiarization and orientation, which offers only marginal utility in transferring skills and knowledge. Each event, taken individually, could easily be construed—and has been construed—as being nothing more than military tourism. During the early periods of engagement in Central Asia, the linkages between the military contact events to the overall security-cooperation objectives were weak. In fairness, this was not unique to US programs in Central Asia. Military contact programs in Europe were primarily based on the concept that "all contacts are good" and there was little overall structure or focus.[30] The wide variety of topics covered by the events in Central Asia, particularly during the 1995 through 2000 period, ensured that many of the events were single flashes of interaction without any reengagement or reinforcement or even a unifying theme.

Military Contact Events

Military contact events are also subject to the systemic inefficiencies of the planning and execution process. DOD, with its Security Cooperation Guidance, and USCENTCOM, with the Theater Security Cooperation Plan, have made great strides in the last seven years in creating deliberate plans with appropriate objectives for security cooperation in Central Asia. The top-down direction, however, stops at this point. When building the annual military contact event plans, USCENTCOM requests nominations from its subordinate commands, the National Guard units, other agencies, and the partner countries. Generally, events that can be viewed as supporting the fairly broad objectives in the Theater Security Cooperation Plan are accepted (although a percentage will not be executed because of scheduling difficulties or funding limitations). Planning officials have admitted that they use the current year's plan as a starting point for the following year's plan. In some cases, similar events are repeated year after year without any understanding of whether those events are have any impact. But, simply accepting nominations for events that *somehow* support the objective does not ensure deliberate forward progress toward the objective.

There are inefficiencies in the execution of military contact events as well. USCENTCOM, and the other unified commands prior to 1999—through subordinate component commands—turns to the military services (primarily the US Army and US Air Force) and the National Guard (through the SPP) to find units to participate in the military contact events. Often the US units tasked to participate are not part of USCENTCOM's normal planning process for the program, so the individuals who actually travel to Central Asia or host delegations from the region have little or no knowledge of the overall US security-cooperation objectives for that particular country or how the event and their specific activities fit into the larger plan. Those individuals often have little knowledge or appreciation of the cultural, political, historic, and economic influences shaping another country's development, and a limited understanding of the size, structure, armament, or capabilities of another nation's military forces. US delegations are seldom briefed on the personalities or positions of the counterparts they will meet in a military contact event. If they are, it is usually upon arrival in country, with little time available to adjust presentations or modify events to meet unexpected circumstances.[31] USCENTCOM provides general guidance to the US team conducting the event, but that guidance generally does not include a contextual framework. As a result, those individuals face great difficulties presenting their information in a context and manner that will translate (literally and figuratively) to their counterparts from Central Asia. This limitation, of course, is much less apparent in the National Guard units that repeatedly engage with their respective partner countries. In fact, some Guardsmen that have been involved in the military contact program since the SPP was established in the early 1990s have had such frequent opportunities that they have become the Defense Department's experts on certain facets of the military forces in Central Asia (fig. 8).

The expansion of the military contact program in the mid-1990s and the high operations tempo of the active duty forces led to an increased reliance on the National Guard through the SPP for the military contact program. While this has many advantages as indicated above, it may also tend to influence the development of the contact program with each country. Each of the five state National Guard organizations has a relatively limited range of capabilities. The plans for military contact events may reflect more of what is available through the National Guard unit rather than what is required to meet specific security-cooperation objectives. This tendency may explain the frequency of artillery unit familiarization visits between Kazakhstan and the Arizona National Guard in the late 1990s, despite a lack of linkage to any of the stated security-cooperation objectives. Likewise, the Arizona National Guard operates F-16 aircraft at the 162d Fighter Wing in Tucson, but does not have transport aircraft, and tends to offer fighter unit familiarization

127

06/12/2004

Figure 8. US Military personnel with the deputy commander of the Kazakhstani Air Force during a transport aviation military contact event, Rep Almaty, Kazakhstan, December 2004 (Reprinted from the author's personal collection.)

events rather than transport unit events, which would be of more use to the Kazakhs.

Additionally, the organizations responsible for the military contact program suffer from an institutional mind-set that focuses more on developing the annual plan and executing a specific event than on ensuring the event achieves its goals. Metrics for the military contact programs, when they exist, usually attempt to measure the quantity of funds expended or the number of events conducted as a percentage of what was planned, rather than the more difficult challenge of evaluating whether the events were useful. Although US participants are required to submit after-action reports following the event, many do not. Apparently most of the reports are not reviewed to determine whether the event was successful in meeting its specific objectives and, if it were reviewed, whether it contributed to the advancement of overall US security-cooperation objectives. Newly established procedures compound the problem—after-action reports for each event are individually forwarded to the Office of the Secretary of Defense, which will try to determine whether the event was successful. Examining each discrete report, however, will not provide the answer. The reports for a series of events having a common objective or objectives should be reviewed together, sequentially, and within context so as to evaluate progress in achieving the events' purpose or purposes.

Because of the vast differences in the size and capabilities of the US armed forces and those of the Central Asian states, some military contact events used to familiarize Central Asian personnel with US operations may not be particularly relevant. For example, military contact events designed to introduce operations or maintenance procedures of particular types of equipment may provide a misleading impression of requirements for support or employment of specific weapon systems. A military contact event that shows the huge US Air Force C-130 transport aircraft Depot Maintenance Center, Warner Robins AFB, Georgia, which is designed to support a fleet of almost 600 aircraft, may not be particularly relevant to the Kazakh Air Force, which hopes to obtain only a handful of these airplanes. Similarly, the series of information exchanges conducted by the US Air Force in Kazakhstan and Uzbekistan in the late 1990s on financial management were probably of little value to defense ministries that use completely different accounting and budgeting systems.

Despite these limitations, military contact events can be very valuable security-cooperation tools if properly planned and integrated into a broader effort. First, they offer a relatively low-cost, low-impact method of exposing large numbers of US and foreign officers to each others' military structures and cultures. A typical familiarization event involves eight to 12 personnel traveling to the other country. Twenty to 30 of these events each year can provide broad familiarity in a relatively positive environment to large numbers of personnel in both countries. Most Central Asian participants in military contact events conducted in the United States have expressed very positive comments about both the information they received and the overall experience of visiting the United States.[32]

Second, military contact programs offer a means of providing "persistent engagement"—repeated interactions with the same partner units and individuals over time—that can build long-term relationships. A series of military contact events can build a "pattern of habitual cooperation." This can be viewed in several ways. A series of events builds the perception within the MOD (or any other ministry) that cooperation with the United States is a routine, normal, and expected pattern of behavior, so that when the United States suggests cooperation in some other fashion, the MOD may be more receptive and inclined to accept the request. The perception of habitual cooperation has a practical side as well as it creates familiarity with US operational practices and requirements and therefore allows the foreign decision makers a context in which to evaluate US requests for greater cooperation. In this regard, the SPP is an invaluable element of a persistent engagement military contact program because of the relative availability of National Guard units. It is often more difficult to use active duty units because of their higher operations tempo. The availability of National Guard units allows USCENTCOM to continue to offer a fairly large number of events with each country each year.

Likewise, a series of events that consistently pairs a US unit and a foreign unit can create an institutional relationship. Like air force sister-squadron pairings, these institutional relationships surpass the personal relationships that may occur, and last well after the normal rotation of personnel wipes out those who started the effort. The NATO Tiger Association, comprised of fighter squadrons with tigers in their squadron patches, has been building institutional ties between NATO air forces since 1959. Again, using the National Guard offers great advantages, as it can create long-term, consistent, reinforcing institutional relationships that can, over time, fundamentally influence the development of its partner unit.

Finally, military contact events can serve as an effective method for introducing or reinforcing the objectives of more complex security-assistance programs: familiarization events prior to the more in-depth training programs, transfers of equipment, tactical exercises, follow-on events to reinforce concepts or practices, exchanges of information on standing operating procedures, or offers of advanced techniques for equipment use. In January 2002, Kazakhstan began receiving HMMWVs purchased through the FMS program, and the following year the Arizona National Guard began a series of contact events with the Kazakhstani Army to develop operational concepts for maintaining the vehicles. This culminated in a series of maintenance workshops in April, May, and August of 2005, leading to the opening of the FMF-funded maintenance center in November 2005.[33] Similarly in 2002, when the Kyrgyzstani MOD inquired about using its FMF funds to refurbish facilities at Koi Tash for a joint training center, the Montana National Guard offered to assist the Kyrgyz military with establishing a noncommissioned officer (NCO) professional development program for the center. In 2004, when the refurbishment plans were finalized, the Montana National Guard began a series of military contact events to help build the necessary course materials.[34] Arizona National Guard efforts in building the HMMWV maintenance center program in Kazakhstan and Montana's support to the NCO professional development program are two good examples of how military contact programs can be successfully integrated with other security-cooperation efforts.

Education and Training Programs

Education and training programs have long been promoted as the most effective means of developing common understanding and the personal and professional relationships between military personnel that help find solutions to international issues and influence the development of foreign military forces. Proponents of education and training programs advocate these efforts (along with other engagement tools) to provide access to current and future foreign military leaders, influence in resolving crises and developing military forces, exposure to US ideals and values, and transfer of specific skills valuable to foreign military forces operating with US forces or in support of US objectives. All of this may be possible, but, the extent to which these objectives are realizable is situation dependent and difficult to measure.

The role of education and training programs in granting access to foreign military leaders is relatively undisputed, if difficult to measure. Foreign graduates of US military training courses are generally favorably influenced by their experience in the United States, and American defense attachés and security-assistance officers often note these positive perspectives translate into a greater willingness on the part of the foreign military officers to meet with their US counterparts or interlocutors. US attachés and SAOs, sometimes only field-grade officers, claim the US training provides "access at the senior ranks of host country military establishments" that they otherwise "wouldn't have or couldn't have without difficulty."[35] These training and education programs also provide a common experience that provides rapport and an ease of communication between US officers and US-trained foreign officers that can otherwise overcome the cultural differences. This access and relationship, although difficult to quantify, are essential ingredients for advancing other aspects of US security-cooperation objectives.

The role of IMET in creating personal and professional relationships that help resolve international crises is often debated. Former USPACOM Commander, Adm Dennis Blair, an otherwise strong proponent of the IMET program, sees less value in this concept: "it is fairly rare that personal relationships made through IMET come into play in solving a crisis."[36] Lincoln Bloomfield Jr., assistant secretary of State for Political-Military Affairs, challenged this perspective in 2004: "There are countless examples of how friendships forged through IMET training have contributed significantly to the resolution of crises and important foreign policy concerns throughout the years."[37] One such example apparently occurred during the September 1991 crisis in Zaire, when a Zairian general officer and IMET graduate permitted the evacuation of 450 Americans from a closed national airport under his control.[38] The reality likely lies somewhere in between—at least a few incidents have been resolved through personal interaction with foreign military officers that have trained in the United States, but those numbers are likely very small compared to the total number of personnel trained through the IMET program. Nonetheless, the number of such situations is probably sufficient to judge that the IMET program has value in this regard.[39]

The evaluation of the relative influence on a specific individual of a training experience in the United States is still subjective. In his 1993 study of the IMET program, John Cope notes: "It is difficult to measure the degree to which a former IMET or FMS student officer or civilian is favorably inclined toward the United States. A graduate may not have made it a part of his

judgment until an issue arises that forces him to make a decision. More than likely, IMET is just one component of a complex
decision process."[40]

A constant objective of US military training and education
programs has been the democratization of foreign military
forces and proponents of the IMET program often argue that
training foreign military students in the United States provides
an opportunity to expose them to American values, ideals, and
culture. They contend that this exposure will, at a minimum,
help the students to understand the United States and hope-
fully entice them to adopt those values and ideals—specifically
the importance of democratic governments, rule of law, free
enterprise economic systems, appropriate civil-military relations, respect for human rights, and the law of armed conflict.
Also, unfiltered access and exposure directly cuts through any
anti-US sentiment that remains. In fact, an important component of the IMET program is designed to do just that. The DOD
Informational Program (DODIP) ensures a certain percentage
of the time a foreign student spends studying in the United
States is dedicated to those topics, reinforced by field trips to
local governmental institutions, religious centers, media, and,
for students attending selected courses, to Washington, DC.[41]
Although a voluntary program, all foreign students are highly
encouraged to participate and the costs are included in the tuition charged to their home country.

However, attending courses in the United States, even when
reinforced by the DOD Informational Program can at most expose foreign military students to American values and culture,
but, the experience cannot guarantee that those students will
adopt those ideals. Some sociologists and social psychologists
have indirectly challenged the premise that US values can be
adopted "through osmosis," the method essentially used by the
DOD Informational Program. It is equally implausible that the
attitudes and behavioral patterns of students attending shorter
courses lasting days, weeks, or even a few months will be so
malleable that they can be systematically altered by the experience.[42] One RAND study concluded:

> The few months a foreign military student spends in the United States
> are unlikely to radically alter his cultural, social, or political views. Inter-
> national military students [IMS] may acquire an improved understand-

ing of the American political system and social culture, and some may develop an affection for the United States, but studies suggest that the majority of IMS will return to their home countries with the same basic *Weltanschauung* [world view] as when they left.[43]

Personal experience suggests that the more culturally, politically, and economically distant the country is from the United States, the more unlikely it is that its military students will be willing or able to internalize US values and ideals.

An even more challenging issue is whether those students who do internalize US values and beliefs can implement them in their own countries. Even if the experience in the United States alters the belief system of a particular student, it does not alter the unique cultural, political, and economic structure in which that student must exist once he or she returns home after training.[44] In many countries in Central Asia, that structure is characterized by clans, political repression, and corruption. That is not to say that such changes cannot take place, but only that if changes do occur, they will do so slowly. Retired Admiral Blair, when he was the USPACOM commander, promoted IMET and other contact programs with closed or problematic military forces such as those in Indonesia precisely because of the potential long-term affect they may have on influencing the development of those forces. He argues that military forces that systematically engage in oppressive practices or human rights abuses become isolated, but engagement can help them "feel kinship with, not isolated from, the norms of more professional militaries."[45] Some observers believe that the decade of US training and education programs in El Salvador helped dramatically reduce the degree to which the military, as an institution, systematically engaged in human rights abuses. Individual officers still committed violations, but they were not condoned or encouraged as before.[46] However, such engagement has not always translated into greater respect for human rights, as case studies of the Philippines have demonstrated.[47] In Central Asia the record is not clear. It is not known whether any of the Uzbekistani forces engaged in the violence at Andijon in May 2005, which primarily came from the Ministry of the Interior, had been exposed to US training programs. On the other hand, US Army colonel Thomas Wilhelm, associate dean for Eurasian Studies at the George C. Marshall Center and a previous defense attaché in Central Asia, noted that Kyrgyzstani alumni of the Center believed that the military contact programs and training and education opportunities offered by the United States helped keep the Kyrgyzstani security services from using force against protestors during the fall of the government in March 2005.[48]

Budgetary constraints have a profound impact on the selection of training and education opportunities, and this selection can have a major impact on the ability to achieve security-cooperation objectives. Maximizing influence, for example, means sending fewer students to the United States for longer, more in-depth, courses that usually last a year or more, such as academies and war colleges, promoting professional development rather than technical skills. Maximizing exposure, alternatively, means sending more students to shorter courses, measured in days, weeks, or a few months. (Even these shorter courses can become longer if the student lacks English-language skills requiring an extended stay at the Defense Language Institute.) These types of courses tend to be focused on the development of specific skills, such as infantry training or resource management. Having mobile training teams or MET travel to Central Asia to present their courses are much more cost effective, but they lack the ability to expose foreign students to American society, culture, and values—a fundamental objective of the IMET program.

Foreign military forces occasionally do not send the most qualified individual to a US training course. Often the candidates whose selection would best benefit the foreign military force lacked the requisite English language skills, so attending a US course implied a commitment of up to a year of English-language training. For longer professional military education courses at war colleges, this could mean a two-year absence, but, unit commanders are often reluctant to send their best officers because the position would remain vacant for that period. Instead, some foreign military leaders view the opportunity for training in the United States a way to reward a favored officer based on their connections to the senior military leadership or as a method to dispose of an unwanted officer.[49]

Training and education programs can improve the skills of a particular individual, but cannot guarantee that the individual will use them appropriately, or at all. One factor is the willingness or ability of the Central Asian armed forces to implement US training on tactics and doctrine. Much of US tactical and operational doctrine, developed for larger, globally-engaged, forces with supporting capabilities such as aviation, advanced communications, and abundant logistics, simply may not be appropriate or applicable for the smaller, less advanced, and underresourced militaries in Central Asia. For example, officers sent to the Air Command and Staff College are taught the fundamentals of developing and executing a joint air campaign employing fighters, bombers, tankers, and intelligence, surveillance, and reconnaissance assets to defeat an integrated-air-defense system—a skill largely unnecessary in Kazakhstan or Uzbekistan. However, increasing interaction with the Central Asian militaries over the past decade has made elements of the US military more familiar with the indigenous training requirements of these forces, and some US units, such as the 5th Special Forces Group and the 6th Special Operations Squadron, are uniquely trained and qualified to modify US tactics and doctrine to meet local needs.

Political factors may also limit the adoption of US tactics and doctrine. For example, efforts to encourage the El Salvadoran armed forces to adopt US counterinsurgency tactics in the early 1980s met with substantial resistance as many Salvadoran officers saw this influence as an infringement on their national sovereignty. Resistance continued during the entire period of US involvement, even as late as 1992, when US training efforts, by then, resulted in over half of the officers in the Salvadoran armed forces having received training in the United States, including every captain and lieutenant. One American officer noted: "the Salvadoran Army has been thoroughly trained in US counterinsurgency tactics, and they can do them well—the problem is getting them to actually use these tactics."[50] Central Asian officers, who prefer strong ties to Russia, perhaps because of having studied in Russian military schools, may see the adoption of US training, tactics, and doctrine as a threat to those ties or as unwanted US influence and interference. While accepting the training, those officers may simply choose not to implement the changes. US training that differs significantly from the legacy Soviet- and Russian-influenced tactics and doctrine will face greater resistance. Units that may want to employ US tactics, but rely on supporting units that do not, will face additional challenges.

Despite the uncertainty over the short- and long-term effectiveness of training and education programs, two factors appear to have a significant impact on the utility of these programs. First, exclusively sprinkling graduates of US training and education programs throughout the foreign military force is counterproductive. They will be isolated and severely hampered in their ability to implement any changes against the legacy and inertia of the existing system. There must be a sufficient number of US-trained military personnel within a specific foreign military unit or organization before US training, tactics, techniques, concepts, or ideals will take hold. The size of the "critical mass" of graduates from US training and education programs will vary depending on the organization. This process must be managed, as experiences in Kazakhstan demonstrate. In 2002, with the aid of the US SAO, the MOD reformed its approach to the IMET program by establishing a specific office to manage foreign training and adopted a personnel administration system to manage the careers of those service members trained overseas. As a result, many of the Kazakhstani IMET graduates—including graduates from the US Military Academy at West Point—have been assigned to the Kazakhstan battalion (KAZBAT) and the mobile forces. This concentrated number of US-trained officers and noncommissioned officers in one place has greatly accelerated the speed and depth of reform in those units.[51]

Second, sending a foreign military member to a single course is not usually an effective method of ensuring that the individual gains and retains the necessary knowledge and skills. To fully utilize the benefits of US training and education programs, they must be reinforced by appropriate refresher or advanced courses. For example, when the Marshall Center, DIILS, DRMI, DISAM, Center for Civil-Military Relations (CCMR), or another educational institution sends an MET to Central Asia for a course or a conference, the MET should also include refresher or advanced training for those foreign military students that have attended the in-residence courses. Alumni programs, such as those maintained by the war colleges and

137

the Marshall Center (the latter since 1998), can also be an effective means of reinforcement.

Most training and education courses are best reinforced by exercises that test the skills and knowledge of the foreign personnel. In the late 1990s, US efforts to focus IMET courses on individuals assigned to the CENTRASBAT unit—those who would then participate in the annual exercise—was a step in that direction. But, since the national elements of the unit were still comprised largely of conscripts, the annual exercise generally had a greater emphasis on basic skills training rather than on reinforcing advanced techniques learned in the United States.

The DTRA's International Counterproliferation Program has developed a simple but effective methodology for reinforcing training through exercises. Each of the three elements of the program—counterproliferation infrastructure planning, Border Security and WMD Investigations, and WMD Evidence Awareness and Management—consists of several training courses followed by an exercise that reinforces and tests the material. These three separate exercises are then followed by an integrated exercise which brings together all of the personnel responsible for a comprehensive proliferation prevention program within that country. Implied within this concept is the need to have the same individuals attend the full set of training courses *and* exercises. The ICP also includes the option to hold regional exercises to promote multinational cooperation as well as follow-up visits and refresher training (fig.9).

Exercises

Exercises offer many benefits in providing or reinforcing advanced skills training or educational concepts, as seen in the SOFEX and JCET events (and as demonstrated in the ICP example above). When properly managed and executed, they can also serve as a useful means of advancing integration with Western military structures via the NATO PfP exercises, promoting regional cooperation in addressing multinational concerns such as terrorism, illegal migration, and drug trafficking through the aptly named Regional Cooperation exercises (formerly known as CENTRASBAT).

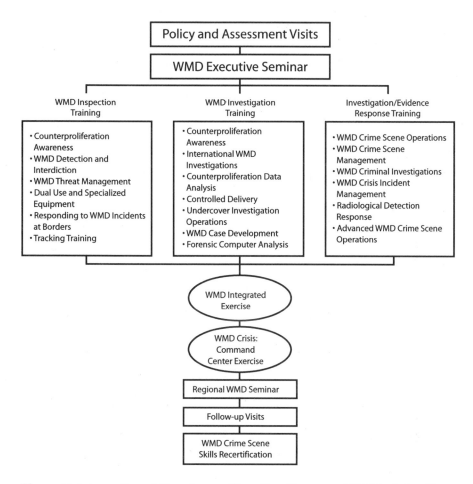

Figure 9. International Counterproliferation Program (ICP) training flow-chart (Adapted from DOD International Counterproliferation Program Briefing, undated, obtained through author correspondence with Defense Threat Reduction Agency, April 2006.)

The special operations exercises are perhaps the most effective exercises for transferring operational capabilities to a foreign military force. They are small, focused, and intended for elite foreign units. They are not intended to provide training on basic skills, but instead on advanced tactical skills. However, occasionally the units they work with in Central Asia are not up to the task. In one instance, the Uzbekistani special forces team leader had not even had basic infantry training.[52] Current operations in Iraq, Afghanistan, and elsewhere have limited the availability of the US special operations forces that conduct these exercises. Many of the SOFEXs and JCETs scheduled from late 2001 through 2003 had to be cancelled. Because they tend to provide training on combat skills, special operations training events also occasionally come under criticism as assisting military forces in nations that routinely abuse human rights, including, according to some observers, Kazakhstan and Uzbekistan.[53]

The larger exercises are among the most complex of security-cooperation activities. Many of them, such as the NATO PfP series or the Regional Cooperation events, take a year or longer to plan and can also be very expensive to plan and execute. The CENTRASBAT 98 exercise involved approximately 450 personnel, including 160 from the United States, in a two-week exercise, but cost over $6 million to conduct.[54] Regional Cooperation 05 cost $1.300 million to train 70 foreign participants.[55] The point is not to measure dollars spent against participants trained, but to emphasize the importance of ensuring the exercises train the right skills to the right participants for the right reasons.

The failure of CENTRASBAT has previously been covered, but two points should be emphasized. First, planners should appreciate that regional cooperation can be encouraged, but it cannot be forced. The participants from the Central Asian states should be responsible for determining lessons learned and shaping the course of subsequent programs and exercises. Second, planners should attempt to limit the "fluff" that tends to accumulate around multinational exercises, such as opening and closing ceremonies, parades, and dignitary visits. These activities often detract from the objectives and can turn the exercise into a showcase event rather than a venue for realistic training.

Equipment Transfers

In most cases, transfers of military weapon systems are usually the most expensive, visible, and politically-sensitive element of US security-cooperation programs. This assertion has proven valid in Central Asia, as well, but on a much reduced scale. The delivery of $2 million worth of armored HMMWVs

140

garners much more publicity and international concern than the $30 thousand visit of financial specialists ready to discuss defense resource management.

However, the amounts and types of equipment provided to the Central Asian states are greatly limited by the available resources. The United States provided just over $115 million in FMF for all five nations through 2005 (almost half of which went to Uzbekistan), over five times the amount of IMET funding provided in that same time period. But the FMF provided to Central Asia is a relatively small amount compared to both the amounts provided to other nations and the cost of most US weapon systems, which greatly limit the types and amounts of military equipment that can be transferred. (The Central Asian states have yet to use national funds to purchase equipment from the United States.) Most of the funding has been spent on relatively small amounts of relatively inexpensive equipment: radios, computers, and communications gear; uniforms, web gear and rucksacks, flight suits, mountaineering gear, body armor, and helmets; language laboratories and training materials; medical and dental equipment; tool kits and sewing machines for parachutes; and security-assistance and assessment teams. There have been only a few transfers of relatively expensive, high-profile equipment: night-vision goggles, patrol boats, HMMWVs, and helicopters.

Providing equipment is no guarantee that the recipient nation will use it effectively, if at all. Uzbekistan has acquired a large number of English-language labs using both IMET and FMF funds, but due to bureaucratic wrangling within the MOD, most of the labs remained in storage for years rather than in use. One lab was hastily installed at the tank academy when there was a rumor of a presidential visit. Another lab was later installed but used to store teaching materials and surplus construction materials.[56]

Equipment that is interoperable with NATO standards often means that the equipment is incompatible with those already in use, by that nation's military forces, particularly the legacy Soviet equipment. Such was apparently the case with radios and communications equipment provided to Kyrgyzstan. According to one Kyrgyz analyst, "The Western communications equipment turned out to be incompatible with the Soviet models used by our army. It was free, I grant you, but it was also use-less."[57] If the US-provided equipment is centralized in one unit, such as KAZBAT, that unit may become increasingly unable to operate with other Kazakh national forces.

Equipment must be properly maintained or it will quickly be-come inoperable. This implies not only the ability to obtain spare parts, but also the establishment of appropriate operational and maintenance procedures and qualitative improvements in the training of operators and maintainers. Unfortunately, this has not always been the case. The five Boston Whaler patrol boats provided under the CTR program in 1995–1996, constituting one-third of Kazakhstan's small Caspian Sea fleet, had broken down by 2001 primarily because the Kazakh sailors used the wrong type of fuel in the engines.[58] According to Kazakh defense officials, the 16 HMMWVs provided to Uzbekistan in 2000 are currently not in working order and the Kazakhs were hoping the United States would recommend that Tashkent send the vehi-cles to Kazakhstan's new HMMWV maintenance center thereby clearly illustrating the lack of regional cooperation between these two neighboring countries.[59] These problems are not unique to equipment provided under the FMS program. Specialized radia-tion detection equipment provided under the various DOD pro-liferation prevention programs also face challenges:

> At a January 2002 IAEA [International Atomic Energy Agency] conference, a DOD official provided information about problems with U.S.-supplied equip-ment. He noted that audits found that detection equipment in several coun-tries had never been used and remained in storage; expensive high-technology equipment was only used in the presence of visiting U.S. delegations; and equipment was going unused because it needed battery replacement, very minor repairs, or major repairs that required out-of-country servicing. The DOD official noted that recipient country officials offered numerous reasons why the equipment was being underutilized or not used at all, including (1) the equipment was too difficult to use; (2) nobody was trained to use it; (3) the equipment would be broken; (4) use of the equipment could cause injuries; (5) repairs were too difficult; (6) no funds had been provided for new batteries; and (7) a lack of knowledge about where or how to send the equipment for re-pairs.[60]

Multilateral Programs

Since the mid-1990s, one of the objectives for the United States has been to increase multinational security-cooperation initiatives and programs in Central Asia wherever and whenever possible. Such activities can help build trust and stability in the region and assist in finding cooperative solutions to intra-regional problems such as border security and disaster re-sponse. However, there are many factors that work against this method and multinational initiatives must be approached with caution or they could prove counterproductive. Planners should appreciate that political and military leaders in Central Asia tend to value their bilateral relationships with the United States more than US-led multilateral relationships within the region and they often view multinational initiatives as detracting from bilateral ties.

Intraregional dynamics and relationships will continue to limit the scope of most US-led multinational programs within Central Asia, primarily with Kazakhstan, Kyrgyzstan, and Ta-jikistan, which at this point seem willing to cooperate. Turk-menistan, citing its "positive neutrality" since independence, has rejected almost all multinational security-cooperation initiatives with the other Central Asian countries and de-clined to participate in either the peacekeeping mission in Tajikistan or the CENTRASBAT program. Ashgabat loses little by not participating in these efforts as it is the most removed from the primary cross-border challenges from Tajikistan, Afghanistan, and China. Turkmenistan instead focuses on bilateral relationships with the United States, Russia, and other neighboring countries, and uses the NATO PfP as its primary multinational forum.

In a different fashion, Uzbekistan has distanced itself over the past few years from security-cooperation relationships with Kazakhstan, Kyrgyzstan, and Tajikistan. While it previously participated with Kazakhstan and Kyrgyzstan in the peace-keeping operation in Tajikistan and in CENTRASBAT, Tash-kent now views these countries as actual or potential hosts of threats to its internal stability. Following the IMU incursions in 1999 and 2000, Uzbekistan has closed its border with Kazakh-stan and Kyrgyzstan. Uzbekistan and Kazakhstan, the largest and most powerful nations in Central Asia, do not even ex-change defense attachés.[61] Uzbekistan has also declined to participate in recent USCENTCOM-sponsored Regional Coop-eration multinational exercises because of the presence of a delegation from Pakistan. Tashkent believes the IMU is using

143

Pakistan as a staging area to rebuild its cadres.[62] Likewise, Kazakhstan, Kyrgyzstan, and Tajikistan view Uzbekistan as a potential regional hegemon.

USCENTCOM recently announced its desire to establish a disaster response center in Kazakhstan. This center can serve as an excellent catalyst for improving regional cooperation in a field that would require a coordinated response should a major terrorist attack or environmental disaster occur in Central Asia. But, the United States should be cautious in establishing additional regional centers. CENTRASBAT and other experiences demonstrate that the Central Asian states are generally reluctant to maintain permanent integrated organizations or establish dependency on a neighboring state for core military requirements such as training. (Kyrgyz willingness to turn to Kazakhstan for military training and education programs is a notable exception.) This experience is not unique to Central Asia. In 1983, the United States established a regional military training center in Puerto Castillo, Honduras, with approximately 120 military advisors to train soldiers from Central American states in counterinsurgency warfare. However, approximately 70 percent of the annual training quotas were reserved for troops from the El Salvadoran armed forces. The remaining 30 percent were distributed among all of the other participating militaries in Central America including the Honduran armed forces. Once the initial honor of being selected to host this regional center wore off, Honduras greatly resented the US program that not only brought soldiers from El Salvador, an historic enemy, onto its soil, but, also reserved the majority of the training quotas for outsiders. Instead of promoting regional cooperation, the regional military training center fostered increased animosity, both regionally and toward the United States. The center was closed in 1985.[63]

Regional centers for "soft" capabilities such as peacekeeping, disaster response, or language training will be more effective in promoting regional cooperation in Central Asia than those designed to promote core military capabilities such as mountain warfare or special operations. Administrative matters, such as training quota allocations and invitations for other nations to participate, should be carefully managed in collaboration with the host nation. While the United States should ensure sufficient funding for the first several years of operation, the host nation should be a collaborative partner and over time assume increasing responsibility for the management and operation of the center, with milestones and measurable criteria in place to ensure consistent progress.

Some of the key US programs for security cooperation, specifically IMET and FMF, are structured to promote bilateral rather than multilateral relationships. IMET funding and procedures are generally structured toward sending individual students to specific courses and offer few venues for multinational activities. While students may benefit from interacting with students from other Central Asian countries while attending US-sponsored training, this cannot be considered a true multinational initiative. Likewise, FMF funding and procedures establish a specific contractual agreement between the United States and a single recipient country for the provision of defense goods and services. Experience with multinational programs such as National Military Command Centers in Eastern Europe suggests that multinational FMS programs can be more complex and offer greater risk than offset by the apparent benefits.

Despite these constraints, appropriate multinational initiatives can be effective in meeting some US security-cooperation objectives in Central Asia. As addressed in the discussion on exercises, regional cooperation cannot be forced, but can be encouraged. In the near term, the United States should pursue a dual-track strategy: continue to develop strong bilateral relationships with each of the five Central Asian states, and use multinational events such as exercises, symposiums, and conferences to foster regional and extra-regional relationships to meet specific needs.

Constraints and Limitations in Perspective

As outlined in this chapter, security-cooperation programs face many challenges, sometimes more so in the unique environment in Central Asia. Security cooperation is an inherently complex and difficult undertaking which requires years of effort and vast amounts of resources to have an impact. Yet they are often executed by organizations which face bureaucratic imperatives that force a short-term perspective and which are granted far fewer resources than they would prefer.

Likewise, these programs must overcome often significant cultural and language differences between the armed forces, and those undertaken by the US military must accommodate overwhelming differences in size, capabilities, and available resources. Beyond the general limitations of time and cost, each of the various security-cooperation activities, military contact events, training and education programs, exercises, and equipment transfers, has specific strengths and weaknesses that must be taken into account when building programs.

However, it is important to put these limitations in perspective. The improved planning process developed under the OSD Security Cooperation Guidance, the USCENTCOM Theater Security Cooperation Plan, and the bilateral five-year plans, as well as the increasing centralization of security-cooperation execution in USCENTCOM and DTRA, has greatly improved the ability of planners and practitioners to weave together the various programs and elements toward a set of more clearly-defined goals. Security-cooperation planners have become innovative in finding methods to match strengths in one program against weaknesses in another. Although military contact programs, training and education opportunities, equipment transfers, and bilateral and multilateral exercises all face inherent limitations in building relationships or improving military capabilities, over time these programs can result in *some* influence and *some* development of capabilities, as the next chapter will show.

Notes

1. Flemming Splidsboel Hansen, "A Grand Strategy for Central Asia," *Problems of Post-Communism* 52, no. 2 (March/April 2005), 46.

2. Cheryl Benard, "Central Asia: 'Apocalypse Soon' or Eccentric Survival?" in Angel M. Rabasa et al., *The Muslim World After 9/11* (Santa Monica, CA: RAND, 2004), 362.

3. Ulrich, *Democratizing Communist Militaries*, 2 (see chap. 2, note 8). Dr. Ulrich's work is the best study of the impact of US security-cooperation programs on military democratization efforts in Eastern Europe and the former Soviet Union.

4. Piotr Dutkiewicz and Plamen Pantev, "Postcommunist Civil-Military Relations in Bulgaria," in *The Evolution of Civil-Military Relations in East-Central*

Europe and the Former Soviet Union, eds. Natalie L. Mychajlszyn and Harald von Riekhoff (Westport, CT: Praeger, 2004), 151.

5. Lahue, "Security Assistance in Kazakhstan," 9–13 (see chap. 4, note 36).

6. Ahmed Rashid, *Jihad: The Rise of Militant Islam in Central Asia* (New York: Penguin Books, 2003), 83.

7. US Central Command (USCENTCOM) interviews (see chap. 5, note 38).

8. Ibid.; and author's personal experience.

9. Rashid, *Jihad: The Rise of Militant Islam*, 74 (see chap. 6, note 6).

10. Briefing, US Security Assistance Officer, US Embassy Dushanbe, Tajikistan, 16 March 2006; author with Defense Language Institute English Language Center (DLIELC), correspondence, January 2006; and USCENTCOM interviews (see chap. 6, note 7).

11. DLIELC correspondence (see chap. 6, note 10); and USCENTCOM interviews (see chap. 6, note 7).

12. Kimberly Marten, "Understanding the Impact of the K2 Closure," *PONARS Policy Memo No. 401*, December 2005, 216, http://www.csis.org/media/csis/pubs/pm_0401.pdf.

13. Ahrari, "The Strategic Future of Central Asia," 160 (see chap. 1, note 1).

14. Maxim Shashenkov, "Central Asia: Emerging Military-Strategic Issues," in *After Empire: The Emerging Geopolitics of Central Asia*, ed. Jed C. Snyder (Washington, DC: National Defense University Press, 1995), 96.

15. Col Assylbek Mendygaliev, Kazakhstani Defense Attaché to the United States, interviewed by the author, September 2005; "DM Ivanov Says Over 800 Kazakhstani Troops Undergo Training in Russia," *Moscow ITAR-TASS*, 8 June 2003; "Kazakhstani Military to Undergo Free Training at Russian Academies," *Moscow ITAR-TASS*, 3 September 2002; "Russia to Export to Kazakhstan $20m [million] Worth of Arms," *Moscow ITAR-TASS*, 12 January 2001; and "254 Kazakhstani Cadets Join Military Schools in Russia," *Moscow ITAR-TASS*, 18 August 2003.

16. "Russia to Supply $3 Million Worth of Weapons to Kyrgyzstan," *ITAR-TASS*, 21 September 2005; "Turkmenistan: Niyazov Says Strategic Partnership with Russia Reaffirmed," *Moscow Interfax*, 18 October 1996; "Tajikistan Asks Russia to Expand Military Experts' Team," *ITAR-TASS*, 22 September 2005; "Russia Considers Free Education for Collective Security Organization Cadets," *Agentstvo Voyennykh Novostey*, 22 June 2005; "Tajikistan grateful to Russia for Help in Forming Army," *Moscow ITAR-TASS*, 22 February 2003; "Uzbekistani to Train Army Officers at Russian Academies," *Moscow ITAR-TASS*, 3 October 2000; "Russia: Russia, Kyrgyzstan to Sign Military Cooperation Deal," *Moscow ITAR-TASS*, 23 November 1998; "Tajikistan: Moscow to Send Contingent of Military Advisors," *Moscow Interfax*, 26 November 1996; "Tajikistan: Russian Military Advisors to Work with Tajik Armed Forces," *Moscow Interfax*, 13 April 1997; "Tajikistani Defense Official Hails Defense Partnership with Russia," *ITAR-TASS*, 14 April 2005; "Russia to Sell Arms to CSTO States at Domestic Prices," *Moscow Interfax*, 18 June 2004; "Seventy Tajikistani Army Officers to Be Trained in Russia," *Moscow ITAR-TASS*, 24 August 2004; and "Kyrgyzstan: Russia to Provide $3 Million Worth of Military Aid," *Moscow ITAR-TASS*, 14 April 2004.

17. "Russia to Sell Arms to CSTO States at Domestic Prices," *Moscow Interfax*, 18 June 2004; "Kyrgyzstan: Russia to Provide $3 Million Worth of Military Aid," *Moscow ITAR-TASS*, 14 April 2004; "Russia, Uzbekistan to Boost Military Cooperation," *Moscow ITAR-TASS*, 27 September 2003; "Russia, Kyrgyzstan Agree on Military Cooperation," *Moscow ITAR-TASS*, 11 September 2001; "Turkmenistan to Exchange Gas for Arms with Russia," *Moscow Interfax*, 14 June 2001; "Russia Gives $1 Million to Kyrgyzstan," *Moscow Interfax*, 29 October 1999; "Russia Sending First Batch of Weapons to Kyrgyzstan," *Moscow ITAR-TASS*, 8 October 1999; "Kyrgyzstani, Russian Defense Ministers Sign Aid Agreement," *Kabar News Agency*, 21 September 2005; "Itar-Tass Provides Further Details of Russian-Uzbek Military Cooperation Agreement," *Moscow ITAR-TASS*, 16 June 2004; and "Tajikistan's Defense Minister Hails Military Relations with Russia," *Moscow ITAR-TASS*, 22 February 2004.

18. "Armenia: Military Cooperation Agreements with Kazakhstan Set," *Yerevan SNARK*, 19 September 1996; "Azerbaijani Leader Hails Military Cooperation Accord with Kyrgyzstan," *Baku Turan*, 2 June 2004; "Turkmenistan Wants Military Training with Azeris," *Baku Turan*, 9 March 2000; "Tbilisi Plant to Repair Warplanes for Turkmenistan," *Moscow ITAR-TASS*, 7 August 1999; "Georgia Repairs 43 Military Aircraft, 8 Helicopters for Turkmen Army," *Moscow ITAR-TASS*, 23 December 2004; "Tajikistan, Belarus Promote Military Cooperation," *Moscow ITAR-TASS World Service*, 16 March 1999; "Turkmenistan May Purchase Advanced Weapons in Belarus," *Moscow Interfax*, 17 May 2002; "Tajikistani Air Defense Officers in Belarus for Training," *BELAPAN*, 16 August 2005; "Belarus Ready to Train Military Personnel from Collective Group States in Universities," *Agentstvo Voyennykh Novostey* Internet Edition, 28 September 2005; "Ukraine: Closer Kazakh-Ukrainian Military Cooperation Discussed," *Moscow ITAR-TASS*, 5 October 1996; "Turkmenistan's President Niyazov Says Army to Be Equipped with Most Advanced Weapons," *Moscow ITAR-TASS*, 6 May 2005; "CIS: Military Cooperation Between Ukraine and Turkmenistan Detailed," *Nezavisimoye Voyennoye Oborzreniye*, 3 June 2005, "Ukrainian, Kazakhstani Defense Ministers Discuss Future Purchases," *Interfax-Ukraine*, 18 November 2005.

19. Author's experience on military contact visit to Almaty, Kazakhstan, December 2004.

20. "Tajikistan Hopes Russia Will Fulfill Obligations on Delivering Military Equipment," *Agentstvo Voyennykh Novostey*, 23 September 2005.

21. Bob Woodward, *Bush at War* (New York: Simon & Schuster, 2003), 172–73.

22. US officials continue to stress the temporary nature of its deployments to Central Asia. Secretary of State Condoleezza Rice reiterated this policy in Astana, Kazakhstan, in October 2005: "I declare that we in America are not seeking a permanent military presence in Kyrgyzstan and anywhere else in other parts of Central Asia." "US Secretary of State Says No Permanent Military Presence Sought in Central Asia," *Interfax-Kazakhstan*, 13 October 2005. These statements were originally provided as a means of assuring Russia and China that the deployments to Central Asia and operations in Afghanistan did not pose a long-term threat to their interests in the region. These con-

cerns are no longer valid. Through the Shanghai Cooperation Organization (SCO), Russia and China have gone on record asking the United States to establish a departure date, but the rationale for staying longer has strengthened by the recognition that the terrorist threat in the region will not be eliminated quickly. This emphasis on the transitory nature of the US presence undermines the perception that the United States has long-term interests in stability and security in the region and limits the ability of security-cooperation programs to achieve their goals. But the Bush administration now recognizes that the war on terrorism will be a long one, lasting generations in the way the Cold War spanned a half century. Central Asia will be the site of continual battles in that war, not only by supporting the operations in Afghanistan but potentially as future safe havens for terrorists. Afghanistan is currently experiencing a resurgence in violence, but eventually the political and military situation will stabilize and the remaining Taliban and terrorist bases will be eliminated. Al-Qaeda, the IMU, and other terrorist organizations will seek out new locations. Geography, repression, corruption, poverty, and a host of educated but unemployed young men make Central Asia an attractive option. Rajan Menon, " 'Greater Central Asia,' Russia, and the West: Challenges and Opportunities for Cooperation," in *Russia's Engagement with the West: Transformation and Integration in the Twenty-First Century*, eds. Alexander J. Motyl, Blair A. Ruble, and Lilia Shevtsova (Armonk, New York: M. E. Sharpe, 2005), 211. Instead of emphasizing when its forces will leave, the United States should underscore how long they will stay and take steps to establish a more permanent presence. Stressing the limited commitment of US security objectives and the temporary nature of US military forces in Central Asia limits other areas of security cooperation because it undermines the perspective that the United States can serve as a reliable long-term security partner. The difference between a permanent base and permanent access to an "operating site" is not lost on the leadership in the region. An operating site allows the United States to introduce forces when Washington sees its own interests threatened, whereas a permanent base commits the United States to assist building long-term stability and security. The best opportunity for this policy shift has already passed. The first official statement outlining a long-term US military presence in Central Asia should have come anytime prior to the US invasion of Iraq when the Central Asian nations and surrounding states would have been more accepting of a more permanent status. But it is not too late, and there are multiple methods of changing the current perceptions. The United States should consider posting exchange officers at Kazakh and Kyrgyz military colleges and academies, including those for noncommissioned officers (NCO) professional development. US forces participating in exercises, both small ones such as JCET or larger ones such as Regional Cooperation, should stage from Manas or the divert bases offered by Kazakhstan. And USCENTCOM should consider expanding its use of the facilities at Dushanbe. By leveraging security-cooperation efforts, the United States can emphasize its long-term commitment to stability and security in Central Asia, which will, in turn, improve the effectiveness of the security-cooperation programs.

23. "U.S. Government Delivers Military Transport Vehicles to Uzbekistan," US Embassy Tashkent Public Affairs Office, 14 February 2000, http://www.use mbassy.uz (accessed 8 March 2006).

24. Defense Security Cooperation Agency, personnel, interviewed by the author, October 2005.

25. USCENTCOM interviews (see chap. 6, note 7).

26. *The Management of Security Assistance* (Wright-Patterson AFB, OH: The Defense Institute of Security Assistance Management, 2001), 77.

27. Defense Security Cooperation Agency Briefing, "DSCA Overview," 6 October 2004, http://www.dsca.mil (accessed 12 November 2005).

28. Author with Defense Security Cooperation Agency, correspondence, September 2005.

29. US Security Assistance Officer, Bishkek, Kyrgyzstan, interviewed by author, March 2006.

30. Ulrich, *Democratizing Communist Militaries*, 57 (see chap. 6, note 3).

31. This inefficiency in the military contact program is also addressed by Kevin Pollpeter, *U.S.-China Security Management: Assessing the Military-to-Military Relationship* (Santa Monica: CA: RAND, 2004), 69.

32. Of course there are exceptions and despite best efforts some participants will gain little from the military contact events. One Uzbek officer on a visit to Shaw AFB, South Carolina, in 2003, told his escorts he did not want to come on the trip and wanted to return home as soon as possible. He also recently had undergone surgery and his medication was in a lost suitcase, but he preferred to suffer rather than ask for assistance. According to his US hosts, "He did not appear to enjoy this visit at all. He did not seem to learn from any selected portion of the itinerary. He did not seem to enjoy the major cultural day activities." It is clear that this officer did not consider this visit to the United States as a positive experience. DLIELC correspondence (see chap. 6, note 10).

33. "U.S. Government and Kazakhstani Military Establish HUMVEE Center in Almaty," US Embassy Almaty Public Affairs Office, 14 November 2005, http://www.usembassy-kazakhstan.freenet.kz (accessed 8 March 2006).

34. Author with Montana National Guard, correspondence, December 2005; and USCENTCOM interviews (see chap. 6, note 7).

35. Cope, *International Military Training and Education*, 25–26 (see chap 2, note 14).

36. Priest, *The Mission*, 233 (see chap. 4, note 1.

37. Lincoln P. Bloomfield Jr., "Education and Training: A Common Foundation for Security," *eJournal USA* 9, no. 3 (November 2004), 6.

38. Cope, *International Military Training and Education*, 27 (see chap. 2, note 14).

39. Despite this assessment, the role of the experience in IMET and other training and education programs in resolving crises is still hit-or-miss. It is questionable whether these personal relationships, when they do exist, could be systematically employed. The US military maintains almost no documentation indicating which foreign military personnel have participated in military contact visits and only limited information on those who have partici-

pated in training and education programs. Those records that do exist are often spread through the various institutions that originally provided the training, and they generally do not provide information on the subsequent utilization of that individual in his or her parent military. US embassies are required to maintain this data and periodically report on the career progression of the graduates of US training, but whether this is routinely accomplished depends largely on the aggressiveness of the successive defense attachés and SAO personnel and the willingness of the foreign nation to provide such information (even though accepting US training quotas requires reporting this data). Because of the relatively short history and small size of the training programs, the attachés and SAOs apparently have had greater success in tracking IMET graduates in Central Asia than their counterparts in other regions.

40. Cope, *International Military Training and Education*, 26–27 (see chap. 2, note 14).

41. DOD Directive 5410.17, *Informational Program for Foreign Military Trainees in the United States*, 1985, 1–4. This document was apparently revised in 2000.

42. Jennifer Morrison Taw, *Thailand and the Philippines: Case Studies in U.S. IMET Training and Its Role in Internal Defense and Development* (Santa Monica, CA: RAND, 1994), 55; and Michael Childress, *Effectiveness of U.S. Training Efforts in Internal Defense and Development: The Cases of El Salvador and Honduras* (Santa Monica, CA: RAND, 1995), 13nb.

43. Childress, *Effectiveness of U.S. Training Efforts*, 10 (see chap. 6, note 42).

44. Ibid., 19.

45. Priest, *The Mission*, 235 (see chap. 4, note 1).

46. Many other observers dispute this assertion, believing that the Salvadoran military continued to institutionally encourage and even carry out human rights abuses through this period. Childress, *Effectiveness of U.S. Training Efforts*, 35 (see chap. 6, note 42).

47. Taw, *Thailand and the Philippines*, 55 (see chap. 6, note 42).

48. Thom Shanker and C. J. Chivers, "Crackdowns in Uzbekistan Reopens Longstanding Debate on U.S. Military Aid," *The New York Times*, 13 July 2005.

49. Lahue, "Security Assistance in Kazakhstan," 12 (see chap. 4, note 36).

50. Childress, *Effectiveness of U.S. Training Efforts*, 23–24, 31 (see chap. 6, note 42).

51. Lahue, "Security Assistance in Kazakhstan," 12 (see chap. 4, note 36).

52. Daniel Byman, *Going to War with the Allies You Have: Allies, Counterinsurgency, and the War on Terrorism* (Carlisle, PA: US Army War College Strategic Studies Institute, 2005), 11.

53. John Rudy and Ivan Eland, "Special Operations Military Training Abroad and Its Dangers," *CATO Institute Foreign Policy Briefing Number 53* (Washington, DC: CATO Institute, 1999), 7.

54. This includes over $5 million in NATO funds and $1.1 million in US-provided Warsaw Initiative Funds. Butler, "U.S. Military Cooperation with the Central Asian States" (see chap 3, note 54).

55. USCENTCOM correspondence (see chap. 3, note 55). Participants included 18 from Kazakhstan, 16 from Kyrgyzstan, 19 from Pakistan, 17 from Tajikistan, and 93 from the United States (including interpreters). Turkmenistan, Russia, and the United Arab Emirates each sent two observers.

56. DLIELC correspondence (see chap. 6, note 10).

57. Igor Grebenshchikov, "Kyrgyz Army in Crisis," Institute for War and Peace Reporting, 14 March 2001, http://www.iwpr.net/?p=rca&s=f&o=177189&apc_state=henirca2001.

58. Kenneth Weisbrode, "Patrol Boat Procurement Makes Waves on the Caspian," *Eurasia Insight*, 17 August 2001, http://www.eurasianet.org/departments/insight/articles/eav071701.shtml; and Defense Threat Reduction Agency personnel, interviewed by author, March 2006.

59. US Security Assistance Officer, US Embassy Almaty, interviewed by author, 22 March 2006.

60. *Nuclear Nonproliferation: US Efforts to Help Other Countries Combat Nuclear Smuggling Need Strengthened Coordination and Planning*, US General Accounting Office Report to the Ranking Minority Member, Subcommittee on Emerging Threats and Capabilities, Committee on Armed Services, U.S. Senate, GAO-02-426 (Washington, DC: Government Printing Office, 2002), 21.

61. Col Assylbek A. Mendygaliev, Defense, Military, and Air Attaché of the Republic of Kazakhstan to the United States and Canada, interviewed by author, 28 November 2005.

62. USCENTCOM personnel, interviewed by author, 27 September 2005.

63. Childress, *Effectiveness of U.S. Training Efforts*, 25–26 (see chap. 6, note 42).

Chapter 7

Measuring Effectiveness

You get what you measure. So we need to figure out what the right measures of effectiveness are in our security cooperation programs.

> —Secretary of Defense Donald Rumsfeld, DOD-DOS (Department of Defense– Department of State) Security Cooperation Conference, April 2006

Security cooperation is one of many tools used by the United States to advance its national-security interests in Central Asia. As outlined in chapter 1, the official Defense Department definition offers some insight to the narrower set of objectives within this rubric: "All Department of Defense interactions with foreign defense establishments to build defense relationships that promote specific US security interests, develop allied and friendly military capabilities for self-defense and multinational operations, and provide US forces with peacetime and contingency access to a host nation."[1] In this sense, it addresses and includes those positive activities that strengthen military ties between the US armed forces and those of allied and partner nations. Security cooperation is not altruistic, nor is it conducted without purpose. Therefore, security cooperation has three objectives: to *build relationships* so that the United States can influence other countries and their military forces, to *develop capabilities* of foreign military forces so they can conduct operations on behalf of the United States, and to *provide access* so that the US military has strategic flexibility to conduct its own operations. Security cooperation is, at its core, specifically intended to achieve specific US national-security objectives.

These objectives are interrelated and often complementary. Programs that contribute toward building capabilities will usually result in stronger relationships, and programs designed to establish relationships can contribute to developing capabilities. However, they can at times be contradictory—for example; creating capabilities for participation in coalition operations can detract from efforts to improve internal defensive capabilities. These objectives should be directly related to the US national-security objectives for the region; but, again, they can be supporting or, at times, contradictory in the actual execution of the programs.

The ability to objectively evaluate the effectiveness of the security-cooperation programs in Central Asia is hindered by several separate but related issues. First, for much of the history of US programs in Central Asia, US security-cooperation objectives were poorly defined, if defined at all. Events, activities, and programs were proposed, planned, and implemented if they could be seen as *supporting* an objective, rather than as a specific advancement integrated with other activities toward the objective (fig. 10). Although planning efforts in the past several years have improved this situation, there are still some programs that still lack specific, measurable objectives and corresponding activities that directly contribute to the advance-

Figure 10. US and Kazakhstani personnel during a transport aviation military contact event, Almaty, Kazakhstan, December 2004 (Reprinted from author's personal collection.)

ment toward a specified goal. It is difficult to measure effectiveness against poorly defined goals.

Second, DOD lacks a readily-accessible, detailed, comprehensive database of security-cooperation activities, including plans, funding levels, and execution reports. The historical survey offered earlier in this paper was compiled from a broad range of sources and, to date, offers the fullest presentation of those activities, but it admittedly does not fully capture all of the US security-cooperation activities in the region since 1993. Almost every DOD agency contacted during the preparation of this paper acknowledged shortfalls in maintaining historical records of its activities, and some admitted to not being able to identify activities and events that had occurred as recently as two or three years ago. It is difficult to measure effectiveness without the historical data that describes what has taken place.

Third, DOD has not yet developed comprehensive criteria for measuring the effectiveness of security-cooperation programs. Previous evaluations, such as the annual reports prepared by the Department of State, have tended to focus on quantities of funding, equipment deliveries, or students trained, punctuated with anecdotes of how a specific effort brought a specific victory. But to fully evaluate effectiveness requires performance metrics measured both before and after the event or series of events. Such a database would include collecting information that many of the countries in Central Asia would consider overly intrusive, such as assessments of the combat capability of special forces units before and after a specific exercise or military contact event. Likewise, it is not clear, as will be described below, that measurable criteria can be developed for some aspects of security cooperation.

Finally, it is at this point impossible to separate the impact of US security-cooperation programs from that of other influences. A positive relationship established through a military cooperation program may be offset by the negative effects of other US policies, such as occurred in Uzbekistan. US military aid may improve the capabilities of a specific unit, but that unit may have also been receiving additional national resources or military aid from another country. Over the past few years, for example, the Kyrgyzstani Army has received mountain warfare training and specialized equipment from the United States,

France, Russia, India, Germany, Turkey, Japan, and South Korea. It would be difficult to ascribe any improvements in its capabilities solely to US security-cooperation efforts. In July 1998, US officials provided equipment and training to the Kazakhstani Border Guards at a transshipment point in Dostyk (formerly called Druzhba) through the ICP. In April 2001, two containers were stopped at this checkpoint because border officials noted they were emitting radiation. Although ICP officials highlight this incident as a success story, it is not clear whether the Kazakhstani officials were using the US-supplied equipment or techniques provided three years earlier, or even if they were the same officials that had participated in the ICP program in 1998.[2]

However, some appreciation of the effectiveness of these programs can be offered even with these constraints. This paper will offer a tentative evaluation of US security-cooperation activities against the three main elements of the definition of security cooperation: building relationships, improving capabilities, and obtaining access.

Building Relationships

As described, security cooperation is at best a highly complex, difficult, and expensive process that takes a long time to achieve successes that are both largely immeasurable and likely transitory. Security-cooperation programs in Central Asia face other limitations, as well, because of the unique environment and scarcity of resources. The DOD is struggling with the concept of measuring the results of security-cooperation programs. How can relationships be quantified? Planners usually count the number of events, number of personnel involved, costs of events, or some other measurable figure, but these statistics bear little relation to the status of the military relationship between the United States and these nations. Security assistance officers are required to report the utilization of IMET graduates within the defense establishments of their countries, and many seek to identify senior foreign leaders who have studied in the United States under the program. But even when this information is available, this method does not capture whether that officer internalized what was taught or even if they had a favorable experience while in the United States. Measuring the improvement in relationships between institutions is also difficult, largely subjective, and perhaps possible only in a relative sense. In any event, as the experience in Uzbekistan shows, the results can be perishable. Other factors can intervene resulting in the immediate severing of all ties and spoiling the relations that had developed over a decade.

Building defense relationships is easily the most important but also the most difficult of the three aspects of security cooperation. An individual senior leader visit, military contact event, or training class in itself does not accomplish much in building significant relationships. But persistent engagement over a long period of time; reinforced with other diplomatic, economic, political, and military activities; can build personal and institutional ties that can translate; at the right time, under the right conditions, and for the right reason; in decisions by foreign governments and military institutions that support specific US security interests. In Central Asia, these broad interests were denuclearization, democratization, and regional cooperation. To date, the scorecard is mixed with some successes and some failures.

By any measure, US efforts to denuclearize Central Asia must be considered a success. Within a few short years, cooperative efforts by the United States and Kazakhstan resulted in both the removal of the nuclear weapons and the destruction of the nuclear infrastructure. Despite his initial reluctance, President Nazarbayev fully accepted the US desire to eliminate the weapons, and now sees Kazakhstan's positive experience in denuclearization as a role model for other states to emulate.[3] Those successes allowed the expansion of the effort to include elimination of chemical and biological weapons and infrastructure throughout the region, generating even more successes: eliminating Soviet-era anthrax inventories buried on the Vozrozhdeniye Island in the Aral Sea and helping to destroy a Soviet chemical weapons research, development, and testing facility at Nukus, Uzbekistan.[4]

But the denuclearization initiative must be considered a success in a different fashion as well. Those early efforts created a pattern of cooperation between the defense institutions of both countries that served as the foundation for the entire structure

157

of collaborative programs throughout the 1990s. It also provided an opportunity for those other programs to develop. The CTR program (since it was intended for the denuclearization effort) provided both funding and a bureaucratic architecture for most of the other programs that began in the 1990s—military contact events, senior leader visits, certain types of exercises and exchanges. If the denuclearization program had not existed or had not been successful, attempts to initiate and develop subsequent cooperation programs would have faced even greater challenges.

The denuclearization effort and the related programs to eliminate chemical and biological weapons and facilities are unique, however. They are inherently destructive, not constructive, and success is measured by what has been eliminated rather than what has been created. It is much more difficult to assess the effectiveness of the military democratization efforts in Central Asia. The military contact program and training and education programs have been the primary tools for this objective. During the first phase, 1993–1995, the difference between the limited resources and the lofty and vague objectives was simply too great to make any progress. As no records are available regarding the military contact events conducted during that period, it is impossible to evaluate whether they contributed to the goals set for them. The training and education programs offer more data but not much more confidence. In that three year period, less than 100 students from Central Asia attended US military training and education programs. Just under half attended courses at the Marshall Center, and others attended English language training.

Inherent in this model is the assumption that the state will continue, albeit possibly erratically, its political reform efforts toward a democratic society, thereby providing both the rationale and the opportunity needed to democratize the armed forces. This is not the case in Central Asia, where all five countries have largely ceased reform efforts (if they had ever started) and many have reversed previous gains. The Central Asian states are no longer democratizing and all have governments of varying degrees of authoritarianism. Nor are most of them likely to restart political reform efforts as long as the current leadership remains in power.

Yet despite the limited resources and vague objectives, military democratization and reform efforts have had some small but measurable successes, particularly in Kazakhstan. According to the US SAO in Almaty, the noncommissioned officer professional development program in Kazakhstan has visibly reduced the practice of *dedovshina* (abuse inflicted on new recruits) in certain units. Also, the Kazakh Ministry of Defense established the position of senior sergeant to the minister of defense, who serves as his advisor on matters relating to enlisted personnel. The senior sergeant was authorized an apartment in Astana and a car with a driver, indicating his influence and power.

US efforts to promote regional cooperation in security and defense matters have also had mixed success. Throughout the late 1990s, these efforts were centered on CENTRASBAT. However, over time CENTRASBAT became a showcase unit with no operational utility. The subordinate companies were never posted to the same garrison, and the command-and-control relationships ensured the unit could never have been effectively used. CENTRASBAT was disbanded by the end of the decade and arguably did more to promote discord than cooperation among the partner nations.

Other programs, however, have had greater success. The conferences, exercises, and workshops used for promoting cooperative responses to natural and environmental disasters and major terrorist attacks have made great progress in helping these militaries appreciate the fact that such events can not be managed unilaterally, and they have already fostered a series of bilateral and multilateral agreements for joint planning and response between these nations. The true measure of effectiveness, however, will come when one of these disasters actually occurs. Likewise, efforts to promote cooperation in border security has had mixed results. Kazakhstan and Kyrgyzstan appear to have increased their cooperative efforts to improve border security, but Uzbekistan has sealed its borders with its neighbors.

Building Military Capabilities

Unfortunately, there is insufficient available information to fully evaluate US efforts to improve the military capabilities of these nations. Quantifying the establishment or improvement in military capabilities is equally difficult. Measuring the improvement in capabilities of foreign military forces through security assistance programs is usually captured in numbers of equipment provided, personnel trained, or exercises conducted. But this does not adequately capture whether that unit is capable of conducting the required mission. Most countries have some method for determining combat readiness, but for security reasons will not share that data with foreign security assistance officers. And the results of the security assistance programs also can be transitory or perishable. Personnel rotate out of the unit and the experience is dispersed, skills erode if they are not practiced and exercised, and equipment breaks if not properly maintained. At this point, it is not feasible to offer a solid evaluation of US efforts to improve border security, proliferation prevention, or counterinsurgency capabilities in these nations. However, a case study of US programs to build peacekeeping capabilities can be offered.

To date, the United States has experienced both success and failure in establishing peacekeeping capabilities in the countries of Central Asia, specifically, Kazakhstan, Kyrgyzstan, and Uzbekistan. In terms of regional cooperation, CENTRASBAT failed, but it did provide the nucleus for subsequent efforts to build peacekeeping units. When CENTRASBAT was disbanded in 2000, Kazakhstan used its company-sized element as the foundation for the formation of a larger unit, the Kazakhstan battalion or KAZBAT. In August 2003, at the request of the United States, Kazakhstan deployed an engineering element of KAZBAT to Iraq, one of the few Muslim countries and the only nation from Central Asia to participate in the post-invasion reconstruction operations. As part of the international division commanded by Poland, the KAZBAT element conducted demining and water-purification duties, and by November 2005 had destroyed over four million pieces of ordnance in the region. Since March 2005, the unit has also trained Iraqi soldiers in explosives disposal. Most of the personnel are graduates of the IMET program and the deputy commander graduated from the US Army Command and General Staff College. The 27 members of the deployed unit, all volunteers for service in Iraq, are rotated every six months, spreading the operational experience throughout the battalion. Kazakhstan's participation in Operation Iraqi Freedom with the KAZBAT unit should be considered a success in coalition building, but KAZBAT's actual operations in Iraq also have been widely praised by US, Polish, and Kazakhstani officials. In the fall of 2005, Kazakhstan was awarded $2 million in CSF to support KAZBAT operations in Iraq. These funds will likely be used to purchase additional HMMWVs and body armor. Similarly, the Kazakhstani Ministry of Defense has requested US assistance to increase KAZBAT to a brigade-sized unit, a proposal that will likely gain support.[5]

Unfortunately, US efforts to build peacekeeping units in Kyrgyzstan and Uzbekistan must be considered a failure. While the status of Uzbekistan's elements of CENTRASBAT is unknown, the Kyrgyzstani element of CENTRASBAT dissipated in 2000–2001, with the equipment and personnel absorbed into other units or otherwise discarded. All the experience, skills, and training gained through participating in CENTRASBAT were lost. At the present, Kyrgyzstan does not have the capability of participating in international peacekeeping operations. In 2006, however, Bishkek requested US aid to establish a new peacekeeping unit in order to participate in international operations. Likewise, Tajikistan has also expressed interest in building a peacekeeping unit. It is unknown whether these requests will gain much support.

Gaining Access and Basing Rights

Many observers cited the decisions by the Central Asian states to provide overflight and basing rights as a vindication of US security-cooperation efforts in the region throughout the 1990s. Some even traced the establishment of basing rights directly to the efforts of particular US units in the region at that time, claiming the relationships established during a specific deployment were an immediate factor in approving the basing of US forces.[6] These claims probably overstate the affect the previous security-cooperation programs had on the ultimate

161

decision to provide access. In fact, it is likely that US security cooperation efforts in Central Asia prior to September 2001 played only a minor and indirect role in this process.

By 2001 the United States had concentrated its security-cooperation efforts on Kazakhstan and Uzbekistan and, to a somewhat lesser extent, Kyrgyzstan. At the other end of the spectrum, the security-cooperation relationship with Turkmenistan was weak and with Tajikistan virtually nonexistent. Proponents of security-cooperation programs and military planners, if asked prior to September 2001 which countries would most likely be willing to offer basing rights and overflight privileges, likely would have identified Uzbekistan, Kazakhstan, and Kyrgyzstan. Few would have considered Turkmenistan and Tajikistan as reasonable candidates given the limited nature of security-cooperation interactions to that point. Despite the lack of previous security cooperation programs, Turkmenistan and Tajikistan generally were as willing as Kazakhstan, Kyrgyzstan, and Uzbekistan to offer support to the United States.

Security-cooperation relationships may be helpful when requesting overflight and basing rights, but the lack of a strong relationship does not prohibit a positive outcome. In fact, officials at the US Embassy in Ashgabat reportedly sent the request to the Turkmenistani Ministry of Foreign Affairs without expecting a positive response and were surprised when it was forthcoming.[7] Similarly, Tajikistan had been left out of US security-cooperation programs throughout the 1990s, when the US military was fostering relationships throughout the rest of the region, because of the turmoil and aftermath of its civil war. There had been few results by September 2001. However, Dushanbe readily offered to host US forces as early as 25 September, two weeks after the attacks in New York and Washington. Secretary of State Colin Powell noted that Tajik president Rahmonov had "given us basically everything we want." Despite having almost no security-cooperation relationship, Dushanbe asked for nothing in return for its support.[8]

Providing overflight and basing privileges is always ultimately a political decision, and military relationships established through previous cooperation efforts are but one factor that may influence that decision. In the authoritarian states in Central Asia, a decision of that importance is ultimately and exclusively left to the president. Uzbekistani president Karimov was certainly knowledgeable of the military ties that had developed since 1995, but he was also aware that the relationship had not developed as quickly or as deeply as he had hoped. Tashkent had been seeking security guarantees from the United States and offering permanent bases since 1995, but Washington had discouraged any attempts to build stronger ties. In short, the security-cooperation programs prior to September 2001 demonstrated the limits of that friendship.

Ultimately, Karimov had other reasons for approving the request, including the strong possibility that the US operations in Afghanistan would eliminate the threat from the IMU and a desire to offset growing US and Western condemnations of Uzbekistan's violations of international norms on human rights. Karimov also saw this request as a new opportunity to gain security guarantees from the United States and help balance the growing Russian influence in Central Asia. Additionally, the Central Asian presidents, including Karimov, were probably influenced by President Bush's declaration that "the nations of the world would either be with us or against us in the war on terrorism." According to General Franks, "They had plenty to gain by joining the coalition, and a lot to lose if they did not."[9] While the promise of additional security aid may have contributed to a positive outcome, a recent RAND study concluded "there is little to suggest that prior contacts had a significant influence on the decision making of the Central Asian leaders."[10]

However, US security-cooperation efforts may contribute to positive decisions for overflight and basing rights in several indirect fashions. First, they permit US officials to understand the personalities and bureaucracies within these countries, which helps identify the right interlocutors when making the requests.[11] Second, they create a pattern of cooperation that foreign political and military leaders can use, presumably favorably, to evaluate the request. It is possible that President Karimov sought advice from military leaders who, through US security-cooperation efforts, were familiar with US capabilities and the likelihood of success.[12] Third, they create a pool of foreign military personnel who are familiar with US operations, equipment, and requirements. These personnel can greatly facilitate the deployment once the political decision has been made. Reportedly, an Uzbek officer who had graduated from the US Air Force's Air Command and Staff College coordinated the requirements between the Ministry of Defense and US Central Command.[13]

Relative Accomplishments

It is important to distinguish the relative progress made by US security-cooperation programs with each of the five Central Asian states. The relationship with Tajikistan, established only in 2001 with actual programs initiated in 2002 is too new to judge. The ties to Turkmenistan have been in existence longer, but are very tenuous. Niyazov's authoritarian control and "positive neutrality" stance ensures few changes are likely under his rule. Given the very limited defense ties prior to 2001, it is difficult to attribute his support for US operations in Afghanistan directly to the security-cooperation programs.

Security-cooperation efforts with Uzbekistan were generally productive, but it is much more difficult to identify specific achievements. Unlike Kazakhstan, Uzbekistan's periodic strategic shifts in foreign policy have hampered strong ties, and the breakdown in the relationship since 2005 has all but destroyed any progress that may have been made. While Uzbekistan provided access for Operation Enduring Freedom, it is unlikely to agree to any US deployments in the foreseeable future.

US security cooperation with Kyrgyzstan has been steady and productive, but efforts with Kazakhstan, by almost any measure, have made the most progress. That relationship had the advantage of starting first and having access to more resources, but other factors also played a major role. The cooperative efforts with Kazakhstan were based on plans that were better defined and the specific objectives, from the Kazakh perspective, remained relatively consistent over time: removal of the nuclear legacy, development of a professional noncommissioned officer corps, improved security for the Caspian area, and development of a peacekeeping unit. Even when CENTRASBAT collapsed, Kazakhstan created its own peacekeeping unit and has employed it in Iraq since 2003.

Notes

1. Joint Publication 1-02, *DOD Dictionary of Military and Associated Terms*, as amended through 22 March 2007, http://131.84.1.34/doctrine/jel/doddict/data/s/04830.html.

2. *United States Department of Defense International Counterproliferation (ICP) Program—Success Stories: Impact of the ICP Program on Proliferation*, Defense Threat Reduction Agency Web site, http://www.dtra.mil (accessed 19 March 2006).

3. Rose Gottemoeller, "Cooperative Threat Reduction Beyond Russia," *The Washington Quarterly* 28, no. 2 (Spring 2005), 149.

4. *Cooperative Threat Reduction History*, Defense Threat Reduction Agency Web site, http://www.dtra.mil/oe/ctr/history.cfm.

5. Defense Security Cooperation Agency correspondence (see chap. 6, note 28); Roger M. McDermott and Col Igor Mukhamedov, "Kazakhstan's Peacekeeping Support in Iraq," *Central Asia–Caucasus Analyst*, 28 January 2004, http://www.cacianalyst.org/view_article.php?articleid=2067 (accessed 20 March 2006); Roger McDermott, "KAZBAT Deployment in Iraq Faces Uncertainty," *Eurasia Daily Monitor* 1, no. 15 (21 May 2004), http://jamestown.org/publications_details.php?volume_id=401&issue_id=2961&article_id=236748 (accessed 20 March 2006); Roger McDermott, "Kazakhstan Suffers First Death of Peacekeeper in Iraq," *Eurasia Daily Monitor* 2, no. 95 (13 January 2005), http://jamestown.org/publications_details.php?volume_id=407&issue_id=3194&article_id=2369080 (accessed 20 March 2006); "Kazakhstan Contribution to Normal Life in Iraq Grows," *Kazakhstan News Bulletin* 5, no. 47 (10 November 2005), http://www.homestead.com/prosites-kazakhembus/November_10.pdf (accessed 20 March 2006).

6. Wooley, "America's Quiet Professionals," 61 (see chap. 4, note 48). My criticism of this perspective extends only to the mischaracterization of the results, and not to the valuable accomplishments of the 6th Special Operations Squadron or other units that have conducted security cooperation activities and built relationships in Central Asia.

7. Olga Oliker and David A. Shlapak, *U.S. Interests in Central Asia: Policy Priorities and Military Roles* (Santa Monica, CA: RAND, 2005), 17.

8. Woodward, *Bush at War*, 148, 178 (see chap. 6, note 21).

9. Franks and McConnell, *American Soldier*, 269 (see chap. 5, note 2).

10. Oliker and Shlapak, *U. S. Interests in Central Asia*, 11–12 (see chap. 7, note 7).

11. Ibid., 11.

12. In a similar fashion, David Welch argues that US security-cooperation activities conducted with Israel in the years prior to Operation Desert Storm were principal factor in Prime Minister Yitzhak Shamir's decision not to respond militarily to Iraq's Scud missile attacks:

> But Israel made it clear that its forbearance depended *principally* on a demonstration of the effectiveness of the American military effort. It was here that the closeness of the relationships between the IDF [Israeli Defense Force], on the one hand, and the United States army and air force, on the other, came into play. These relationships had developed and matured over several decades of close

collaboration in a wide variety of fields. Here could be found the crucial elements missing in the political relationship: trust and a spirit of genuine co-operation. Several Israelis interviewed for this study insist that without these close relationships, Israel's political leaders could never have been persuaded to set aside—if only temporarily—the country's long-standing and deeply ingrained policy of military self-reliance. The IDF's growing conviction that American soldiers and pilots could get the job done made it much easier for Shamir to give them the time to try.

David A. Welch, "The Politics and Psychology of Restraint: Israeli Decision-Making in the Gulf War," in Janice Gross Stein and Louis W. Pauly, eds., *Choosing to Cooperate: How States Avoid Loss* (Baltimore, MD: The Johns Hopkins University Press, 1993), 168.

13. Goldstein, "Making the Most of Central Asian Partnerships," 84 (see chap. 3, note 53).

Chapter 8

Prospects

*The sands of Central Asia are littered with the bones of
Westerners in a hurry.*

—British diplomat at the end of the nineteenth century

In testimony before the House of Representatives Subcommittee on the Middle East and Central Asia on 26 April 2006, Deputy Assistant Secretary of Defense James C. MacDougall reiterated the three interrelated national-security interests—political and economic reform, energy and regional economic cooperation, and security—described by Assistant Secretary of State Daniel Fried in October 2005. He then outlined in greater detail the three core goals for US security relationships in Central Asia: supporting the war on terrorism, strengthening regional border security and reducing the risk of the proliferation of weapons of mass destruction, and promoting and assisting with regional defense sector reform.[1] These three goals are largely a continuation of the objectives initiated at various points in the history of US security-cooperation programs in the region since 1993, but they also serve as a road map for US effort over the next several years.

The historical review and discussion on constraints presented in earlier chapters suggest that the United States has experienced both successes and failures with its security-cooperation programs in Central Asia over the past 13 years. The efforts that have made the most progress are those that resulted from improvements in planning and integration of the various programs, while the less successful are characterized by disjointed activities against diffuse objectives. As such, there are specific lessons from these experiences that can help guide future programs.

Central Asia will retain its strategic importance to the United States for many decades. The national-security objectives for this region have remained consistent for the past 12 years and will remain constant for many more, but they will likely grow in

167

urgency over the next 10 to 15 years. Yet, despite the relatively large amounts of security-cooperation funding at various stages since 1993, the United States has never dedicated sufficient resources to achieve many of its security-cooperation objectives in Central Asia. Current funding levels in almost every category—the CN program is the sole exception—show a slow, steady decrease since the highs of 2002, and in relative terms they pale in comparison with funding offered to other, arguably less strategic, regions of the world. As a result, there have been a relatively modest number of successes for an increasing number of disparate objectives.

Funding for current security-cooperation efforts are the seeds for the relationships and capabilities of the future. Given the strategic importance of the region, US funding should be dramatically increased, commensurate with an increase in funding for programs that support political and economic reform. Unfortunately, other budgetary concerns, including the response to Hurricane Katrina and the ongoing operations in Iraq, ensure any increases will be incremental. With or without additional funding, the United States must restructure its security-cooperation efforts in Central Asia so they are increasingly integrated, focused, and persistent. This chapter offers five specific recommendations that will assist policy makers and security-cooperation planners to get the most effect out of the existing resources.

Integrate Efforts within the Defense Department

Two independent organizational changes within the DOD helped consolidate US security-cooperation efforts in Central Asia. First, the establishment of DTRA in late 1998 integrated the denuclearization and counterproliferation activities of the OSIA, the DSWA, and the OSD's CTR Program Office and Chemical and Biological Warfare Program Office. Second, the 1999 publication of the revised Unified Command Plan (UCP) assigned the diverse military contact and exercise efforts of the USEUCOM, the USACOM, and the USPACOM to the USCENT-COM. Coming simultaneously with the beginning of a period of reassessment, these two separate bureaucratic changes significantly contributed to providing greater structure and focus to these programs in the region. Likewise, over the following years, several factors helped link the USCENTCOM's military engagement activities and the DSCA's security-assistance programs, including internal changes within the USCENTCOM, the creation in several of the countries of the SAOs (which are responsive to both organizations), and the publication of the DOD's Security Cooperation Guidance.

Despite these improvements, the DOD's efforts remain somewhat disjointed. For example, the USCENTCOM, DTRA, and OSD are all conducting activities designed to improve the security of the borders of the Central Asian states, justified as supporting proliferation prevention, CN, counterterrorism, or US operations in Afghanistan. But these activities are not fully synchronized or integrated. As previously mentioned, some DOD organizations use definitional debates to avoid such coordination: "Officials in OSD's Counter-proliferation Policy office refused to admit that activities intended to improve the maritime security capabilities of Azerbaijan and Kazakhstan in support of counter-proliferation would be included under the definition of Security Cooperation and declined to integrate their program formally with other DOD Security Cooperation efforts."[2] The relationship between the USCENTCOM and the DTRA has recently grown stronger and each organization has taken steps to synchronize their programs, but more can and should be done.

Likewise, both USEUCOM and USJFCOM invite the Central Asian states to participate in the NATO PfP exercises, often without consulting the USCENTCOM to determine whether the objectives of the exercise are consistent with the USCENTCOM's Theater Security Cooperation Plan or whether funding is available. When the nations agree to participate, the USCENTCOM—the command responsible for building relations with these military forces—is placed in the awkward position of having to either decline the request or divert resources from other higher priority programs. Similarly, other defense organizations occasionally engage in security-cooperation activities in Central Asia without coordinating those efforts through the USCENTCOM. Such efforts also divert host nation resources and energies, and have the potential to embarrass the DOD by making it apparent to the foreign nation (often the same cadre of officers works all these issues with foreign interlocutors) that the various commands do not communicate with each other.

To facilitate this integration, the secretary of defense should grant the USCENTCOM the full authority and responsibility to coordinate and orchestrate all DOD security-cooperation efforts in Central Asia, including those conducted by the DTRA, DSCA, other defense agencies, other unified commands, and the military services. Along with the responsibility and authority, the OSD should transfer funding for many of these programs—specifically those used for the military contact programs—directly to the USCENTCOM for planning and execution. In other cases, such as the DTRA's proliferation prevention and biological and chemical weapons elimination programs, the USCENTCOM and the DTRA should institutionalize procedures to ensure programs and funding are executed in a manner consistent with the DOD Security Cooperation Guidance and the USCENTCOM Theater Security Cooperation Plan. While the regulations governing the use of each source of funding may limit the ability to redirect resources to higher priority objectives, having a single lead agency responsible for synchronizing, integrating, and deconflicting the various programs will dramatically improve the effectiveness of these efforts and provide greater opportunities for the United States to achieve its security-cooperation objectives in Central Asia.

The OSD should also task the USCENTCOM to establish a comprehensive security-cooperation database that captures and retains all relevant information for all activities, regardless of which organization funds, manages, and executes them. (Multiple databases currently exist, but they are usually narrowly focused on a specific activity and difficult for all members of the security-cooperation community to access.) All defense organizations, military services, and unified commands would be required to populate this database appropriately. Over time, the analysis of the information in such a database would permit a more effective evaluation of the total range of US security-cooperation activities in the region and offer additional suggestions for improvement.

Integrate Efforts within the US Government

Some observers have suggested the current explanation of security cooperation, as broad as it is, should be expanded. Col Albert Zaccor, US Army, a senior fellow at the Atlantic Council of the United States, proposes the following definition: "Security Cooperation refers to all USG [US government] assistance provided to foreign law enforcement, security, and defense establishments in support of national defense, security, and foreign policy objectives."[3] Using this definition, however, would require a much more complete integration of the various efforts of the entire US government than is evident today, but such an approach is needed.

Despite the scarcity of resources, US security-cooperation efforts are poorly integrated across the US government. In many cases, a variety of US government organizations have established separate programs with varying objectives that all tend toward the same goal. For example, at least six separate federal departments are conducting proliferation prevention, CN, or counterinsurgency programs in Central Asia, all of which include some aspect of improving border security. However, these programs are poorly integrated. This observation is not new—a Government Accounting Office report in 2002 made the following assessment:

> U.S. assistance efforts to combat nuclear smuggling are divided among six federal agencies—the Departments of Energy, State, and Defense; the U.S. Customs Service; the Federal Bureau of Investigation (FBI); and the U.S. Coast Guard. . . . U.S. assistance is not effectively coordinated and lacks an overall government-wide plan to guide it. Although an interagency group, chaired by the State Department, exists to coordinate U.S. assistance efforts, the six agencies that are providing assistance do not always coordinate their efforts through this group. As a result, the Departments of Energy, State, and Defense have pursued separate approaches to installing radiation detection equipment at other countries' border crossings; consequently, some countries' border crossings are more vulnerable to nuclear smuggling than others.[4]

Some of the US embassies located in Central Asia have started conducting regular staff meetings to deconflict and synchronize the security-cooperation initiatives executed by the various US government agencies. This is a superb initiative and should be encouraged. But its limits should also be recognized—the representatives of the different federal agencies that serve on the embassy staffs are trying to ensure that planned activities and programs do not interfere with each other. What is required is a broader integration at the agency level, before the programs are pushed out to the embassies.

The OSD should spearhead a concerted effort to fully integrate the US government security-cooperation efforts in Central Asia. The first attempt, the CASI announced by the State Department in April 2000, was a step in the right direction but only partially met this goal as it simply loosely linked several programs under an umbrella concept rather than forcing the integration of the programs. CASI has apparently been abandoned, having not been mentioned in State Department reports since 2003. Likewise, the OSD-initiated first-ever DOD-DOS Security Cooperation Conference held in Washington, DC, in April 2006, highlighted on a broader scale the need for integrating security-cooperation programs between these two agencies. But much work lies ahead on actually building the procedures and authorities necessary to fully synchronize those efforts. As they develop, other US government agencies must be drawn in to the effort. Although this integration is necessary in all of the regions in which the United States conducts security-cooperation activities, Central Asia is an ideal location to initiate these efforts.

Integrate Efforts with NATO and Allied and Partner Nations

Throughout the 1990s, NATO was a reluctant and seldom-seen player in the security-cooperation efforts in Central Asia. Kazakhstan, Kyrgyzstan, Turkmenistan, and Uzbekistan had joined the Partnership for Peace program, but PfP offered little more than a handful of training seminars and courses and a convenient source of funding for US or Turkish-sponsored national activities. Often the distinction between national activities and PfP programs was muddied by the use of the term "in the spirit of PfP," which meant that the initiatives were national in nature but consistent with NATO's objectives. CENTRASBAT is a prime example—carried out "in the spirit of PfP." It was not sponsored by NATO but by the United States. Even NATO leaders were sometimes confused: one remarked at the CENTRASBAT 97 exercise that "this will be the first time we've [NATO] had such a military exercise in Central Asia," and was immediately corrected by his more astute colleagues.[5]

Central Asia leaders were also hesitant about investing in new military relationships with NATO. Alliance membership was never a real option, so there was no prospect of meaningful security guarantees. Other factors also limited interest. Kazakhstan was cautions about any initiatives that might irritate its relationship with Russia, Turkmenistan stood behind its "positive neutrality" foreign policy, and Tajikistan did not join PfP because of its ongoing civil conflict. Instead, the Central Asian states have preferred bilateral ties with the United States, Turkey, and Germany over institutional ties with NATO.[6]

NATO's involvement in Afghanistan in 2003 changed the dynamics of these relationships, and now both NATO and many of the Central Asian states are seeking greater interaction. Kazakhstan leads this trend, asking in November 2002 for assistance in military reform and strengthening KAZBAT's capabilities, and then in November 2005 signing an Individual Partnership Action Plan (IPAP), the most comprehensive web of ties with NATO ever agreed to by a Central Asian state. NATO's links to Kyrgyzstan and Turkmenistan are also growing rapidly, and Tajikistan's entry into PfP in 2002 offers new opportunities. NATO's relationship with Uzbekistan was increasingly robust until the Andijon incident and the resulting harsh criticisms of Karimov by the international community.

The United States should strongly encourage increased NATO security-cooperation activities in Central Asia, and should also seek to better integrate its programs with those conducted by NATO. The NATO PfP program offers a proven model for defense reform and new perspectives on counterterrorism, counterinsurgency, CN, and proliferation prevention. Increased interaction with and by NATO will help decrease Russian military influence and solidify linkages to Euro-Atlantic institutions.

But leveraging NATO's activities in the region is not the only opportunity. During the 1990s, Turkey and Germany were the only other two Western nations with significant security-cooperation programs in Central Asia. Since the end of 2001,

173

however, a number of other Western nations have recognized the strategic importance of the region, largely as a result of deploying military units to Central Asian nations to support operations in Afghanistan. Some of these nations, including the United Kingdom, Germany, and France, have established formal security-cooperation programs, with both bilateral efforts and via the NATO PfP program, with a number of the Central Asian states. A summary of these third-nation efforts is shown in appendix D. Most of these nations share the same fundamental objectives in Central Asia as the United States, so these third-country relationships offer opportunities to reinforce and reemphasize US programs. According to Ms. Heidi Reisinger, an analyst in the Military Policy Directorate of the Ministry of Defense in Berlin, Germany is promoting goals almost identical to those of the United States: stability through democracy and the rule of law, regional cooperation through economic growth, trustworthy relationships in the effort against terrorism, crime, and narcotics smuggling, and reform of the armed forces.[7] Some efforts have been made by the United States, German, and Turkish officials in Kazakhstan to synchronize their security-cooperation efforts, and these initiatives should be encouraged and expanded.[8] The United States should establish a forum by which key allied nations, including Turkey, Germany, the United Kingdom, and France, can deconflict and synchronize their bilateral security-cooperation efforts in Central Asia.

The United States should also seek collaborative security-cooperation efforts with nontraditional partners. For example, the United States should encourage Kazakhstan, Kyrgyzstan, Tajikistan, and Uzbekistan to continue to send cadets to India's National Defense Academy.[9] While sending cadets to non-US military schools does not build specific ties with the United States, the curriculum of these institutions are usually consistent with the broader US objectives of military democratization in that they promote officer professionalism and increase the quantity of officers with English-language skills.

Initiatives to integrate US security-cooperation efforts with the programs of NATO and other nations are not without complications, however. As a means of controlling the relationships, Russia has been pushing to force NATO to work through the

CSTO when dealing with the Central Asian states. So far NATO has resisted. Additionally, synchronizing US, NATO, and Western European security-cooperation programs could lead to inadvertently de-emphasizing a US objective of establishing partnerships based on mutual respect and overemphasizing the patron-client relationship normally created by assistance efforts. With careful management, however, these risks can be mitigated.

Focus Security-Cooperation Efforts on Kazakhstan

The United States will have the greatest opportunities for success if, over the next decade, it focuses its security-cooperation programs in the region of Kazakhstan as it offers the best prospects for evolution into a strategic partner in Central Asia. While none of the governments in Central Asia could be considered liberal democracies and all of the populations enjoy fewer freedoms than they had during the last years of the Soviet Union, Kazakhstan and Kyrgyzstan stand in a different class than the brutal authoritarian regimes in Turkmenistan and Uzbekistan. While the results of the December 2005 elections in Kazakhstan are disappointing, only Kazakhstan and Kyrgyzstan have functioning civil societies, have the least repressive policies against opposition groups, and are most likely to adopt democratic reforms, if only slowly.

Economically, Kazakhstan's oil wealth brings both resources to potentially implement defense reform and modernization, and an increased US interest in ensuring the strategic security of the energy resources. Almaty has also demonstrated a desire to increase its collaborative efforts, and its history with past programs shows a level of success unmatched in the region. Only Kazakhstan and Uzbekistan have the wherewithal to absorb and implement programs that can eventually lead to significant defense capabilities, and for the immediate future the cooperative efforts in Uzbekistan will remain limited. Additionally, focusing on Almaty will offer tangential benefits to Kyrgyzstan, because of that country's reliance on Kazakhstan, and possibly Tajikistan. Also, success with Kazakhstan may help establish a model to which other nations can aspire.

Kazakhstan remains the only viable choice in Central Asia, also by process of elimination. While Uzbekistan remains the other potential regional power and besides Kazakhstan the only state able to absorb increased security assistance, Tashkent's decision to sever most cooperative ties and its authoritarian government ensure that it will not be a viable partner as long as Karimov remains in power. Likewise, Turkmenistan's repressive regime and foreign policy based on "positive neutrality" limits both Ashgabat's attraction as a partner and receptiveness to increased cooperation. Kyrgyzstan and Tajikistan, while important for regional stability, lack the ability to absorb significant amounts of security assistance.

US officials have noted that Kazakhstan has the potential to be a regional leader in promoting tolerance and respect for human rights, using its energy resources to power economic growth and possibly even advancing democratic reform.[10] The United States should support that potential by focusing its security-cooperation efforts on its relationship with Kazakhstan and dedicating the majority of security-cooperation funds allocated for Central Asia to bilateral programs with Almaty.

Focus Security-Cooperation Efforts on a Limited Range of Objectives

The DOD has made great progress over the past several years in basing its security-cooperation programs on a limited set of objectives and targeted on specific units to create useful capabilities and real relationships. The most significant improvements in the development and execution of security-cooperation programs over the past twelve years have come through the creation of the OSD Security Cooperation Guidance, the USCENT-COM Theater Security Cooperation Plan, and the bilateral five-year plans. These planning documents have brought focus and a set of objectives to what was otherwise a relatively chaotic set of activities. The review of the history of security cooperation in the region continues to suggest that too few resources are chasing too many objectives in too many countries.

In each country, the US should narrow down its efforts to a few narrowly defined, measurable objectives (table 7). There

176

Table 7. Proposed focus areas for US security cooperation in Central Asia

	Kazakhstan	Kyrgyzstan	Tajikistan	Turkmenistan	Uzbekistan
Denuclearization (including biological and chemical weapon elimination)	X				X
Democratization (PME Programs)	X	X	X	X	X
Democratization (officer and NCO professional development)	X	X			
Regional Cooperation (disaster response and border security)	X	X	X	X	X
Military Capabilities (peacekeeping)	X				
Military Capabilities (border security)	X	X	X	X	X
Military Capabilities (counterterrorism and counterinsurgency)	X	X			

should be no more than six to seven in Kazakhstan and two to five in each of the others. The key is a limited number of clearly defined and measurable objectives. The relationships will develop as the United States delivers on meaningful capabilities.

An important aspect of focusing on a limited number of objectives is ensuring that these efforts do not get sidetracked or overtaken by well-meaning but secondary offers of assistance. Col Thomas Wilhelm, now at the Marshall Center in Germany, recounts this anecdote that occurred while he served as a defense attaché in Central Asia:

> My favorite story is of a US Air Force general who desperately wanted to provide a "deliverable" at the end of his visit. So while standing at the host nation's airbase, he waved his arms and said that he would send out an airfield safety survey team. His arms were waving over the tarmac and huts of a base that was long dead with the corpse stripped bare and a squadron of aircraft that was being scraped for metal. Sheep were grazing in the potholes of the tarmac. The host nation air force officers, however, were bobbing their heads enthusiastically, though their air force did not and would not have a single flying aircraft. It was welcome "cooperation" all the same because it gave them distraction and influence at the General HQ level, and, they (wrongly) thought leverage to ask for EDA C-130s, etc. It had the summing effect of delaying the

177

process of getting on with the painful growth of real transformation, which involved changing their concept of their air force completely.[11]

DOD senior officials and security-cooperation planners must temper desires to frequently shift resources, constantly provide "deliverables," or initiate new programs to meet new objectives. Instead, they should remained focused on a limited number of clearly defined objectives within the broader goals of denuclearization and WMD elimination, promoting military democratization and regional cooperation, and improving specific military capabilities. Security cooperation is a slow, deliberate process that takes long-term commitment. Through persistent engagement, these programs will have the greatest opportunity for long-term success.

Denuclearization and WMD Elimination

The elimination of the nuclear weapons arsenal and infrastructure in Kazakhstan and subsequent efforts to destroy biological and chemical weapons infrastructure in Kazakhstan and Uzbekistan stand as the hallmarks of success for security cooperation in Central Asia. However, some of these long-term programs have not been fully completed, and the rise of terrorism as the primary threat to the United States brings greater urgency to these efforts. The United States must continue to locate, identify, safeguard, and destroy these weapons and the infrastructure, technology, and materials used to produce them. Currently, this objective should be a focus area for Kazakhstan and Uzbekistan, but security-cooperation planners should remain open to the possibility that previously unidentified weapons or materials may be found in any of the other Central Asian states.

Democratization

In all countries in the region, the United States should continue to emphasize programs and initiatives that promote democratization of the armed forces, while recognizing those efforts will likely meet with only modest success for a long time. Until the governments of the Central Asian states truly adopt democratic principles, promote human rights, and eliminate corruption throughout the political structures, there will be

178

little leeway for broader military reform, even if the senior military leadership in one or more of the nations presses for it. But that should not deter maintaining democratization as a major objective for US security-cooperation programs. To support this goal, the United States should promote courses offered by the Marshall Center, DIILS, CCMR, DRMI, and other institutions that can assist the Central Asian states to transform their militaries into ones that are responsive to civilian control and legislative oversight, are subject to budget and defense planning transparency, and are realistically sized and funded. Additionally, the United States should offer increased opportunities for cadets and officers from Central Asia to study in US academies and war colleges.

Promoting democratization should be the primary objective for security-cooperation programs in Turkmenistan, where United States efforts will remain limited for the immediate future. The military contact program will be the primary vehicle for interaction, although the United States also can continue to engage the Turkmenistani military via the existing modest joint exercises and limited training and education programs. Given Niyazov's authoritarian style and desire to keep foreign influences at a minimum, this level of cooperation is not likely to change until his regime ends. Niyazov will cling to power until the very end, and his "cult of personality," constant shuffling of ministers and advisors, and weak constitutional framework have prevented the emergence of any potential successor and will likely result in internal instability when Niyazov passes from the scene.[12] The United States should shape its security-cooperation efforts toward preparing for this succession period by engaging all security services in Turkmenistan, not just the military, with contact events and training programs that build personal relationships and promote strong command-and-control functions, the role of security forces in domestic politics, and the appropriate uses of force in succession crises. In this way, the United States may be able to mitigate the possibility of internal conflict and influence the nature of the post-Niyazov regime.[13]

Likewise, the United States should also be preparing for the eventual succession of Karimov in Uzbekistan. As in Turkmenistan, the US security-cooperation program should seek to build ties with and eventually influence the officer corps of the

armed forces and other security services.[14] In the interim, however, the United States should use security-cooperation programs to offset the increasing anti-Western and anti-US sentiments developing in Uzbekistan. Cooperative efforts in this
regard should be characterized as "strategic engagement" much
as was conducted with the Soviet Union in the late 1980s, Russia in the early 1990s, and China today: aiming "to alter the
perception within these countries' armed forces of the US/the
West as a threat, for example by explaining Western intentions
and capabilities, emphasizing common interests and highlight-
ing the shared challenges facing military professionals."[15] Already there exists a core of officers in Uzbekistan with a Western outlook, although they are likely to remain marginalized as
long as Karimov remains in power.[16]

One important element of promoting democratization in Uzbekistan should be to reinstate IMET funding for Uzbekistan,
with restrictions. Following the December 2004 decision not to
certify that Uzbekistan had made progress on protecting human rights, Tashkent was prohibited from using FMF and IMET
funds, and did not receive any in 2005 or 2006. While a restriction on using FMF funds is appropriate to ensure US military
equipment is not used for repression, restricting the use of
IMET funds eliminates one of the most valuable methods the
United States has available to influence current and future
leaders in the military and other security services. Instead,
Congress should permit the use of these funds, but mandate
they may only be used for E-IMET courses—those that have
been specifically identified as promoting the concepts of democracy, civilian rule of law, civilian control of the military,
and internationally recognized standards of human rights.
Continued engagement, at the right level, for the right reasons,
and with the right methods is the only way to modify or mitigate the increasing repression in Uzbekistan, and it will help
ensure that in the post–Karimov era there are civilian and military leaders at all levels who understand and appreciate American perspectives on these issues. To promote this effort, DOS
and DOD should seek a limited waiver to the Congressional restriction on using IMET funds for Uzbekistan. The waiver would
permit Uzbekistani personnel to attend specific E-IMET courses
that directly promote the establishment of a professional mili-

tary force, appropriate civil-military relations, and respect for human rights.

Unlike in the other three countries, promoting military democratization in Kazakhstan and Kyrgyzstan should include support for officer and noncommissioned officer professional development programs. The United States has already devoted over a decade to these efforts, and Almaty and Bishkek continue to request support for these efforts. To discontinue these efforts would undermine the relationships that have been built, create the impression that democratic military professionalism is not important, and foster the perception that the United States can be an unreliable security partner. Likewise, these programs have made some progress, and experience in Bulgaria suggests that military democratization and reform efforts in the absence of political reform can build a reservoir of military leaders that understand and appreciate the value of these concepts, and military reform can progress very rapidly once the need for fundamental political reform is accepted. Therefore, the United States should reinforce the officer and noncommissioned officer development programs in Kazakhstan and Kyrgyzstan.

Regional Cooperation

The disaster response and border security cooperative initiatives under the IWER program and the Regional Cooperation exercises have made progress in promoting regional cooperation. These programs should be continued and expanded. In particular, the DOD should continue to encourage Turkmenistan and Uzbekistan to participate in these forums, although their desire and involvement may be limited. Similarly, the United States should extend these programs to include delegations from China, India, Russia, and Afghanistan as the other regional players that can both support and benefit from improved regional cooperation in Central Asia.

The USCENTCOM has also begun to establish regional centers of excellence in Central Asia. The first to be announced was the Disaster Preparedness Center, which will likely be situated in Kazakhstan as early as 2007. This center can serve as an excellent method for improving regional cooperation in a field that would require a coordinated response should a major terrorist attack or environmental disaster occur in Central Asia. Col Dan Groeschen, the chief of the Central Asian Branch at USCENTCOM, envisions other such centers of excellence in the region, including ones for noncommissioned officer professional development, modeling and simulation, and language training. The DOD should encourage and fund the establishment of centers for noncombat-related activities as a means of promoting regional cooperation.

Military Capabilities

The United States should also continue to develop certain force capabilities within Central Asia. In all countries, this effort should primarily be devoted to improving integrated border security capabilities that address WMD proliferation prevention, CN, and counterinsurgency considerations (including maritime security in Kazakhstan and Turkmenistan). The programs should be geared to improve the specific military capabilities of small, relatively autonomous units. These programs must be executed with a strong understanding of how those capabilities will fit into the larger force structure of the country, and must ensure an appropriate sustainment plan for training and logistics.

In most cases, however, the United States should avoid expanding its efforts beyond border security, for in doing so it will spread its limited resources too thin and decrease the likelihood that these specific capabilities will be achieved. There are exceptions: in Kazakhstan, the United States should support the expansion of the KAZBAT peacekeeping forces and the development rapid response forces (including special operations forces with counterinsurgency and counterterrorism capabilities). In Kyrgyzstan, the United States should support counterinsurgency and counterterrorism forces, but should not promote the reestablishment of a peacekeeping unit.

Persistent Engagement

As it focuses on these key security-cooperation objectives, US planners should seek to integrate these efforts over time for *persistent engagement.* Long-term development plans should integrate military contact visits, mobile training and education teams, training courses in the United States, and appropriate weapons and equipment purchases to provide depth to those capabilities. Exercises and deployments should be crafted to evaluate and reinforce those capabilities. These activities must not only be integrated and reinforcing within the broader set of objectives, they must also be scheduled and executed over an appropriate period of time to ensure persistent, recurring interaction with a defined set of recipients within each country. In short, this means creating and executing a deliberate, time-phased, event-driven plan to "meet" the objective. Since security cooperation takes a long time to have an effect, these plans (one for each country) must have a five-year forward planning horizon and at least a three-year back assessment window.

Notes

1. Statement of James C. MacDougall, deputy assistant secretary of Defense for Eurasia, before the House Committee on International Relations, Subcommittee on the Middle East and Central Asia, 26 April 2006, http://www.foreignaffairs.house.gov/archives/109/27230.pdf (accessed 4 May 2006).

2. Zaccor, *Security Cooperation and Non-State Threats*, 34 (see chap. 1, note 7).

3. Ibid., 7.

4. *Nuclear Nonproliferation*, 2–3 (see chap. 6, note 60).

5. Bhatty and Bronson, "NATO's Mixed Signals," 132 (see chap. 3, note 25).

6. Ibid., 133; "Turkmenistan: Official Says NATO Respects Turkmenistan's Neutrality," *Moscow ITAR-Tass*, 3 July 1998; "NATO Chief Favours Closer Military Ties with Turkmenistan," *Moscow Interfax*, 18 January 2001; "NATO Ready to Help Uzbekistan in Army Reforms," *Moscow Interfax*, 19 March 2002; "Kazakh President Reaffirms Benefits of Cooperation with NATO," *Moscow Interfax*, 22 November 2002; "Xinhua 'Roundup': NATO Seeks to Expand Military Presence in Central Asia," *Beijing Xinhua*, 17 July 2003; "NATO Seeks to Step Up Partnership with Turkmenistan," *Moscow ITAR-TASS*, 16 August 2003; "NATO Meeting Urges Uzbekistan to Be Open About Army," *Tashkent UzReport.com Internet Text*, 26 February 2004; "NATO Ready to Expand Security Cooperation with Kyrgyzstan," *Moscow Agentstvo Voyennykh Novostey Internet Text*, 19 October 2004; "Uzbekistani President Hails Ties with NATO," *Tashkent Uzbek Radio 1*, 20 October 2004; "NATO Envoy Visits Uzbekistan, Outlines Cooperation Plans," *Agentstvo Voyennykh Novostey Internet Text*, 14 March 2005; and "Kazakhstan, NATO to Prepare Signing of Individual Partnership Action Plan," *Interfax*, 11 November 2005.

7. Author with Military Policy Directorate, Ministry of Defense, Federal Republic of Germany, correspondence, March 2006. For those who read German, Ms. Reisinger's statement is as follows:

DEU setzt tatsächlich auf Ausbildung. Vorrangiges Ziel bleibt die Schaffung von Stabilität durch Förderung von Demokratie, Rechtstaatlichkeit, wirtschaftlicher Entwicklung und regionaler Kooperation sowie der Ausbau vertrauensvoller Beziehungen als gemeinsame Basis für den Kampf gegen den internationalen Terrorismus, die Organisierte Kriminalität und den internationalen Drogenhandel. Gerade die Streitkräfte der zentralasiatischen Staaten spielen dabei eine wichtige Rolle: Neben der Sicherung der Region stellen sie ein Instrument der multilateralen Zusammenarbeit mit Partnern in der Region als auch euroatlantischen Strukturen dar und sind zudem wichtiger Bestandteil der staatlichen Entwicklung: Sowohl ihr innerer Zustand wie auch ihre Einbettung in rechtsstaatliche und demokratische Strukturen stellen einen wichtigen Faktor dar. Unterstützung der Streitkräftereform wird damit auch als ein bedeutender Beitrag zur Entwicklung und auch Stabilisierung der Region insgesamt gesehen.

8. Sergey V. Golunov, "Border Security in Kazakhstan: Threats, Policies, and Future Challenges," *Journal of Slavic Military Studies* 18, no. 1 (Spring 2005), 51; and Lahue, "Security Assistance in Kazakhstan," 13 (see chap. 4, note 36).

9. "India: Defense Academy to Update Training Curriculum Following Committee Report," *New Delhi Force*, 22 June 2005.

10. Fried, *A Strategy for Central Asia*, (see chap. 1, note 3).

11. Marshall Center correspondence (see chap. 5, note 36).

12. Eugene B. Rumer, "Central Asian Leadership Succession: When, Not If," *Institute for National Strategic Studies Strategic Forum Number 203* (Washington, DC: National Defense University, December 2003), 2–4.

13. Steven Sabol, "Turkmenbashi: Going it Alone," *Problems of Post-Communism* 50, no. 5 (September/October 2003), 55.

14. Rumer, "Central Asian Leadership Succession," 2–4 (see chap. 8, note 12).

15. Cottey and Forster, *Reshaping Defense Diplomacy*, 16 (see chap. 1, note 5).

16. Svante Cornell, "The United States and Central Asia: In the Steppes to Stay?" *Cambridge Review of International Affairs* 17, no. 2 (July 2004), 248.

Chapter 9

Conclusion

Here's what I learned: our potential partner countries want respect more than cooperation, and they are willing to work to get deserved respect. Giving them stuff is just symbolic and plays into the current power games. Giving them our ideas is giving them nothing. But giving them respect by finding out what they could possibly do right and concentrating on it, gives them something most haven't truly had: success. And if you give someone success, they will become a true and devoted partner.

—Col Thomas Wilhelm, USA

US security-cooperation activities with the Central Asian states span just over a dozen years, having started in 1993. From modest beginnings, the United States slowly built a web of ties to the military forces of the Central Asian nations. Progress was slow and uneven, largely due to limited funding, the involvement of a diverse and often uncoordinated set of US government agencies in the activities, multiplying objectives, and the effect of outside factors, such as reversals in democratic reform and the insurgent attacks in the region in 1999 and 2000. This development went through three distinct stages prior to the turning point of 11 September 2001, and two more stages afterward.

Through these 13 years, US national-security policy makers have introduced various security-cooperation programs to meet changing and multiplying national-security objectives for the region. Generally, those programs sought to achieve US objectives in denuclearization and proliferation prevention, democratization and military reform, regional cooperation, and improving military capabilities. These security-cooperation efforts were limited by a variety of factors, including the lack of political and economic reform in the region, Russian influence through bilateral cooperation agreements and multilateral security institutions, constrained resources, diffuse objectives

185

and multiplying recipients, and US policies that restrained commitment to Central Asia. Each of the programs available to US planners had strengths and weaknesses, but these programs were not always integrated in a fashion to achieve the best results. The linkages between the specific activities and the ultimate objectives have not always been constant and still may not always be clear. As a result, the United States has had mixed results in building relationships, developing capabilities, and providing access. Much has been done over the last eight years to improve the planning, coordination, and execution of these programs. These programs are generally evolving in the right direction, but there is still room for improvement. The United States should focus its efforts on Kazakhstan, more closely integrate the existing security-cooperation programs within the Department of Defense and across the US government, leverage the assistance programs of NATO partners, and seek to employ a strategy of persistent engagement against a limited number of clearly defined objectives.

In the years ahead, Central Asia will remain a critical region in America's long war against terrorism. Security cooperation has been and can be a valuable tool in building relationships with allies and partners, developing capabilities of foreign militaries so they can join in this endeavor, and providing access so American forces can take the war to the enemy.

Appendix A

US Security-Cooperation
Funding in Central Asia

Policy without funding is just a dream.

—Anonymous

Figures

Figure		Page
A.1	Trends in cooperative threat reduction (CTR) program funding.	191
A.2	Trends in CTR program defense and military contacts (DMC)	193
A.3	Trends in CTR program biological and chemical weapon elimination and proliferation prevention	195
A.4	Trends in international military education and training (IMET) program	198
A.5	Trends in foreign military financing (FMF)	200

Tables

Table		Page
A.1	CTR program funding	189
A.2	CTR program DMC funding	192
A.3	CTR program biological and chemical weapon elimination and proliferation prevention	194
A.4	ICP funding	196

Table		Page
A.5	IMET program funding.	197
A.6	FMF program funding	199
A.7	FMS agreements	201
A.8	FMS deliveries	202
A.9	Regional Defense Counterterrorism Fellowship (RDCTF) program	203
A.10	Counternarcotics (CN) program	204

Table A.1. Cooperative Threat Reduction (CTR) program funding for Central Asia, 1993–2006

(In US$s)	1993	1994	1995	1996	1997	1998	1999	2000
Strategic offensive arms elimination	–	14,962,637	43,143,697	1,386,341	–	–	–	–
Government-to-government Communications link	–	2,199,433	111,501	–	–	–	–	–
Weapons of Mass Destruction (WMD) infrastructure elimination	–	1,405,818	9,785,165	22,849,899	–	–	–	–
Emergency response	–	3,987,859	–	–	–	–	–	–
Material control and accounting	–	4,625,106	2,984,011	14,276,910	–	–	–	–
Export control	–	2,185,874	4,930,310	–	–	–	–	–
Defense conversion	–	14,999,138	2,142,446	–	–	–	–	–
Science and Technology Center	–	–	9,000,000	–	–	–	–	–
Defense enterprise fund	–	–	7,000,000	–	–	–	–	–
Biological warfare proliferation prevention	–	–	–	–	–	5,000,000	–	–
Nukus Chemical Research Facility elimination	–	–	–	–	5,862,925	–	–	–
Total	0	44,365,865	79,097,130	38,513,150	5,862,925	5,000,000	0	0

Table A.1. CTR program funding for Central Asia, 1993–2006 (Continued)

(In US$s)	2001	2002	2003	2004	2005	2006	Total
Strategic offensive arms elimination	–	–	–	–	–	–	59,492,675
Government-to-government Communications link	–	–	–	–	–	–	2,310,934
WMD infrastructure elimination	–	3,500,000	4,510,000	–	–	–	42,050,882
Emergency response	–	–	–	–	–	–	3,987,859
Material control and accounting	–	–	–	–	–	–	21,886,027
Export control	–	–	–	–	–	–	7,116,184
Defense conversion	–	–	–	–	–	–	17,141,584
Science and Technology Center	–	–	–	–	–	–	9,000,000
Defense enterprise fund	–	–	–	–	–	–	7,000,000
Biological warfare proliferation prevention	–	–	–	–	–	–	5,000,000
Nukus Chemical Research Facility Elimination	–	2,500,000	–	–	–	–	8,362,925
Total	0	6,000,000	4,510,000	0	0	0	183,349,070

(*Source:* Ms. Jeannie Borden, Cooperative Threat Reduction Office, Defense Threat Reduction Agency, Fort Belvoir, VA. [See also fig. A.1.])

Note: Totals shown are for fiscal years. Amounts for 2005 and earlier are budgeted; for 2006 are estimated. This chart does not identify all of the CTR funding executed in Central Asia, but only that funding which was specifically designated for projects in the region. Additional CTR funding may have come from regional programs applicable to the entire former Soviet Union. This table does not include funding for defense and military contacts, which is identified separately. All funds shown here were allocated for projects in Kazakhstan except for those allocated for the Nukus Chemical Research Facility in Uzbekistan. Some elements, such as material control and accounting, were transferred out of the CTR program and continued under the Department of Energy. See John M. Shields and William C. Potter, eds., *Dismantling the Cold War: U.S. and NIS [newly independent states] Perspectives on the Nunn-Lugar Cooperative Threat Reduction Program* (Cambridge, MA: Center for Science and International Affairs, 1997), for more information on the specific programs within CTR.

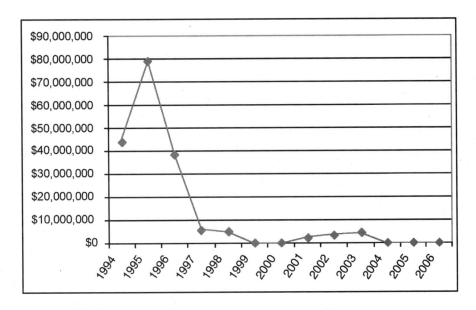

Figure A.1. Trends in CTR program funding for Central Asia, 1994–2007
(Adapted from table A.1.)

Table A.2. CTR program DMC funding for Central Asia, 1993–2006

(In US$s)	Kazakhstan	Former Soviet Union	Former Soviet Union (Counterproliferation)
1993	–	–	–
1994	470,862	494,386	–
1995	400,856	3,175,437	–
1996	759,650	955,543	–
1997	–	7,934,594	1,882,000
1998	–	7,337,000	2,000,000
1999	–	–	–
2000	–	2,000,000	–
2001	–	8,714,864	285,000
2002	–	6,949,000	–
2003	–	10,300,000	–
2004	–	945,625	–
2005	–	7,963,000	–
2006	–	8,000,000	–
Total	1,631,368	64,769,449	4,167,000

(*Source*: Ms. Jeannie Borden, Cooperative Threat Reduction Office, Defense Threat Reduction Agency, Fort Belvoir, VA. [See also fig. A.2.])

Note: Totals are shown for fiscal years. Amounts for 2005 and earlier were budgeted, for 2006 are estimated. Until 1997 DOD maintained separate funding lines for DMC in Russia, Ukraine, Belarus, Kazakhstan, and other former Soviet Union. In 1997 these funding lines were merged.

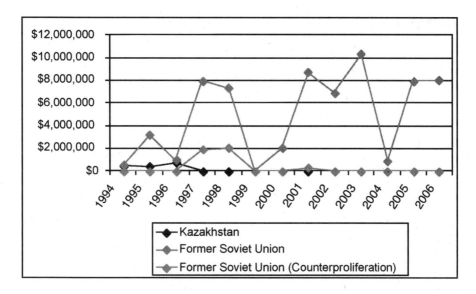

Figure A.2. Trends in CTR program DMC funding for Central Asia, 1993–2007 (Adapted from table A.2.)

Table A.3. CTR program biological and chemical weapon elimination and proliferation prevention funding, 1993–2006

(In US$s)	Kazakhstan biological weapons proliferation prevention	Uzbekistan Nukus Chemical Research Facility elimination	Former Soviet Union biological weapons proliferation prevention (BWPP)	Former Soviet Union (except Russia) chemical weapons proliferation prevention (WMD-PPI)
1993	–	–	–	–
1994	–	–	–	–
1995	–	–	–	–
1996	–	–	–	–
1997	–	5,862,925	4,899,808	–
1998	5,000,000	–	2,000,000	–
1999	–	–	2,000,000	–
2000	–	–	30,000,000	–
2001	–	2,500,000	27,000,000	–
2002	–	–	24,100,000	–
2003	–	–	67,390,000	39,800,000
2004	–	–	67,750,000	29,400,000
2005	–	–	68,699,000	36,700,000
2006	–	–	60,849,000	40,600,000
Total	5,000,000	8,362,925	354,687,808	146,500,000

(*Source*: Ms. Jeannie Borden, Cooperative Threat Reduction Office, Defense Threat Reduction Agency, Fort Belvoir, VA. [See also fig. A.3.])

Note: Totals are shown for fiscal years. Amounts for 2005 and earlier were budgeted, for 2006 are estimated. Only those amounts in the first two columns were specifically allocated for programs in Central Asia. Amounts for BWPP and WMD-PPI were executed throughout the Former Soviet Union, including Central Asia, but specific allocations by country are not available.

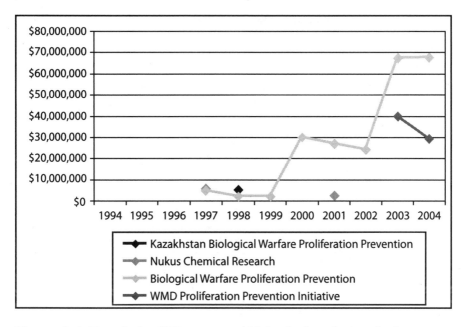

Figure A.3. Trends in CTR program biological and chemical weapon elimination and proliferation prevention funding, 1994–2004 (Adapted from table A.3.)

Table A.4. ICP funding, 1995–2005

(In US$s)	Kazakhstan	Kyrgyzstan	Tajikistan	Turkmenistan	Uzbekistan
95-99	1,121,000	465,000	0	600,000	873,000
2000	109,000	65,000	0	0	187,000
2001	195,000	154,000	56,000	56,000	521,000
2002	120,000	550,000	30,000	0	500,000
2003	1,200,000	500,000	0	0	1,190,000
2004	160,000	0	0	0	850,000
2005	444,000	0	10,000	0	0
Total	3,349,000	1,734,000	96,000	656,000	4,121,000

(*Source*: Office of the Coordinator of US Assistance to the Newly Independent States, US Department of State, *U.S. Government Assistance To and Cooperative Activities with the New Independent States of the Former Soviet Union, FY2000 Annual Report* (Washington, DC: Department of State, 2001), Appendix 1; ibid., *FY 2001 Annual Report* (Washington, DC: Department of State, 2002), Appendix 1; ibid., *FY2002 Annual Report* (Washington, DC: Department of State, 2003), Appendix 1; ibid., *FY2003 Annual Report* (Washington, DC: Department of State, 2004), Appendix 1; and ibid., *FY2004 Annual Report* (Washington, DC: Department of State, 2005), Appendix 1.)

Note: Totals are shown for fiscal years. Amounts for 2004 and earlier are as expended.

Table A.5. IMET program funding for Central Asia, 1993–2007

(In US$s)	Kazakhstan	Kyrgyzstan	Tajikistan	Turkmenistan	Uzbekistan
1993	163,000	–	–	–	–
1994	90,000	50,000	–	50,000	–
1995	97,000	60,000	–	118,000	95,000
1996	388,000	231,000	–	213,000	293,000
1997	389,000	257,000	–	262,000	286,000
1998	587,000	336,000	–	336,000	457,000
1999	383,000	383,000	–	261,000	526,000
2000	550,000	350,000	–	300,000	500,000
2001	583,000	380,000	–	258,000	494,000
2002	893,000	600,000	259,000	388,000	880,000
2003	872,000	1,068,000	339,000	216,000	1,104,000
2004	1,233,000	1,047,000	351,000	340,000	484,000
2005	997,000	1,039,000	348,000	389,000	–
2006	990,000	1,089,000	346,000	297,000	–
2007	1,085,000	1,085,000	370,000	395,000	–
Total	9,300,000	7,975,000	2,013,000	3,823,000	5,119,000

(*Source*: For 1993 through 2004, from the Bureau of European and Eurasian Affairs, US Department of State. For 2005 through 2007, from *Congressional Budget Justification for Foreign Operations, Fiscal Year 2007* (Washington, DC: Department of State, 2006), 215–216. [See also fig. A.4.])

Note: Totals are shown for fiscal years. Amounts for 2005 and earlier were expended, for 2006 are estimated, and for 2007 are as requested.

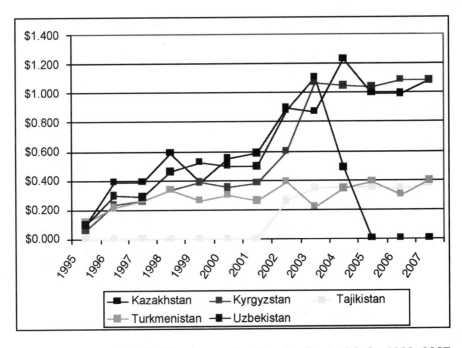

Figure A.4. Trends in IMET program funding for Central Asia, 1993–2007
(Adapted from table A.5.)

Table A.6. FMF program funding for Central Asia, 1993–2007

(In US$s)	Kazakhstan	Kyrgyzstan	Tajikistan	Turkmenistan	Uzbekistan
1993	–	–	–	–	–
1994	–	–	–	–	–
1995	–	–	–	–	–
1996	–	–	–	–	–
1997	1,500,000	800,000	–	500,000	1,000,000
1998	2,250,000	1,350,000	–	450,000	1,550,000
1999	1,800,000	1,550,000	–	600,000	1,650,000
2000	1,500,000	1,000,000	–	600,000	1,500,000
2001	1,900,000	1,846,000	–	699,000	2,445,000
2002	4,750,000	11,000,000	3,700,000	–	36,207,000
2003	2,900,000	3,900,000	–	690,000	8,600,000
2004	2,980,000	4,075,000	1,995,000	500,000	–
2005	4,960,000	1,984,000	496,000	694,000	–
2006	3,465,000	1,881,000	495,000	297,000	–
2007	3,500,000	1,500,000	250,000	250,000	–
Total	31,505,000	30,886,000	6,936,000	5,280,000	52,952,000

(*Source*: For 1993 through 2004, from the Bureau of European and Eurasian Affairs, US Department of State. For 2005 through 2007, from *Congressional Budget Justification for Foreign Operations, Fiscal Year 2007* (Washington, DC: Department of State, 2006), 215–216. [See also fig. A.5])

Note: Totals are shown for fiscal years. Amounts for 2005 and earlier were expended, for 2006 are estimated, and for 2007 are as requested.

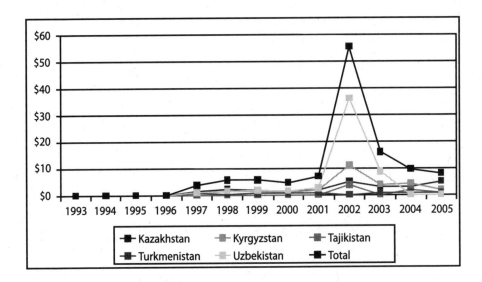

Figure A.5. Trends in FMF program funding for Central Asia, 1993–2005.
(Adapted from table A.6.)

Table A.7. FMS agreements for Central Asia, 1993–2004

(In US$s)	Kazakhstan	Kyrgyzstan	Tajikistan	Turkmenistan	Uzbekistan
1993	–	–	–	–	–
1994	–	–	–	–	–
1995	–	–	–	–	–
1996	–	–	–	–	–
1997	–	–	–	–	–
1998	165,000	–	–	–	1,401,000
1999	–	776,000	–	–	2,613,000
2000	2,430,000	872,000	–	657,000	34,000
2001	130,000	–	–	–	1,786,000
2002	5,951,000	7,516,000	–	962,000	27,408,000
2003	1,317,000	4,751,000	1,804,000	603,000	16,046,000
2004	3,050,000	7,417,000	1,759,000	–	4,347,000
Total	13,043,000	21,332,000	3,563,000	2,222,000	53,635,000

(*Source*: *Foreign Military Sales, Foreign Military Construction Sales, and Military Assistance Facts* (Washington, DC: Defense Security Cooperation Agency, 2004), 4–7, 13.)

Note: Totals are shown for fiscal years. These figures indicate the value of defense goods and services the United States agreed to provide under the foreign military sales program at the time of the signature by both parties of the letter of offer and acceptance (LOA). Depending on the type of equipment or services, actual deliveries may come weeks, months, or years later. Totals may not add due to rounding. The 2002 amount for Kazakhstan includes $5,951,000 in foreign military construction sales (FMCS); the 2004 amount for Kyrgyzstan includes $5,561,000 in FMCS.

Table A.8. FMS deliveries for Central Asia, 1993–2004

(In US$s)	Kazakhstan	Kyrgyzstan	Tajikistan	Turkmenistan	Uzbekistan
1993	–	–	–	–	–
1994	–	–	–	–	–
1995	–	–	–	–	–
1996	–	–	–	–	–
1997	–	–	–	–	–
1998	–	–	–	–	–
1999	21,000	–	–	–	25,000
2000	110,000	726,000	–	–	2,354,000
2001	–	690,000	–	–	348,000
2002	3,086,000	2,250,000	–	–	3,126,000
2003	2,371,000	2,746,000	1,159,000	1,823,000	33,971,000
2004	2,466,000	4,722,000	390,000	381,000	1,717,000
Total	8,054,000	11,135,000	1,550,000	2,204,000	41,541,000

(*Source: Foreign Military Sales, Foreign Military Construction Sales, and Military Assistance Facts* (Washington, DC: Defense Security Cooperation Agency, 2004), 20–23, 28–29.)

Note: Totals are shown for fiscal years. These figures indicate the value of defense goods and services the United States delivered under the FMS program. Totals may not add due to rounding. The 2002, 2003, and 2004 amounts for Kazakhstan include $51,000, $1,957,000, and $1,369,000, respectively, in FMCS; the 2004 amount for Kyrgyzstan includes $5,561,000 in FMCS.

Table A.9. RDCTF program funding for Central Asia, 1993–2006

(In US$s)	Kazakhstan	Kyrgyzstan	Tajikistan	Turkmenistan	Uzbekistan
1993	–	–	–	–	–
1994	–	–	–	–	–
1995	–	–	–	–	–
1996	–	–	–	–	–
1997	–	–	–	–	–
1998	–	–	–	–	–
1999	–	–	–	–	–
2000	–	–	–	–	–
2001	–	–	–	–	–
2002	–	–	–	–	–
2003	70,000	12,000	50,000	–	3,000
2004	164,000	120,000	202,000	–	42,000
2005	251,000	123,000	86,000	–	113,000
2006	175,000	175,000	175,000	–	200,000
Total	660,000	430,000	513,000	0	358,000

(*Source*: Mr. Hussam Bader, CTFP Office, Office of the Secretary of Defense, Washington, DC.)

Note: Totals are shown for fiscal years. Amounts for 2005 and earlier were expended, for 2006 are estimated.

Table A.10. CN program funding for Central Asia, 1993–2005

(In US$s)	Kazakhstan	Kyrgyzstan	Tajikistan	Turkmenistan	Uzbekistan	Central Asia Regional
1993	–	–	–	–	–	–
1994	–	–	–	–	–	–
1995	–	–	–	–	–	–
1996	–	–	–	–	–	–
1997	–	–	–	–	–	–
1998	–	–	–	–	–	–
1999	–	–	–	–	–	–
2000	–	–	–	–	–	–
2001	–	–	–	–	230,000	–
2002	–	–	–	–	213,000	–
2003	–	–	500,000	–	6,564,000	351,000
2004	–	–	–	–	581,000	462,000
2005	–	5,270,000	9,629,000	4,879,000	47,000	705,000
Total	0	5,270,000	10,129,000	4,879,000	7,635,000	1,518,000

(*Source*: Mr. Mark Pirritano, Counternarcotics Office, Office of the Secretary of Defense, Washington, DC.)

Note: Totals are shown for fiscal years. Amounts for 2005 and earlier were expended. Data for FY 2002 and earlier are incomplete since many files were lost in September 2001.

Appendix B

US Security Cooperation Training Programs in Central Asia

Figures

Figure   *Page*

B.1   Trends in Central Asian military students
        trained in the IMET program   208

B.2   Trends in Central Asian military
        students trained in Defense Language
        Institute English Language Center
        (DLIELC)   209

B.3   Trends in Central Asian military and
        civilian students trained in the George C. Marshall
        European Center for Strategic Studies   211

Tables

Table   *Page*

B.1   Central Asian military students trained
        in the IMET program   207

B.2   Central Asian military and civilian
        students trained in DLIELC   209

B.3   Central Asian military and civilian
        students trained in Marshall Center   210

B.4   Central Asian attendance at US war
        colleges   212

Table		Page
B.5	Central Asian military and civilian students trained in Defense Institute for International Legal Studies (DIILS)	213
B.6	Central Asian military and civilian students trained in Defense Resource Management Institute (DRMI)	214
B.7	Central Asian military and civilian students trained in Center for Civil-Military Relations (CCMR)	215
B.8	Central Asian attendance at US service academies	216
B.9	Central Asian invitations to the Aviation Leadership Program (ALP)	217
B.10	Central Asian military and civilian students trained in Defense Institute of Security Assistance Management (DISAM)	218

Table B.1. Central Asian military students trained in the IMET program, 1993–2007

	Kazakhstan	Kyrgyzstan	Tajikistan	Turkmenistan	Uzbekistan
1993	8	–	–	–	–
1994	2	1	–	1	–
1995	32	2	–	3	5
1996	93	15	–	9	77
1997	14	63	–	10	6
1998	16	92	–	11	80
1999	11	13	–	6	14
2000	18	9	–	8	33
2001	12	11	–	5	1
2002	57	16	–	9	75
2003	27	59	100	4	75
2004	46	30	124	5	4
2005	36	26	5	30	–
2006	36	28	5	23	24
2007	43	30	6	23	56
Total	451	395	240	147	450

(*Source*: Compiled from *Congressional Budget Justification for Foreign Operations, 1995 through 2007*, Department of State, Washington, DC. [See also fig. B.1.])

Note: Totals are shown for fiscal years. Numbers for 2006 are estimated and those for 2007 are projected. A single individual may be counted more than once by attending a sequence of courses, such as completing an English language refresher class prior to entering a technical training curriculum.

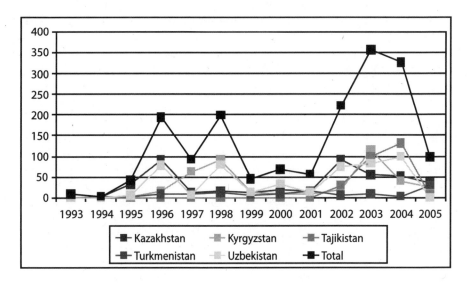

Figure B.1. Trends in Central Asian military students trained in the IMET program, 1993–2005 (Adapted from table B.1.)

Table B.2. Central Asian military and civilian students trained in DLIELC resident courses, 1993–2005

	Kazakhstan	Kyrgyzstan	Tajikistan	Turkmenistan	Uzbekistan
1993	2	–	–	–	–
1994	–	1	–	–	–
1995	3	2	–	2	2
1996	8	4	–	4	9
1997	10	1	–	–	–
1998	11	–	–	–	–
1999	12	4	–	2	5
2000	17	6	–	1	6
2001	13	7	–	6	–
2002	24	14	2	2	2
2003	25	16	3	4	9
2004	54	20	6	4	–
2005	28	29	6	9	–
Total	207	104	17	34	33

(*Source*: Office of Resident Studies, DLIELC, Lackland AFB, TX. [See also fig. B.2.])

Note: Totals are shown for calendar years when students began English language training.

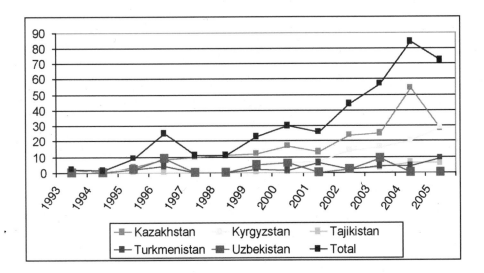

Figure B.2. Trends in Central Asian military students trained in DLIELC resident courses, 1993–2005 (Adapted from table B.2.)

Table B.3. Central Asian military and civilian students trained in Marshall Center resident courses, 1993–2005

	Kazakhstan	Kyrgyzstan	Tajikistan	Turkmenistan	Uzbekistan
1993	–	–	–	–	–
1994	2	4	2	3	4
1995	5	6	5	2	8
1996	5	8	2	4	8
1997	6	7	2	4	7
1998	10	10	8	4	14
1999	7	12	10	2	14
2000	12	12	13	3	15
2001	12	12	11	2	14
2002	9	16	14	2	11
2003	13	24	18	–	23
2004	20	18	27	7	32
2005	19	20	27	9	15
Total	120	149	139	42	165

(*Source*: Graduate Support Office, George C. Marshall European Center for Strategic Studies, Garmisch, Germany. [See also fig. B.3.])

Note: Totals are shown for calendar years.

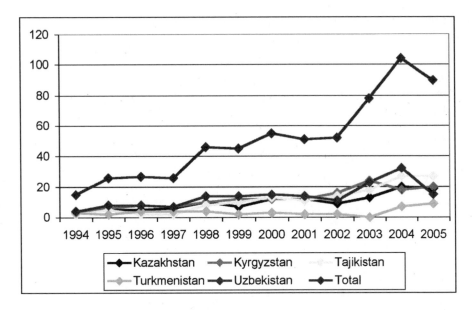

Figure B.3. Trends in Central Asian military and civilian students trained in Marshall Center resident courses, 1994–2005. (Adapted from table B.3.)

Table B.4. Central Asian attendance at US war colleges, 1993–2005

	Kazakhstan	Kyrgyzstan	Tajikistan	Turkmenistan	Uzbekistan
1993	–	–	–	–	–
1994	–	–	–	–	–
1995	–	–	–	–	–
1996	–	–	–	–	–
1997	CGSC, CNSC	–	–	–	ACSC
1998	CNSC, ACSC	–	–	–	ACSC
1999	CGSC	–	–	–	–
2000	CGSC	–	–	CGSC	CGSC
2001	CGSC	–	–	–	ACSC
2002	CGSC, ACSC	CGSC	–	CGSC	–
2003	CGSC	CGSC	–	CGSC	–
2004	CGSC, ACSC, ICAF	CGSC	–	–	CGSC, ACSC
2005	NWC	CGSC	–	–	–
Total	14	4	0	3	6

(*Sources*: LTC Jim Fain, International Military Student Office, US Army Command and General Staff College, Fort Leavenworth, KS; Alice Deery, International Military Student Office, Naval War College, Newport, RI; Lt Col Paul Bigelow, International Military Student Office, Air War College, Maxwell AFB, AL; John Charlton, International Military Student Office, National War College, Washington, DC.)

Note: Courses are for an academic year; year of graduation is indicated.

College of Naval Staff and Command (CNSC)
Air Command and Staff College (ACSC)
Industrial College of the Armed Forces (ICAF)
National War College (NWC)

Table B.5. Central Asian military and civilian students trained in DIILS resident courses or by METs, 1993–2005

	Kazakhstan	Kyrgyzstan	Tajikistan	Turkmenistan	Uzbekistan
1993	–	–	–	–	–
1994	–	–	–	–	–
1995	–	–	–	–	–
1996	74*	–	–	–	62**
1997	–	55†	–	–	–
1998	–	56††	–	2	46‡
1999	–	–	–	–	–
2000	–	–	–	–	–
2001	2	1	–	–	–
2002	1	–	–	–	–
2003	2	63‡‡	–	–	–
2004	–	–	36§	–	–
2005	1	–	–	–	–
Total	80	175	36	2	108

(*Source*: Walter Monroe, Academic Director, DIILS, Newport, RI.)

*MET "Disciplined Military Operations" in September 1996.
**MET "Military Justice" in September 1996.
†MET "Military Justice" in June 1997.
††MET "Peace Operations" in May 1998 (55 participants).
‡MET "Peace Operations" in June 1998.
‡‡METs "Military Justice" in May 2003 (55 participants) and "Combating Terrorism" in May 2003 (7 participants).
§METs "Military Justice" in March 2004 (20 participants) and "Developing a Professional Military" in April 2004 (16 participants).

Table B.6. Central Asian military and civilian students trained in DRMI resident courses or by METs, 1993–2006

	Kazakhstan	Kyrgyzstan	Tajikistan	Turkmenistan	Uzbekistan
1993	–	–	–	–	–
1994	–	–	–	–	–
1995	–	–	–	–	–
1996	–	1	–	–	1
1997	1	1	–	–	26*
1998	1	2	–	–	–
1999	1	–	–	1	–
2000	–	–	–	–	1
2001	2	–	–	–	16**
2002	2	2	–	–	–
2003	1	1	–	–	–
2004	–	–	23***	–	–
2005	–	1	–	–	–
2006	1	2	–	–	–
Total	9	10	23	1	44

(*Source*: Walter Monroe, Academic Director, DIILS, Newport, RI.)

*MET in December 1997.
**MET in August 2001 (15 participants).
***MET in June 2004.

Table B.7. Central Asian military and civilian students trained in CCMR resident courses or by METs, 1993–2005

	Kazakhstan	Kyrgyzstan	Tajikistan	Turkmenistan	Uzbekistan
1993	–	–	–	–	–
1994	–	–	–	–	–
1995	–	–	–	–	–
1996	–	–	–	–	–
1997	–	–	–	–	–
1998	–	–	–	–	–
1999	–	–	–	–	–
2000	–	–	–	–	–
2001	–	–	–	–	–
2002	–	–	–	–	–
2003	–	4*	7**	–	3***
2004	–	–	4	–	–
2005	–	–	–	–	–
Total	0	4	11	0	3

(*Source*: Christina Matei, International Programs Office, CCMR, Monterrey, CA.)

*MET "Civil Military Responses to Terrorism"
**MET "Civil Military Responses to Terrorism" (4 participants)
***MET "Civil Military Responses to Terrorism"

Table B.8. Central Asian attendance at US service academies, 1993–2008

	Kazakhstan	Kyrgyzstan	Tajikistan	Turkmenistan	Uzbekistan
1993	–	–	–	–	–
1994	–	–	–	–	–
1995	–	–	–	–	–
1996	–	–	–	–	–
1997	–	–	–	–	–
1998	–	USMA (Enter)	–	–	–
1999	–	–	–	–	–
2000	USMA (Enter)	–	–	–	–
2001	USMA (Enter)	–	–	–	–
2002	–	USMA (Graduate)	–	–	–
2003	USMA (Enter)	USNA (Enter) USAFA (Enter)	–	–	–
2004	USMA (Graduate)	USMA (Enter) USMA (Enter)	–	–	–
2005	USMA (Graduate)	–	–	–	–
2006	–	–	–	–	–
2007	USMA (Graduate)	USNA (Graduate) USAFA (Graduate)	–	–	–
2008	–	USMA (Graduate) USMA (Graduate)	–	–	–
Total	3	5	0	0	0

(*Sources*: Service Academy Exchange Program Coordinator [SAEPC], USMA [US Military Academy]; SAEPC, USNA [US Naval Academy]; and SAEPC, USAFA [US Air Force Academy].)

Note: Courses are for four academic years and both year of entrance and year of graduation are indicated.

Table B.9. Central Asian invitations to the ALP, 1996–2005

	Kazakhstan	Kyrgyzstan	Tajikistan	Turkmenistan	Uzbekistan
1996					
1997					
1998					X
1999	----------	----------	----------	----------	----------
2000	----------	----------	----------	----------	----------
2001	----------	----------	----------	----------	----------
2002					X
2003	X			X*	X
2004	X	X			X
2005					X**
Total	2	1	0	1	5

(*Source*: Office of the Deputy Under Secretary of the Air Force, International Affairs.)

*Invitation was declined.
**Invitation was declined.

Note: Due to the increased requirement for flight training quotas for US Air Force pilots, ALP was in abeyance between 1999 and 2001.

Table B.10. Central Asian military and civilian students trained in DISAM resident courses or by METs, 1993–2006

	Kazakhstan	Kyrgyzstan	Tajikistan	Turkmenistan	Uzbekistan
1993	–	–	–	–	–
1994	–	–	–	–	–
1995	–	1	–	–	–
1996	–	–	–	–	–
1997	–	–	–	–	–
1998	–	1	–	–	1
1999	–	–	–	–	–
2000	2	1	–	1	–
2001	–	–	–	–	–
2002	39*	–	–	–	1
2003	–	–	3	–	2
2004	7	–	16**	–	2
2005	2	1	–	–	–
2006	3	–	–	1	–
Total	53	4	19	2	6

(*Source*: Kenneth Martin, International Programs Office, DISAM, Wright-Patterson AFB, OH.)

*Includes 34 trained by a MET.
**Includes 15 trained by a MET.

Appendix C

Expanded International Military Education and Training Program

The following list represents training and education programs and courses that qualify under the expanded international military education and training program as meeting Congressional intent to promote understanding of democracy and civilian rule of law, increase appreciation for internationally recognized standards of human rights, improve military justice systems, contribute to responsible defense resource management, and foster cooperation between military and law enforcement personnel in counternarcotics efforts.[1] These courses range from training classes lasting only a few days to graduate programs lasting up to two years. Some of the courses may be taught in-country by mobile training teams or mobile education teams. This listing should be viewed as representative rather than comprehensive.

Military Professional Development

National Defense University Advanced Management Program
National War College International Fellows Program
Industrial College of the Armed Forces International Fellows
  Program
NATO Staff Officer Orientation Course
International Senior Officer Staff Course
Inter-American Defense College Hemispheric Defense and Security Course
Inter-American Air Force Academy (IAAFA) Company Grade
  Professional Development Course
IAAFA Noncommissioned Officer Professional Development
  Course

Civil-Military Relations

Establishing Democratic Civil-Military Relations and the Rule
  of Law Course

219

Civil-Military Relations Course
Democratic Sustainment Course
Equal Opportunity Staff Advisors Course
Human Rights Instructor Course
Defense Equal Opportunity Management Institute Course
Civil-Military Operations Course
Civil-Military Responses to Terrorism
Intelligence and Democracy Course
Civil-Military Strategy for Internal Development Course—Latin
    America
Civil-Military Strategy for Internal Development Course—Africa
Civil-Military Strategy for Internal Development Course—Central
    and Eastern Europe
Civil-Military Strategy for Internal Development Course—Middle
    East
Civil-Military Strategy for Internal Development Course—Asia/
    Pacific
Civilian Control of the Armed Forces in a Democracy Course
Civil-Military Cooperation: Support of Multinational and Inter-
    agency Relief in Reconstruction Operations
Civil Affairs/Civil-Military Cooperation Support of Information
    Operations
Master of Arts Program in International Security and Civil-
    Military Relations

Defense Reform

Defense Restructuring Course
International Defense Transformation Course
International Defense Management Course
Executive Program in Defense Decision Making

National Security Affairs

Master of Arts Program in International Security Studies: De-
    fense Decision Making & Planning
Master of Arts Program in International Security Studies: Se-
    curity Building in Post-Conflict Environments
Master of Arts Program in National Security Affairs—Middle
    East, Africa, South Asia

Master of Arts Program in National Security Affairs—Far East, Southeast Asia, Pacific

Master of Arts Program in National Security Affairs—Europe and Former Soviet Union

Master of Arts Program in National Security Affairs—Western Hemisphere

Peacekeeping

Planning Peace Operations Course

Peacekeeping for Decision Makers Course

Preparing for Peacekeeping Deployments: Negotiating Effective Support Agreements with International Organizations

Preparing for Peacekeeping Deployments: Reviewing Inter-ministerial Peacekeeping Roles and Missions

Preparing for Peacekeeping Deployments: Reviewing Ministry of Defense and Defense Headquarters Peacekeeping Roles and Missions

Preparing for Peacekeeping Deployments: Adopting Task Lists and Standard Operating Procedures

Military Law

International Operational Law Course

Marine Corps Law of War Course

Judge Advocate General (JAG) Officer Basic Course

JAG Officer Graduate Course

JAG Officer Military Judge Course

JAG Operational Law Seminar

JAG Contract Attorney's Course

JAG Law of War Workshop

IAAFA Rule of Law and Disciplined Military Operations Course

Conducting Military and Peacekeeping Operations in Accord with the Rule of Law Course

Military Law Development Program

International Law of Military Operations

Legal Aspects of Counter Terrorism

Maritime Law Enforcement (MLE)

International Maritime Officer Course
MLE Boarding Officer Course
Advanced MLE Boarding Officer Course
Counternarcotics MLE Boarding Officer Course
Advanced Counternarcotics MLE Boarding Officer Course
Counternarcotics MLE Instructor Course
Fisheries MLE Boarding Officer
MLE Boarding Team Member Course
MLE On-the-Job Training Course
Maritime Operations Planning and Management
Maritime Commerce Control and Infrastructure Development
    Course
Model Maritime Service Code Course

Medical and Disaster Response

Medical Strategic Leadership Program
Executive Health Care Resource Management Course
Health Resource Management Course
Health Systems Development Course
Nursing Administration Course
Disaster Planners Course
Preparation, Response, and Consequence Management in Di-
    sasters: Mental Health Aspects Course
Leadership Course in Regional Disaster Response and Trauma
    System
Leadership Program in Disaster Public Health and Public
    Health System
Leadership Course in HIV/AIDS [Human Immuno-deficiency
    virus/Acquired Immune-Deficiency Syndrome] Program De-
    velopment Course
HIV/AIDS Planning/Policy Development Course

Defense Resource Management

Defense Resources Management Course
International Defense Management Course
Senior International Defense Management Course

Multiobjective Decision Making Course
Departmental Resource Management and Logistics Course
Multinational Logistics Course
Security Assistance Management Resource Planning & Management Course
Principles of Defense Acquisition Management Course
International Defense Acquisition Negotiations Course
International Shipyard Management Course
Principles of Defense Procurement and Contracting Course
Principles of Government Contract Law Course
Budget Preparation, Execution, and Accountability Course
Financial Integrity, Accountability, and Transparency Course
Streamlining Government through Outsourcing, Privatization and Public-Private Partnership Course
Base Realignment, Closure and Economic Redevelopment Course
Graduate Program in Logistics Management
Master of Arts Program in Systems Management
Master of Science Program in Cost Analysis
Master of Science Program in Manpower Systems Analysis
Master of Science Program in Financial Management
Master of Science Program in Information Systems Technology
Master of Science Program in Resource Planning and Management for International Defense
Master of Science Program in Acquisition and Contract Management
Master of Science Program in Systems Acquisition Management

Note

1. This list was derived from *The Expanded IMET Handbook*, 1-68. It is a listing of courses that qualify as expanded-IMET if the student is a civilian. Duplicate listings and entries representing precourse surveys have been eliminated. Department of Defense Manual 5105.38-M, *Security Assistance Management*, 346.

Appendix D

Allied Security Cooperation Efforts in Central Asia

Turkey was the first NATO nation to seriously engage in military cooperation in Central Asia, an effort strongly encouraged by the United States. In the wake of the dissolution of the Soviet Union, Turkish leaders in Ankara, particularly Pres. Turgut Ozal, emphasized the historic cultural, ethnic, linguistic, and religious links to build ties with Kazakhstan, Kyrgyzstan, Turkmenistan, and Uzbekistan. (Tajikistan, with its ethnic Persian, Farsi-speaking population, was largely ignored.) Turkish military officials immediately offered to assist in establishing the necessary military establishments and train officers for these new armed forces, and enrollments at Turkish military academies began as early as 1992. Most of the Central Asian states were ambivalent about extensive military ties with Turkey, and Ankara soon found it lacked the resources to make its proposals appear more attractive. Turkmenistan was largely the exception and the first to take advantage of this offer, sending 30 military cadets for training in 1992. By April 1993 over 300 Turkmen cadets and junior officers had been trained in Turkey. By 1998 over 1,000 Turkmen military personnel had been trained and in that year alone 100 to 120 officers from the Ministry of Defense (MOD) and another 60 from the State Border Services were in Turkey. Turkmenistan continued to receive the majority of Turkey's attention. As of January 2006 Turkey had trained 1,299 personnel from Turkmenistan, 426 from Uzbekistan, 401 from Kyrgyzstan, 383 from Kazakhstan, and three from Tajikistan.[1]

Turkey's influence eventually began to be felt in the rest of Central Asia as well. Turkey and Kazakhstan signed an agreement on military technical cooperation and military training in 1996. Ankara began providing military equipment in 1998 and established a language center in Almaty in 1999 large enough for 27 students to study simultaneously. In 2001 Turkey offered communications equipment, computers, and map-printing equipment in April, followed in August with a ten-year, $10 million aid program that would eventually include two patrol boats, additional communications gear, and vehicles for Kazakhstan's special forces. Along with this program was the establishment of a Turkish general staff technical representation office in Almaty, supplementing the defense attaché office which had been established earlier. Turkish forces also began training Kazakh special forces in Turkey and in Kazakhstan. By 2005 over $6.500 million in aid had been provided since 1998, including 24 Land Rover vehicles (including four that could be used as ambulances), 92 portable radios, and another $900 thousand was promised for 2006.[2]

Following the IMU incursions in the summer of 1999, Turkey began to ramp up its military aid to Kyrgyzstan. In December 1999, Turkey extended $210 thousand in military aid to Bishkek, including communications gear and logistical material sufficient to outfit 3,000 soldiers. Two weeks after this initial offer came another for $700 thousand worth of communications equipment and in June 2000 another $1 million for communications gear and uniforms was presented. In 2000 Turkish special forces began training with the Kyrgyz special forces in counterinsurgency, counterterrorism, and mountain warfare operations, conducting three to four exercises each year. Another $1 million in aid was delivered in 2001, including $300 thousand worth of uniforms, night vision goggles, and infrared sights for sniper rifles in October, and $750 thousand in 2004, including clothing, mobile kitchens and baths, computers, and other equipment. Turkey's aid to Kyrgyzstan in 2005 was over $1 million and included twelve all-terrain vehicles, including three ambulances.[3]

Although Uzbek military personnel had been training in Turkey since the early 1990s, the security relationship between the two countries also expanded in 2000 when Turkey and Uzbekistan signed a military-cooperation agreement and began special forces training exercises and military contact events. Over $1.5 million worth of military clothing was sent from Turkey to Uzbekistan in 2001, and another $1.500 million in military aid was provided in 2002. In December 2004, Ankara provided $648 thousand worth of military equipment, including 16 Land Rover all-terrain vehicles. Uzbekistan has been somewhat dissatisfied with Turkey's assistance, however, preferring higher-quality US or Russian equipment.[4]

Like Turkey, Germany was among the first of the European nations to establish bilateral military relationships in Central Asia, but its efforts were much more modest. Throughout the early 1990s, Berlin played an active role in the region, particularly in Kazakhstan and Kyrgyzstan, because of the large ethnic German population in those countries.[5] In this period, the bulk of Germany's efforts were conducted with Kazakhstan, and it wasn't until after September 2001 that Uzbekistan figured more prominently in Berlin's programs. In all cases, however, Germany's security-cooperation efforts in Central Asia were a function of opportunity rather than a deliberate program designed to serve long-term operational interests.[6] In the beginning, Germany leveraged its large stock of former East German military equipment and Soviet-trained officers to build relationships, including providing a large quantity of trucks to Kazakhstan in the early 1990s. Germany provided a patrol boat to Kazakhstan in 1995–1996, and at some points in the late 1990s had a more extensive security-cooperation relationship with Kazakhstan than did the United States. In 1996 the German defense ministry sent over $26 million worth of surplus military supplies to Uzbekistan, and in May 2001 it donated approximately $120 thousand worth of medical equipment, uniforms, and night vision devices to Kyrgyzstan in response to the Islamic extremist incursions of the previous two years. In 1997 the *Bundeswehr* began a long-term training program for Uzbek armor, artillery, signals, and air defense officers, and by February 2002, some 50 Uzbek officers had trained at the *Bundeswehr* Academy. By 2003 the two countries discussed expanding the training programs to include mountain warfare and pilot training. These efforts undoubtedly played a role in Tashkent's decision to allow the *Luftwaffe* to use a base at Termez in the southern part of the country to support the German contingent in Afghanistan. In 2004 Germany also expanded its relationship with Kazakhstan hosting 17 Kazakh military students at its military university, academy, and officer schools.[7]

The United Kingdom initiated its formal programs in Central Asia with the exchange of defense attachés with Kazakhstan in the summer of 2001, and subsequently has developed a fairly extensive program of security cooperation in that country. The Kazakhstani minister of defense paid his first official visit to the United Kingdom in January 2003, and two months later the two nations held their first bilateral cooperation working group in Almaty. Since then, the working group has met twice a year to focus on the five key areas of cooperation: noncommissioned officer training; cooperation with the airmobile forces; and training of peace support operations instructors, military police, and naval forces. The United Kingdom is providing Royal Navy specialist assistance at the new Kazakhstani naval academy in Aktau, and has also provided a variety of training courses in the United Kingdom, British training facilities in the Czech Republic and in Kazakhstan, and a 10-day seminar, Defense Administration in a Democratic Society, offered by the Defense Academy of the United Kingdom in Almaty in September 2004. The British defense attaché also sponsors a military English language program that consists of seminars and computer training facilities in various locations throughout the country including the Ministry of Defense.[8]

The hallmark of the military cooperation effort between the United Kingdom and Kazakhstan is the annual Steppe Eagle exercise, first conducted in July 2003. The first evolution of this exercise included 500 Kazakhstani airborne troops, elements of the KAZBAT, Scots Guards from the United Kingdom, and US Special Forces (which were in Kazakhstan to participate in the Zhardem exercise). The scenario was based on an insurgency incursion into southern Kazakhstan. Steppe Eagle 2004 was held in August in Kapchagai with 164 members of the 3d Motorized Infantry Battalion of the Princess of Wales Regiment, KAZBAT, and Kazakhstani airborne and air defense units (including Su-27 fighters, Mi-8 helicopters, and An-12 cargo aircraft), in a scenario based on antiterrorism and peacekeeping operations. United States participation was limited due to ongoing operations in Iraq. Steppe Eagle 2005 was held in September, again at Kapchagai, with a similar scenario to the first two iterations of the exercise. Members of the Arizona National Guard participated for the United States.

The United Kingdom also has a defense attaché in Uzbekistan whose responsibilities include coordinating and implementing the annual program of cooperative defense activities. This program, which was initiated in November 2001 during a visit of British defense secretary Geoffrey Hoon to Tashkent, included a proposal to train Uzbek officers in British military colleges such as the Royal Military Academy at Sandhurst. Sr Lt Polatjon Sotvoldiyev, the first Uzbek officer to attend, won the coveted Overseas Award as the best foreign student during the eleven-month program in August 2004. Uzbek minister of defence Kodir Gulamov paid an official visit to the United Kingdom in late October 2003, and Gen Sir Michael Jackson, chief of the General Staff, British Ministry of Defence, made a reciprocal visit to Tashkent in May 2004. Following the events at Andijon, the British program in Uzbekistan was dramatically reduced and now consists primarily of an English language program. The United Kingdom MOD also sponsors a military-focused English language program in Tajikistan.[9]

France had established some very tentative military relationships in Central Asia in the 1990s, but its efforts surged in early 2002 with the introduction of French combat forces into the region for operations in Afghanistan. Paris focused its security-cooperation efforts on Tajikistan and Kyrgyzstan, the two countries that agreed to host French forces. Defense Minister Alain Richard, meeting with Tajik president Emomali Rahmonov in Dushanbe on 2 January 2002, stated his desire to set up long-term military cooperation between the two countries.[10] Within six months, the two countries were conducting a joint airborne and mountain warfare exercise near the capital. In September Tajik officers were invited to observe mountain infantry exercises in France. These bilateral exercises, usually focusing on mountain warfare, have continued at least twice a year since. Tajik officers are also attending French language courses, attending French military schools, and receiving instruction from visiting French military instructors.[11] French bilateral security cooperation with Kyrgyzstan progressed along similar lines, with agreements starting in 2002 that grew to include the training of Kyrgyz service members in France, including at staff colleges, and the provision of mountain warfare, medical, and French language training in Kyrgyzstan. France has also donated excess military equipment, including navigation aids and vehicles, after its deployments to Manas.[12]

In addition, other NATO nations are starting to initiate military relationships in Central Asia, albeit at a much smaller scale. Greece, Poland, Belgium, and Lithuania have all established cooperation programs with Uzbekistan of varying types. Most include personnel visits and information exchanges, occasionally through the NATO Partnership for Peace program. The Greek agreement, which was signed in 1998, also includes the offer of training Uzbek officers at Greek military academies.[13] It is unclear how active any of these programs remain after the strong European reaction to the events in Andijon in May 2005, but it is likely they are continuing, possibly on a smaller scale.

European nations are not the only possible US partners for security cooperation in Central Asia. Asian nations, as well, are seeking to establish security ties to the region. India has been the most active, developing military links with all of the Central Asian states except Turkmenistan. The primary drivers are energy and security. As India must import over 70 percent of its energy requirements, it constantly seeks new suppliers to support its rapidly expanding population and growing economy. The strategic concerns over Pakistan and China also play a major role—India views improved ties with Central Asia as a means to outflank its two major rivals. In this regard, Delhi often works cooperatively with Moscow to build security ties to Central Asia, ensuring it will not face resistance from Russia.[14] India began building military ties in 1997 with a defense cooperation agreement with Kyrgyzstan, but little was done over the next few years except for occasional military contacts and a few training opportunities. In 2003, however, India offered to send instructors to Kyrgyzstan to train special operations units, and indicated a desire to purchase weapons produced in Kyrgyzstan, although the specifics were not made public. Delhi soon began providing mountain training, English language instruction, and quotas for its military academies, the costs of which are covered by India.[15] Delhi's ties with Tajikistan were boosted by a visit of Tajik defense minister Col Gen Sherali Khayrulloyev in December 2001, in which the two sides agreed that India would help reconstruct Ayni Air Base, just outside of Dushanbe. A February 2002 reciprocal visit by Indian air force commander Vice Marshal S. K. Jain brought offers for new navigation and landing aids for the facility and plans to train Tajik pilots in Indian trainer aircraft there. The program has since grown to include Russian assistance.[16] India is also upgrading Tajikistan's Soviet and Russian military equipment, providing English language instruction, and training Tajik troops. India's ties with Uzbekistan and Kazakhstan are less extensive, involving a few exercises and training opportunities, but they also include weapons purchases—Il-76 tanker-transport aircraft from Uzbekistan and torpedoes from Kazakhstan.[17]

A few other Asian nations have made tentative steps toward security-cooperation relationships with the Central Asian states. Pakistan had provided flight training to the Turkmen air force in the late 1990s, but Ashgabat was dissatisfied with the quality of training and cancelled the program. The Turkmenistani State Border Service, however, continued to send officers to Pakistan for training. More recently, Islamabad, concerned about being strategically outflanked by India, began discussions with Tajikistan to explore options for military and technical cooperation in August 2005.[18] South Korea, which had deployed medical troops to support the coalition operations out of Manas and Japan, one of the largest aid donors in Kyrgyzstan, also started small military-cooperation programs with Kyrgyzstan in late 2005.[19]

Notes

1. Gareth M. Winrow, "Turkey and Central Asia," in Roy Allison and Lena Jonson, eds., *Central Asian Security: The New International Context* (Washington, DC: Brookings Institution Press, 2001), 199, 207–8; Bess A. Brown, "National Security and Military Issues in Central Asia," in Bruce Parrott, ed., *State Building and Military Power in Russia and the New States of Eurasia, The International Politics of Eurasia*, vol. 5 (Armonk, New York: M. E. Sharpe, 1995), 236, 247; Olcott, Central Asia's Second Chance, 53, 73–74 (see chap. 4, note 10); Bhatty and Bronson, "NATO's Mixed Signals in the Caucasus and Central Asia," 135 (see chap. 3, note 25); Trip Report, McCarthy, (see chap. 3, note 15); and "Turkish Armed Forces Military Training Support to Friendly, Allied Armies Detailed," *Anatolia*, 2 January 2006.

2. "Turkish Armed Forces Opens Language Center in Almaty," *Ankara Anatolia*, 17 September 1999; "Kazakhstan: Turkey to Give Aid for Military Defense," *Moscow Interfax*, 24 December 1999; "Turkish Armed Forces Donates 2 Trucks of Equipment, Devices to Kazakh Army," *Ankara Anatolia*, 24 April 2001; "Kazakhstan Receives $10 Million Military Assistance from Turkey," *Moscow Interfax*, 3 August 2001; "Kazakhstan, Turkey Agree on Need to Revise Defense Cooperation Agreements," *Moscow Interfax*, 21 September

2001; "Turkey: TSK Grants Military Equipment worth $1.3 Million to Kazakh Army," *Anatolia*, 10 June 2005; "Turkey Donates Military Equipment to Kazakhstan," *Almaty Interfax-Kazakhstan*, 10 June 2005; and "Kazakhstan's Defense Minister, Turkish Chief of Staff Discuss Cooperation Prospects," *Agentstvo Voyennykh Novostey*, 16 June 2005.

3. Olga Oliker and Thomas S. Szayna, eds., *Faultlines of Conflict in Central Asia and the South Caucasus: Implications for the U.S. Army* (Santa Monica, California: RAND, 2003), 202; "Turkey to Extend Military Aid to Kyrgyzstan," *Ankara Anatolia*, 12 December 1999; "Turkey to Provide Military-Technical Aid to Kyrgyzstan," *Moscow ITAR-TASS*, 13 December 1999; "Turkey to Give Kyrgyzstan $1 Million to Aid Armed Forces," *Moscow Interfax*, 15 June 2000; "Turkish Instructors Supervising Kyrgyzstani Servicemen's Mountain Training," *Bishkek Kabar News Agency*, 18 June 2003; "Turkey to Provide Material assistance to Kyrgyzstani military," *Moscow ITAR-TASS*, 21 May 2003; "Turkey to Extend Military, Technical Aid to Kyrgyzstan," *Ankara Anatolia*, 9 November 2004; "FYI-Turkey to Give $1 Million to Kyrgyzstan for Military Reforms," *AKIpress Internet Version*, 18 October 2005; and "Delivery of Turkish Military Equipment Donations to Kyrgyzstan Reported," *Anatolia*, 28 November 2005.

4. Robert McDermott, "The Armed Forces of the Republic of Uzbekistan 1992–2002: Threats, Influences, and Reform," *Journal of Slavic Military Studies* 16, no. 2 (June 2003), 42–43; Oliker and Szayna, *Faultlines of Conflict*, 202 (see app. D, note 3); Olcott, *Central Asia's Second Chance*, 191 (see chap. 4, note 10); "Turkish Military Delegation Goes to Tashkent Under Cooperation Accord," *Ankara Anatolia*, 20 November 2001; "Uzbek President Supports Greater Military Cooperation with Turkey," *Tashkent Uzbek Radio*, 19 December 2003; and "Turkey Extends Military Aid of $648,000 to Uzbekistan," *Ankara Anatolia*, 21 December 2004.

5. Olcott, *Central Asia's Second Chance*, 80 (see chap. 4, note 10).

6. German Military Policy Directorate correspondence (see chap. 8, note 7).

7. McDermott, "The Armed Forces of the Republic of Uzbekistan." 43 (see app. D, note 4); Oliker and Szayna, *Faultlines of Conflict*, 207 (see app. D, note 3); Kenzhetaev, "Kazakhstan's Military-Technical Cooperation with Foreign States" (see chap. 4, note 41); "Uzbekistan: Troops Begin Long-term Military Training Program in Germany," *Moscow Interfax*, 11 April 1997; Bhatty and Bronson, "NATO's Mixed Signals." 136 (see chap. 3, note 25); and "Germany to Help Uzbekistan Train Army Officers," *Moscow Interfax*, 10 August 2003.

8. Roger McDermott, "Kazakhstan's Western Military Cooperation Sparks Tensions with Russia," *Jamestown Foundation Eurasia Daily Monitor* 1, no. 50, 13 July 2004; British Embassy, Kazakstan, http://www.britishembassy.gov.uk (accessed 2 March 2006); and "Kazakhstan: UK Defense Experts to Train Central Asian Military Officers, Experts," *Almaty Interfax-Kazakhstan*, 3 September 2004.

9. "Uzbekistan: UK Defense Secretary Pledges Expansion of Military Ties," *Moscow Interfax*, 14 November 2001; "Uzbekistani Serviceman Gets Top Military Award in UK's Royal Academy," *Tashkent Khalq Sozi*, 13 August 2004;

British Embassy, Uzbekistan, http://www.britishembassy.gov.uk (accessed 2 March 2006); and British Council, Uzbekistan, http://www.britishcouncil .org, (accessed 2 March 2006).

10. "French Defense Minister says wants military cooperation with Tajiks," Paris *Agence France-Presse (AFP)*, 2 January 2002.

11. "Tajikistani, French Troops Begin Joint Exercise Near Dushanbe," *Moscow ITAR-TASS*, 26 July 2002; "France to Help Train Tajikistani Servicemen," *Moscow Interfax*, 29 July 2002; "France to Hold Joint Military Exercises with Tajikistan—Defense Minister," *Paris AFP*, 14 December 2003; and "Tajikistan: President, French Defense Minister Discuss Military Cooperation," *Avesta*, 19 December 2005.

12. "Kyrgyzstan: President, French Defense Minister Discuss Military Aid, Cooperation," *Moscow Interfax*, 3 June 2002; "France Transfers $200,000 of Military Equipment to Kyrgyzstan," *Moscow Interfax*, 15 October 2002; "Kyrgyzstan, France Sign Agreement on Military Cooperation," *Bishkek Kabar News Agency*, 4 October 2004; and "Kyrgyzstan, France to Expand Military Cooperation," *AKIpress*, 5 December 2005.

13. "Greece: Greek-Uzbek Military Cooperation Agreement Signed," *Athens News Agency*, 19 November 1998; "Lithuania, Uzbekistan Lay Groundwork for Military Cooperation," *Tallinn BNS*, 24 September 2002; "Uzbekistan, Poland to Develop Military Cooperation," *Moscow Interfax*, 21 October 2002; and "Belgian Top Military Official Visits Uzbekistan to Boost Cooperation," *Tashkent Uzbek Television First Channel*, 25 November 2004.

14. "AFP: India, Uzbekistan Agree; to Increase Defense Ties with Exercises," *AFP*, 5 April 2005; and "Russia, India Agree on Military Cooperation in Central Asia," *Moscow ITAR-TASS*, 4 December 2004.

15. "India, Kyrgyzstan to Develop Military Contacts," *Moscow ITAR-TASS World Service*, 23 February 1999; "India, Kyrgyzstan to Develop Military-Technical Cooperation," *Moscow Interfax*, 31 January 2003; "Indian Military Delegation in Kyrgyzstan to Discuss Bilateral Cooperation," *Bishkek Kabar News Agency*, 13 March 2004; and "Kyrgyzstani Defense Minister, Indian Envoy Discuss Boosting Military Ties," *Kabar News Agency Internet Version*, 19 November 2005; "Kyrgyzstani, Indian Defense Ministries Considering Joint Drills," *Kabar News Agency*, 2 December 2005.

16. "Tajikistani Defense Minister to visit India," *Moscow ITAR-TASS*, 18 December 2001; "India, not France, to Help Refurbish Strategic Tajik Airfield," *Moscow Interfax*, 2 February 2002; "India Extends Strategic Reach with 'First' Overseas Military Base in Tajikistan," *Bangalore Deccan Herald*, 19 October 2004; and "Defense Minister Ivanov Says Russia, India May Share Airbase in Tajikistan," *Moscow ITAR-TASS*, 5 December 2005.

17. "India Defense Minister Comments on value of working visit to Uzbekistan," *Moscow ITAR-TASS*, 1 March 2003; "AFP: India, Uzbekistan Agree," (see app. D, note 14); "Kazakhstan Offers Improved Torpedoes to Indian Navy," *New Delhi: The Asian Age*, 24 February 2002; and "Kazakhstani, Indian Leaders Sign Agreement on Military Cooperation," *Moscow Interfax*, 3 June 2002.

18. Trip Report, McCarthy (see chap. 3, note 15); and "Tajikistani Minister, Pakistani Envoy Discuss Afghan Situation, Military Ties," *ASIA-PLUS*, 17 August 2005.

19. "Kyrgyzstani Defense Minister, Japanese Envoy Discuss Military Cooperation," *AKIpress*, 2 September 2005; and "Kyrgyzstani Defense Minister, South Korean Envoy Mull Cooperation," *AKIpress*, 28 October 2005.

Abbreviations

6 SOS	6th Special Operations Squadron
ACSC	Air Command and Staff College
AECA	Arms Export Control Act of 1976
AETC	Air Education and Training Command
AFMC	Air Force Materiael Command
AFSAC	Air Force Security Assistance Center
ALP	Aviation Leadership Program
BWG	bilateral working groups
BWPP	biological weapons proliferation prevention
CADRE	College of Aerospace Doctrine, Research and Education
CASI	Central Asia Border Security Initiative
CCMR	Center for Civil-Military Relations
CENTRASBAT	Central Asian peacekeeping battalion
CFE	conventional forces in Europe
CGSC	Command and General Staff College
CIS	Commonwealth of Independent States
CN	counternarcotics
CNSC	College of Naval Staff and Command
CSF	Coalition Solidarity Funds
CSTO	Commonwealth Security Treaty Organization
CTR	cooperative threat reduction
DIA	Defense Intelligence Agency
DIILS	Defense Institute for International Legal Studies
DISAM	Defense Institute of Security Assistance Management
DLIELC	Defense Language Institute English Language Center
DMC	defense and military contacts
DOD	Department of Defense
DRMI	Defense Resource Management Institute

DRMS	Defense Resource Management Studies
DSCA	Defense Security Cooperation Agency
DSWA	Defense Special Weapons Agency
DTRA	Defense Threat Reduction Agency
DTSA	Defense Technology Security Administration
DOD-DOS	Department of Defense–Department of State
DHS	Department of Homeland Security
DODIP	DOD Informational Program
EDA	Excess Defense Articles
E-IMET	Expanded IMET
EXBS	export control and related border security
FAA	Foreign Assistance Act of 1961
FAO	Foreign Area Officers
FBI	Federal Bureau of Investigation
FMCS	foreign military construction sales
FMF	foreign military financing
FMS	foreign military sales
FSU	Former Soviet Union
GTEP	Georgia Train and Equip Program
HEU	highly enriched uranium
HMMWV	high mobility multipurpose wheeled vehicle
IAAFA	Inter-American Air Force Academy
IAEA	International Atomic Energy Agency
ICAF	Industrial College of the Armed Forces
ICBM	intercontinental ballistic missile
ICP	International Counterproliferation Program
IISS	International Institute for Strategic Studies
IMET	international military education and training
IMSO	International Student Management Office
IMU	Islamic Movement of Uzbekistan
INF	Intermediate-range Nuclear Forces
IPAP	Individual Partnership Action Plan
IPP	Individual Partnership Program

ISR	intelligence, surveillance, and reconnaissance
ITAR	International Traffic in Arms Regulation
IWER	International Workshop on Earthquake Response
IWER	International Workshop on Emergency Response
JAG	Judge Advocate General
JCET	Joint Combined Exchange Training
JCTP	Joint Contact Team Program
KAZBAT	Kazakhstan battalion
LOA	letter of offer and acceptance
MET	mobile education teams
MLE	Maritime Law Enforcement
MOD	Ministry of Defense
MTT	mobile training teams
NATO	North Atlantic Treaty Organization
NIS	newly independent states
NPS	Naval Postgraduate School
NWC	National War College
OEF	Operation Enduring Freedom
OSCE	Organization for Security and Cooperation in Europe
OSD	Office of the Secretary of Defense
OSIA	On-Site Inspection Agency
PASS	Program in Advanced Security Studies
PfP	Partnership for Peace
PME	professional military education
RCC	Regional Coordination Center
RDCTF	Regional Defense Counterterrorism Fellowship
RHIBS	rigid-hull inflatable boats

SAEPC	Service Academy Exchange Program Coordinator
SAO	Security Assistance Officer
SATFA	Security Assistance Training Field Activity
SCO	Shanghai Cooperation Organization
SDE	senior developmental education
SFG	special forces group
SSD	safe and secure dismantlement
SOFEX	special operations forces exercise
SPP	State Partnership Program
START	Strategic Arms Reduction Treaty
TCA	Traditional CINC Activities
UCP	Unified Command Plan
US	United States
USACOM	US Atlantic Command
USAFA	US Air Force Academy
USARCENT	US Army Central Command
USCENTAF	US Central Command Air Forces
USCENTCOM	US Central Command
USCS	US Customs Service
USEUCOM	US European Command
USG	US government
USJFCOM	US Joint Forces Command
USMA	US Military Academy
USMARFORCENT	US Marine Component Central Command
USNA	US Naval Academy
USNAVCENT	US Naval Forces Central Command
USPACOM	US Pacific Command
USSOCCENT	US Special Operations Command Central
USSOCPAC	US Special Operations Command Pacific
WIF	Warsaw Initiative Fund
WMD	weapons of mass destruction
WMD-PPI	Weapons of Mass Destruction Proliferation Prevention Initiative

Selected Bibliography

Ahrari, Ehsan. "The Strategic Future of Central Asia: A View from Washington." *Journal of International Affairs* 56, no. 2 (Spring 2003), 157–66.

Akbarzadeh, Shahram. *Uzbekistan and the United States: Authoritarianism, Islamism & Washington's Security Agenda.* London: Zed Books, 2005.

Allison, Roy, and Lena Jonson, eds. *Central Asian Security: The New International Context.* Washington, DC: Brookings Institution Press, 2001.

Bhatty, Robin, and Rachel Bronson. "NATO's Mixed Signals in the Caucasus and Central Asia." *Survival* 42, no. 3 (Autumn 2000), 129–46.

Blank, Stephen J. *After Two Wars: Reflections on the American Strategic Revolution in Central Asia.* Carlisle, PA: US Army War College Strategic Studies Institute, 2005.

———. *The Future of Transcaspian Security.* Carlisle, PA: US Army War College Strategic Studies Institute, 2002.

Bloomfield, Lincoln P., Jr. "Education and Training: A Common Foundation for Security." *eJournal USA* 9, no. 3 (November 2004), 6–8.

Bohr, Annette. "Regionalism in Central Asia: New Geopolitics, Old Regional Order." *International Affairs* 80, no. 3 (May 2004), 485–502.

Brandt, Craig M., and Mark T. Ahles. "Defense Institute of Security Assistance Management Mobile Education Team Travels to Kazakhstan." *DISAM Journal of International Security Assistance Management* 25, no. 1 (Fall 2002/Winter 2003), 19–21.

Bureau of European and Eurasian Affairs, US Department of State. *U.S. Government Assistance to and Cooperative Activities with Eurasia, Fiscal Year 2001.* Washington, DC: Department of State, 2002.

———. *U.S. Government Assistance to and Cooperative Activities with Eurasia, Fiscal Year 2002.* Washington, DC: Department of State, 2003.

———. *U.S. Government Assistance to and Cooperative Activities with Eurasia, Fiscal Year 2003.* Washington, DC: Department of State, 2004.

————. *U.S. Government Assistance to and Cooperative Activities with Eurasia, Fiscal Year 2004*. Washington, DC: Department of State, 2005.

Burghart, Daniel L., and Theresa Sabonis-Helf, eds. *In the Tracks of Tamerlane: Central Asia's Path to the 21st Century*. Washington, DC: National Defense University Press, 2004.

Burles, Mark. *Chinese Policy toward Russia and the Central Asian Republics*. Santa Monica, CA: RAND, 1999.

Butler, Kenley. *U.S. Military Cooperation with the Central Asian States*. Monterey, CA: Center for Nonproliferation Studies, Monterey Institute of International Studies, 17 September 2001.

Byman, Daniel. *Going to War with the Allies You Have: Allies, Counterinsurgency, and the War on Terrorism*. Carlisle, PA: US Army War College Strategic Studies Institute, 2005.

Chicky, Jon E. "A Military Strategy for Central Asia," Unpublished paper, US Army War College Strategy Research Project, March 2004.

Childress, Michael. *The Effectiveness of U.S. Training Efforts in Internal Defense and Development: The Cases of El Salvador and Honduras*. Santa Monica, CA: RAND, 1995.

Chivers, C. J. "Long Before War, Green Berets Built Military Ties to Uzbekistan," *New York Times*, 25 October 2001.

Clancy, Tom, Gen Tony Zinni (retired), and Tony Koltz. *Battle Ready*. New York: G. P. Putnam's Sons, 2004.

Clarke, Duncan L., Daniel B. O'Connor, and Jason D. Ellis. *Send Guns and Money: Security Assistance and U.S. Foreign Policy*. Westport, CT: Praeger Publishers, 1997.

Cole, Ronald H., Walter S. Poole, James F. Schnabel, Robert J. Watson, and Willard J. Webb. *The History of the Unified Command Plan, 1946–1999*. Washington, DC: Joint History Office, 2003.

Collins, Kathleen. "Clans, Pacts, and Politics in Central Asia." *Journal of Democracy* 13, no. 3 (July 2002), 137–52.

Congressional Budget Justification for Foreign Operations: Fiscal Year 2001. Washington, DC: Department of State, 2000.

Congressional Budget Justification—Foreign Operations: Fiscal Year 2002. Washington, DC: Department of State, 2001.

Congressional Budget Justification—Foreign Operations: Fiscal Year 2003. Washington, DC: Department of State, 2002.

Congressional Budget Justification—Foreign Operations: Fiscal Year 2004. Washington, DC: Department of State, 2003.

Congressional Budget Justification—Foreign Operations: Fiscal Year 2005. Washington, DC: Department of State, 2004.

Congressional Budget Justification—Foreign Operations: Fiscal Year 2006. Washington, DC: Department of State, 2005.

Congressional Budget Justification—Foreign Operations: Fiscal Year 2007. Washington, DC: Department of State, 2006.

Congressional Presentation for Building Democracy: Fiscal Year 1995. Washington, DC: Department of State, 1994.

Congressional Presentation for Foreign Operations: Fiscal Year 1997. Washington, DC: Department of State, 1996.

Congressional Presentation for Foreign Operations: Fiscal Year 1998. Washington, DC: Department of State, 1997.

Congressional Presentation for Foreign Operations: Fiscal Year 1999. Washington, DC: Department of State, 1998.

Congressional Presentation for Foreign Operations: Fiscal Year 2000. Washington, DC: Department of State, 1999.

Congressional Presentation—Foreign Operations: Fiscal Year 1996. Washington, DC: Department of State, 1995.

Cooperative Threat Reduction Annual Report to Congress, Fiscal Year 2004. Washington, DC: Defense Threat Reduction Agency, 2003.

Cooperative Threat Reduction Annual Report to Congress, Fiscal Year 2005. Washington, DC: Defense Threat Reduction Agency, 2004.

Cooperative Threat Reduction Annual Report to Congress, Fiscal Year 2006. Washington, DC: Defense Threat Reduction Agency, 2005.

Cope, John A. *International Military Education and Training: An Assessment,* McNair Paper, no. 44. Washington, DC: National Defense University Press, 1995.

Cornell, Svante. "The United States and Central Asia: In the Steppes to Stay?" *Cambridge Review of International Affairs* 17, no. 2 (July 2004), 239–54.

Cossaboom, Robert T. *The Joint Contact Team Program: Contacts with the Former Soviet Republics and Warsaw Pact Nations, 1992–1994.* Washington, DC: Joint History Office, 1997.

241

Cottey, Andrew, and Anthony Forster. *Reshaping Defense Diplomacy: New Roles for Military Cooperation and Assistance.* London: Oxford University Press, 2004.

Danopoulos, Constantine P., and Daniel Zirker, eds. *Civil-Military Relations in the Soviet and Yugoslav Successor States.* Boulder, CO: Westview Press, 1996.

Director of Strategy and Plans, US Joint Chiefs of Staff. *Bilateral Military Contact Plans, Planning Reference Book.* 2000 Joint Chiefs of Staff/Office of the Secretary of Defense Planning Conference for the NIS [Newly Independent] Peacetime Engagement, Washington, DC, June 1999.

———. *Planning Reference Book,* 1999 Joint Chiefs of Staff Planning Conference for the NIS Peacetime Engagement, Washington, DC, May 1998.

———. *Planning Reference Book.* 2000 Joint Chiefs of Staff/Office of the Secretary of Defense Planning Conference for the NIS Peacetime Engagement, Washington, DC, June 1999.

———. "Central Asia Border Security Initiative (CASI) Background Paper," undated, in *Addendum to the Peacetime Engagement Planning Reference Book.* 2001 Joint Chiefs of Staff/Office of the Secretary of Defense Russia-Eurasia Policy and Strategy Conference, Washington, DC, 2–6 April 2001.

———. *Peacetime Engagement Planning Reference Book.* 2001 Joint Chiefs of Staff/Office of the Secretary of Defense Russia-Eurasia Policy and Strategy Conference, Washington, DC, 2–6 April 2001.

Directorate of Defense Trade Controls, US Department of State. *International Traffic in Arms Regulations (ITAR).* http://www.pmddtc.state.gov/itar_index.htm.

Doran, James. "Americans Covertly Training Kazakh Troops." *Times of London,* 30 March 2002.

Foreign Military Sales, Foreign Military Construction Sales, and Military Assistance Facts. Washington, DC: Defense Security Cooperation Agency, 2004.

Foreign Military Training and DoD Engagement Activities of Interest in Fiscal Years 1999 and 2000, 1. Washington, DC: Department of State, 2000.

Foreign Military Training in Fiscal Years 2000 and 2001, 1. Washington, DC: Department of State, 2001.

Foreign Military Training in Fiscal Years 2001 and 2002, 1. Washington, DC: Department of State, 2002.

Foreign Military Training in Fiscal Years 2002 and 2003, 1. Washington, DC: Department of State, 2003.

Foreign Military Training in Fiscal Years 2003 and 2004, 1. Washington, DC: Department of State, 2004.

Foreign Military Training in Fiscal Years 2004 and 2005, 1. Washington, DC: Department of State, 2005.

Franken, Sara Bette. "Regional Defense Counterterrorism Fellows Program." *DISAM Journal of International Security Assistance Management* 26, no. 1 (Fall 2003), 12–14.

Franks, Tommy, and Malcolm McConnell. *American Soldier.* New York: HarperCollins Pulishers Inc., 2004.

Gareyev, Col Shamil'. "Military Cooperation: Uzbekistan and the U.S.A." *Asia-Pacific Defense Forum*, Winter 1997, 12–15.

Garnett, Sherman W., Alexander Rahr, and Koji Watanabe. *The New Central Asia: In Search of Stability—A Report to the Trilateral Commission.* New York: The Trilateral Commission, 2000.

General Accounting Office. *Nuclear Nonproliferation: US Efforts to Help Other Countries Combat Nuclear Smuggling Need Strengthened Coordination and Planning.* US General Accounting Office Report to the Ranking Minority Member, Subcommittee on Emerging Threats and Capabilities, Committee on Armed Services, US Senate, GAO-02-426. Washington, DC: Government Printing Office, 2002.

Giragosian, Richard. "The US Military Engagement in Central Asia and the Southern Caucasus: An Overview." *Journal of Slavic Military Studies* 17, no. 1 (March 2004), 43–77.

Gleason, Gregory. *The Central Asian States: Discovering Independence.* Boulder, CO: Westview Press, 1997.

Goldstein, Lyle J. "Beyond the Steppe: Projecting Power into the New Central Asia." *Journal of Slavic Military Studies* 17, no. 2 (April–June 2004), 183–213.

———. "Making the Most of Central Asian Partnerships." *Joint Forces Quarterly* no. 31 (Summer 2002), 82–90.

Golunov, Sergey V. "Border Security in Kazakhstan: Threats, Policies and Future Challenges." *Journal of Slavic Military Studies* 18, no. 1 (Spring 2005), 31–58.

Goodman, Glenn W., Jr. "Low-Key Spadework by Green Berets Reaps Valuable Benefits for War in Afghanistan." *Armed Forces Journal International*, January 2002, 60.

Gottemoeller, Rose. "Cooperative Threat Reduction beyond Russia." *Washington Quarterly* 28, no. 2 (Spring 2005), 145–58.

Grebenshchikov, Igor. "Kyrgyz Army in Crisis." *Reporting Central Asia* no. 44, 14 March 2001. http://www.iwpr.net/?p=rca &s=f&o=177189&apc_state=henirca2001.

Griffard, Bernard F. "Enhancing Regional Stability and Security in Central Asia: Implementing the US Central Command Disaster Preparedness Program." *Center for Strategic Leadership Issue Paper* 10-04. Carlisle, PA: US Army War College Center for Strategic Leadership, 2004.

———. "Promoting Stability in Central Asia." *Center for Strategic Leadership Issues Paper* 6-01. Carlisle, PA: US Army War College Center for Strategic Leadership, 2001.

Griffard, Bernard F., Bert B. Tussing, and Lt Col Curtis Turner. "Strengthening Regional Cooperation in Central Asia: Central Asian States Disaster Response Conference 2003." *Center for Strategic Leadership Issue Paper* 12-03. Carlisle, PA: US Army War College Center for Strategic Leadership, 2003.

Griffard, Bernard F., and Kent H. Butts. "Responding to Environmental Challenges in Central Asia and the Caspian Basin." *Center for Strategic Leadership Issue Paper* 3-01. Carlisle, PA: US Army War College Center for Strategic Leadership, 2001.

Groves, John R. "PfP and the State Partnership Program: Fostering Engagement and Progress." *Parameters* 29, no. 1 (Spring 1999), 43–53.

Hansen, Flemming Splidsboel. "A Grand Strategy for Central Asia." *Problems of Post-Communism* 52, no. 2 (March/April 2005), 45–54.

Harahan, Joseph P., and Capt Robert J. Bennett. *Creating the Defense Threat Reduction Agency.* Washington, DC: Defense Threat Reduction Agency, 2002.

Hughes, Edward L., Kent H. Butts, Bernard F. Griffard, and Arthur L. Bradshaw Jr., eds. *Responding to Environmental Challenges in Central Asia and the Caspian Basin.* Carlisle,

PA: Center for Strategic Leadership, US Army War College, 2001.

Joint Chiefs of Staff. *National Military Strategy of the United States.* Washington, DC: Government Printing Office, 1992.

Kazakhstan: Reducing Nuclear Dangers, Increasing Global Security. Washington, DC: Embassy of Kazakhstan, 2004.

Kazemi, Leila. "Domestic Sources of Uzbekistan's Foreign Policy, 1991 to the Present." *Journal of International Affairs* 56, no. 2 (Spring 2003), 205–16.

Kenzhetaev, Marat. "Kazakhstan's Military-Technical Cooperation with Foreign States: Current Status, Structures, and Prospects." *Eksport Vooruzheiy Journal,* no.1 (January/February 2002), http://mdb.cast.ru (accessed 6 March 2006).

Khaitov, Ata. "A New Role for Russia: Niazov's Best Friend." *Jamestown Foundation Russia & Eurasia Review* 2, no. 3 (4 February 2003), 1–4.

———. "Central Asian Responses to the Iraq Crisis: Hopes and Fears." *Jamestown Foundation Russia & Eurasia Review* 2, no. 5 (5 March 2003), 1–5.

Kucera, Joshua. "CENTCOM Sets Up Disaster Management Centre." *Janes' Defense Weekly,* 1 March 2006.

Lahue, Lt Col William. "Security Assistance in Kazakhstan: Building a Partnership for the Future." *DISAM Journal of International Security Assistance Management* 25, no. 1 (Fall 2002/Winter 2003), 6–18.

Levgold, Robert, ed. *Thinking Strategically: The Major Powers, Kazakhstan, and the Central Asian Nexus.* Cambridge, MA: The MIT Press, 2003.

Mandelbaum, Michael. *Central Asia and the World: Kazakhstan, Uzbekistan, Tajikistan, Kyrgyzstan, and Turkmenistan.* New York: Council on Foreign Relations, 1994.

MacFarlane, S. Neil. *Western Engagement in the Caucasus and Central Asia.* London: Royal Institute of International Affairs, 1999.

Management of Security Assistance, 21st Edition. Wright-Patterson AFB, OH: Defense Institute of Security Assistance Management, 2001.

McCoy, William H., Jr. *Senegal and Liberia: Case Studies in U.S. IMET Training and Its Role in Internal Defense and Development.* Santa Monica, CA: RAND, 1994.

McDermott, Roger. "The Armed Forces of the Republic of Uzbeki-
    stan, 1992–2002: Threats, Influences, and Reform." *Journal
    of Slavic Military Studies* 16, no. 2 (June 2003), 27–50.
———. *Countering Global Terrorism: Developing the Anti-Terrorist
    Capabilities of the Central Asian Militaries.* Carlisle, PA: US
    Army War College Strategic Studies Institute, 2004.
———. "Kazakhstan Suffers First Death of Peacekeeper in Iraq."
    Eurasia Daily Monitor 2, Issue 9 (13 January 2005), http://
    jamestown.org/publications_details.php?volume_id=407
    &issue_id=3194&article_id=2369080 (accessed 20 March
    2006).
———. "KAZBAT Deployment in Iraq Faces Uncertainty." *Eurasia
    Daily Monitor* 1, Issue 15 (21 May 2004), http://jamestown
    .org/publications_details.php?volume_id=401&issue
    _id=2961&article_id=236748 (accessed 20 March 2006).
McDermott, Roger, and Col Igor Mukhamedov. "Kazakhstan's
    Peacekeeping Support in Iraq." *Central Asia—Caucasus
    Analyst,* 28 January 2004, http://www.cacianalyst.org/
    view_article.php?articleid=2067 (accessed 20 March 2006).
Mott, William H., IV. *United States Military Assistance: An Em-
    pirical Perspective,* Westport, CT: Greenwood Press, 2002.
Motyl, Alexander J., Blair A. Ruble, and Lilia Shevtsova, eds.
    *Russia's Engagement with the West: Transformation and
    Integration in the Twenty-First Century.* London: M. E.
    Sharpe, 2005.
Mychajlszyn, Natalie L., and Harald von Riekhoff, eds. *The Evo-
    lution of Civil-Military Relations in East-Central Europe and
    the Former Soviet Union.* Westport, CT: Praeger Publishers,
    2004.
Naumkin, Vitaly V. *Radical Islam in Central Asia: Between Pen and
    Rifle.* New York: Rowman & Littlefield Publishers, Inc., 2005.
Office of the Coordinator of US Assistance to the Newly Inde-
    pendent States, US Department of State. *U.S. Government
    Assistance To and Cooperative Activities with the New Inde-
    pendent States of the Former Soviet Union, FY 2000 Annual
    Report.* Washington, DC: Department of State, 2001, Ap-
    pendix 1.
———. *U.S. Government Assistance To and Cooperative Activi-
    ties with the New Independent States of the Former Soviet*

Union, FY 2001 Annual Report. Washington, DC: Department of State, 2002, Appendix 1.

———. *U.S. Government Assistance To and Cooperative Activities with the New Independent States of the Former Soviet Union, FY 2002 Annual Report.* Washington, DC: Department of State, 2003, Appendix 1.

———. *U.S. Government Assistance To and Cooperative Activities with the New Independent States of the Former Soviet Union, FY 2003 Annual Report.* Washington, DC: Department of State, 2004, Appendix 1.

———. *U.S. Government Assistance To and Cooperative Activities with the New Independent States of the Former Soviet Union, FY 2004 Annual Report.* Washington, DC: Department of State, 2005, Appendix 1.

Olcott, Martha Brill. *Central Asia's Second Chance.* Washington, DC: Carnegie Endowment for International Peace, 2005.

———. "The Great Powers in Central Asia." *Current History,* October 2005, 331–35.

———. *Kazakhstan: Unfulfilled Promise.* Washington, DC: Carnegie Endowment for International Peace, 2002.

———. "Taking Stock of Central Asia." *Journal of International Affairs* 56, no. 2 (Spring 2003), 3–17.

Oliker, Olga, and David A. Shlapak. *U.S. Interests in Central Asia: Policy Priorities and Military Roles.* Santa Monica, CA: RAND, 2005.

Oliker, Olga, and Thomas S. Szayna, eds. *Faultlines of Conflict in Central Asia and the South Caucasus: Implications for the U.S. Army.* Santa Monica, CA: RAND, 2003.

O'Malley, William D., and Roger N. McDermott. "Kyrgyzstan's Security Tightrope: Balancing Its Relations with Moscow and Washington." *Journal of Slavic Military Studies* 16, no. 3 (September 2003), 72–111.

Pannier, Bruce. "Kyrgyzstan: Bishkek Presents New Air-Base Terms to U.S.-Led Coalition." *Radio Free Europe/Radio Liberty,* 25 January 2006. http://www.rferl.org/features article/2006/01/e377d17f-622a-41e0-b9ea-1c9d4698 b453.html.

Parrott, Bruce. *State Building and Military Power in Russia and the New States of Eurasia.* Armonk, NY: M. E. Sharpe, 1995.

Pikulina, Marina. *Uzbekistan in the Mirror of Military Security: A Historical Preface to Current Events*. Surrey, United Kingdom: The Conflict Studies Research Centre, November 1999.

Pollpeter, Kevin. *U.S.-China Security Management: Assessing the Military-to-Military Relationship*. Santa Monica, CA: RAND, 2004.

Polyakov, Leonid I. *U.S.-Ukraine Military Relations and the Value of Interoperability*. Carlisle, PA: US Army War College Strategic Studies Institute, 2005.

Priest, Dana. *The Mission: Waging War and Keeping the Peace with America's Military*. New York: W. W. Norton & Co., 2004.

Rabasa, Angela, Cheryl Benard, Peter Chalk, C. Christine Fair, Theodore W. Karasik, Rollie Lal, Ian O. Lesser, David E. Thaler, eds. *The Muslim World After 9/11*. Santa Monica, CA: RAND, 2004.

Rashid, Ahmed. *Jihad: The Rise of Militant Islam in Central Asia*. New York: Penguin Books, 2003.

Reynolds, Jeffrey C., Arthur L. Bradshaw Jr. Kent Hughes Butts, and Bernard F. Griffard, eds. *Partnering for Environmental Security Cooperation in Central Asia and the Caspian Basin*. Conference Report. Carlisle, PA: US Army War College Center for Strategic Leadership, 2002.

Reynolds, Jeffrey C., and Kent Hughes Butts. "Partnering for Environmental Security Cooperation in Central Asia and the Caspian Basin." *Center for Strategic Leadership Issues Paper 02-02*. Carlisle, PA: US Army War College Center for Strategic Leadership, 2002.

Rudy, John, and Ivan Eland. "Special Operations Military Abroad and Its Dangers." *CATO Institute Foreign Policy Briefing* no. 43, 22 June 1999. http://www.cato.org/pubs/fpbriefs/fpb53.pdf.

Rueckert, George L. *On-Site Inspection in Theory and Practice: A Primer on Modern Arms Control Regimes*. Westport, CT: Praeger Publishers, 1998.

Rumer, Eugene B. "Central Asian Leadership Succession: When, Not If." *Strategic Forum* no. 203. Washington, DC: National Defense University Institute for National Strategic Studies, December 2003.

———. "Filling the Void: The United States in Central Asia." *Foreign Service Journal* 80, no. 4 (April 2003), 1–5.

———. "Flashman's Revenge: Central Asia after September 11." *Strategic Forum* no. 195. Washington, DC: National Defense University Institute for National Strategic Studies, December 2002.

Sabol, Steven. "Turkmenbashi: Going it Alone." *Problems of Post-Communism* 50, no. 5 (September/October 2003), 48–57.

Shanker, Thom, and C. J. Chivers. "Crackdown in Uzbekistan Reopens Longstanding Debate on U.S. Military Aid." *New York Times*, 13 July 2005.

Sherwood-Randall, Elizabeth. "Building Cooperative Security Ties in Central Asia." *Stanford Journal of International Relations* 3, no. 2 (Fall/Winter 2002). http://www.stanford.edu/group/sjir/3.2.06_sherwoodrandall.html.

Shields, John M., and William C. Potter, eds. *Dismantling the Cold War: U.S. and NIS Perspectives on the Nunn-Lugar Cooperative Threat Reduction Program.* Cambridge, MA: The MIT Press, 1997.

Smith, Dianne L. *Breaking Away From the Bear.* Carlisle, PA: US Army War College Strategic Studies Institute, 1998.

———. *Opening Pandora's Box: Ethnicity and Central Asian Militaries.* Carlisle, PA: US Army War College Strategic Studies Institute, 1998.

Snyder, Jed C., ed. *After Empire: The Emerging Geopolitics of Central Asia.* Washington, DC: National Defense University Press, 1995.

Sokolsky, Richard, and Tanya Charlick-Paley. *NATO and Caspian Security: A Mission Too Far?* Santa Monica, CA: RAND, 1999.

Stein, Janice Gross, and Louis W. Pauly, eds. *Choosing to Cooperate: How States Avoid Loss.* Baltimore, MD: The Johns Hopkins University Press, 1993.

Szayna, Thomas S., Adam Grisson, Jefferson P. Marquis, Thomas-Durell Young, Brian Rose, and Yuna Huh. *US Army Security Cooperation: Toward Improved Planning and Management.* Santa Monica, CA: RAND, 2004.

Taw, Jennifer Morrison. *Thailand and the Philippines: Case Studies in U.S. IMET Training and Its Role in Internal Defense and Development.* Santa Monica, CA: RAND, 1994.

Ulrich, Marybeth Peterson. *Democratizing Communist Militaries: The Case of the Czech and Russian Armed Forces*. Ann Arbor, MI: University of Michigan Press, 1999.

US Department of Defense. *Quadrennial Defense Review Report*. Washington, DC: Government Printing Office, 2001.

———. *Quadrennial Defense Review Report*. Washington, DC: Government Printing Office, 2006.

US Department of Defense and US Department of State, *Foreign Military Training and DOD Engagement Activities of Interest in Fiscal years 1999 and 2000*. vol. 1. Washington, DC: Government Printing Office, 2000.

———. *Foreign Military Training in Fiscal Years 2000 and 2001*. vol. 1. Washington, DC: Government Printing Office, 2001.

———. *Foreign Military Training in Fiscal Years 2001 and 2002*. vol. 1. Washington, DC: Government Printing Office, 2002.

———. *Foreign Military Training in Fiscal Years 2002 and 2003*. vol. 1. Washington, DC: Government Printing Office, 2003.

———. *Foreign Military Training in Fiscal Years 2003 and 2004*. vol. 1. Washington, DC: Government Printing Office, 2004.

———. *Foreign Military Training in Fiscal Years 2004 and 2005*. vol. 1. Washington, DC: Government Printing Office, 2005.

Ward, Adam, ed. "Uzbekistan Casts Out America: Setback or Opportunity for Washington?" *IISS* [International Institute for Strategic Studies] *Strategic Comments* 11, no. 6 (August 2005), 1–2.

Weisbrode, Kenneth. *Central Eurasia: Prize or Quicksand?* New York: Oxford University Press, 2001.

White House. *A National Security Strategy for a New Century*. Washington, DC: Government Printing Office, 1997.

———. *A National Security Strategy for a New Century*. Washington, DC: Government Printing Office, 1998.

———. *A National Security Strategy for a New Century*. Washington, DC: Government Printing Office, 1999.

———. *A National Security Strategy of Engagement and Enlargement*. Washington, DC: Government Printing Office, 1994.

———. *A National Security Strategy of Engagement and Enlargement.* Washington, DC: Government Printing Office, 1995.

———. *National Security Strategy of the United States.* Washington, DC: Government Printing Office, 1991.

———. *National Security Strategy of the United States.* Washington, DC: Government Printing Office, 1993.

———. *National Security Strategy of the United States of America.* Washington, DC: Government Printing Office, 2002.

Williamson, Joel E., and Jennifer D. P. Moroney. "Security Cooperation Pays Off: A Lesson from the Afghan War." *DISAM Journal of International Security Assistance Management* 24, no. 3 (Spring 2002), 79–82.

Wishnick, Elizabeth. *Strategic Consequences of the Iraq War: U.S. Security Interests in Central Asia Reassessed.* Carlisle, PA: US Army War College Strategic Studies Institute, 2004.

Woodward, Bob. *Bush at War.* New York: Simon & Schuster, 2002.

———. *Plan of Attack.* New York: Simon & Schuster, 2004.

Wooley, Lt Gen Michael W., USAF. "America's Quiet Professionals: Specialized Airpower—Yesterday, Today, and Tomorrow." *Air and Space Power Journal* 19, no. 1 (Spring 2005), 59–66.

Zaccor, Col Albert, USA. *Security Cooperation and Non-State Threats: A Call for an Integrated Strategy.* Washington, DC: Atlantic Council of the United States, August 2005.

Zhasuzakov, Col S. A. "JCET Balance Kayak 97—Kazakhstan and the U.S.: Training Together." *Asia-Pacific Defense Forum,* (Summer Special Supplement) 1998.

GPO U.S. GOVERNMENT PRINTING OFFICE: 2007–626-312